The Golden Age of Russian Literature

by Ivar Spector

The Golden Age of Russian Literature

by Ivar Spector

Essay Index Reprint Series

 BOOKS FOR LIBRARIES PRESS
FREEPORT, NEW YORK

First Published 1939
Reprinted 1971

INTERNATIONAL STANDARD BOOK NUMBER:
0-8369-2298-0

LIBRARY OF CONGRESS CATALOG CARD NUMBER:
70-156720

PRINTED IN THE UNITED STATES OF AMERICA

TO MY WIFE

Preface

THIS WORK is the product of courses in Russian Literature offered in the Departments of English and Oriental Studies at the University of Washington, Seattle, during the academic years 1931-39. While the author has often been asked by students and teachers of literature to publish his lectures, and thus make them available to a larger audience beyond the University campus, it is, however, due to his wife's insistence and to her concrete assistance, that this work has finally been accomplished.

Although many books have been written on Russian literature, no work known to the author has yet appeared which adequately meets the needs of American college students, whose knowledge of this field is for the most part fragmentary and superficial.

The purpose of this book, therefore, is to present the subject of Russian literature to the American student and reader as a unit, and as a natural outgrowth and development of Russian environment. Only those authors have been chosen whose contributions are of national and universal significance. Many others might have been included, but these, by general consensus of opinion, are considered as most representative of the Golden Age of Russian Literature.

The bibliography is necessarily selective rather than exhaustive. It is designed to serve as a guide for collateral reading, and hence only a limited number of carefully selected titles has been included.

All dates given are those of the Gregorian calendar (N. S.), although the Julian calendar (O. S.) was in vogue in Russia until February 14, 1918.

The English spelling of Russian names is either phonetic or transliterated. In spite of the fact that there exists a gentleman's agreement on this subject, it has never been universally observed. For this reason, the author has deemed it advisable to use the phonetic spelling, except in the case of excerpts quoted from other sources, where the original spelling has been retained. For example the author has written Tchekhov instead of Chekhov; Tchatsky instead of Chatsky; Dostoyevsky instead of Dostoevsky, etc.

I. S.

University of Washington

Table of Contents

Key to Russian Names

RUSSIANS, as a rule, have no middle names, but in ordinary conversation, men and women are addressed by the given name followed by the patronymic. For example, if a man's Christian name is Anton and his father's name is Pavel, he is called Anton Pavlovitch, meaning Anton, the son of Pavel. If a woman's name is Anna and her father's name is Ivan, it is customary to address her as Anna Ivanovna, meaning Anna, the daughter of Ivan.

Russian given names have many diminutives. The following list covers the names most extensively used in Russian literature:

Full Given Name	Diminutive
Agráfina	Grúshenka, Grúnya
Alexánder	Sásha, Sáshenka
Alexéy, (Alexis)	Alyósha
Anastásya	Nástya
Avdótya (Eudoxia)	Dúnya
Borís	Bórya, Bórenka
Daryá	Dásha, Dáshenka
Dimítri (Dmítri)	Mítya
Elizavéta (Elizabeth)	Líza, Lízanka
Fyódor (Feodor)	Fédya
Grigóry (Gregory)	Grísha
Ilyá	Ilyúsha
Iván (John)	Ványa
Katerína (Catherine)	Kátya, Katiúsha
Nikolái (Nicholas)	Kólya
Márya	Másha
Natálya	Natásha
Péter (Pyótr)	Pétya
Sergéy	Seryózha
Sóphya	Sónia
Tatyána	Tánya, Tánitchka
Vladímir	Volódya

Introduction

*J*T IS CUSTOMARY to speak of the nineteenth century either as the classical or the golden age in Russian literature. Strictly speaking, however, this age extends from the publication of Fonvisin's *The Minor (The Young Hopeful)* in 1782 to the death of Maxim Gorky in 1936. Thus classical Russian literature covers a period of approximately a century and a half. Gorky definitely seals the classical age.

This classical age, contrary to prevailing opinion, does not mark the birth of Russian literature—but rather its rebirth, which with some justification may be termed the Renaissance. The few ancient Russian manuscripts extant in the field of theology, homiletics, and poetry, and particularly that literary gem, the *Tale of the Host of Igor*, prove beyond a doubt that in the pre-Mongolian period, 862-1243, the ancestors of the Russian people created a literature of a high type. During the era of Mongolian supremacy, 1243-1480, the Dark Ages of Russian political and cultural development, innumerable manuscripts and historical records were destroyed or lost to posterity. Archeological research may yet bring more of them to the light of day. It was not until the reign of Ivan the Terrible, 1530-84, at the close of the Rurik dynasty, that Russia made any serious attempt to reassert herself politically or culturally. Unfortunately the Time of Troubles, 1598-1613, which brought foreign invasion and civil strife in its train, frustrated a promising Russian literary revival. During the reign of Peter the Great, 1682-1725, no outstanding original Russian literature was produced. By opening a window to the West, Peter introduced an age of imitation, adaptation, and translation, which lasted with few exceptions until the close of the eighteenth century.

It was Catherine the Great, 1762-96, who laid the foundation for a national literary awakening. Although

German herself by origin, and a follower of Peter the
Great, she, unlike Peter, did not allow herself to become
a slave to the policy of westernization. Catherine's famous
Nakaz of 1768 was directly responsible for the produc-
tion of the first genuine Russian comedy, *The Minor*, by
Fonvisin, followed by *The Choice of a Tutor* in 1792.

The Russian literary Renaissance proper, however,
owed its origin to two major forces: one cultural, the
other political. The first was the appearance in the year
1800 of the manuscript of the *Tale of the Host of Igor*,
which created a stir in Russian literary circles, and which
inspired Russian authors to cast aside their foreign
models in order to emulate the quality of work produced
by their ancestors. In the second place Russian literature
owed a great deal to the Napoleonic Wars. During the
French invasion of Russia there came a strong reaction
against foreign influence in general—against French influence in particular. In spite of the fact that the Russian
officers who fought Napoleon spoke French among themselves, the bulk of the Russian people despised it. Following the trend of popular opinion, and stimulated by the
discovery of ancient manuscripts, Russian authors chose
Russian themes as their literary medium during the
golden age. The founder and the most outstanding leader
of this Russian national literary Renaissance was Alexander Sergeyevitch Pushkin, 1799-1837.

When we speak of Russian literature we mean the
novel. Unlike other literatures, where poetry occupies the
most prominent place, in Russia it is prose. For various
reasons, the Russian genius expressed itself much better
in prose. The majority of Russian writers considered
poetry as entertaining literature—but Russian literature
as a whole is not entertaining. It is closely interwoven
with current events and deals with problems of utmost
importance to the individual, to the nation, or to society
as a whole. The most significant reason for this phe-
nomenon was the censorship that existed in Russia during the period in question. In Russia writers were not

permitted to express themselves directly on any controversial subject. Much material, which in other countries
would have found its way into scientific or theological
journals—in Russia, found an outlet in fiction as the
medium of expression. For example, it was impossible to
have the same debates and discussions over the condition
of the serfs in Russia as occurred in the United States
over the abolition of slavery. Russian champions of
emancipation had to resort to fiction—to novels and short
stories in which they discussed the pros and cons of the
problem. It will suffice to mention Gogol's *Dead Souls,*
Turgenev's *Memoirs of a Sportsman* or Pisemsky's works.
In the light of this situation there is perhaps no such
thing as Russian fiction, for each novel dealt with the
burning issues of the day. In other words, if one were
to substitute the real names for the fictitious names one
could easily reproduce an important part of Russian history in the nineteenth century. In this connection we do
well to remember that the reading public in Russia during
the period, although few in number in proportion to the
total population, was, generally speaking, a highly intelligent group, capable of grasping the underlying facts behind the so-called fiction.

Although the novel occupies the most prominent place
in Russian literature, we can hardly afford to overlook
the rôle of the drama. In brief, classical Russian drama
is a purely secular institution. Unlike the drama of
western Europe, whose beginnings are traceable to the
church, the Russian classical drama was founded and
developed outside the church; in fact, it was established
and flourished in spite of the church.

While the novel afforded a medium for the highest
expression of Russian tragedy, the genius of Russian
drama lay in the comedy. For this reason, in Russian
literature the novel and the play are closely interwoven
and inseparable—the one complementing the other.
Closer examination reveals, moreover, that the technical
structure of the best Russian fiction was based upon the

play. In view of these facts it is not surprising to find that practically every Russian novelist of renown was also a playwright and *vice versa*.

The novel reflected life as it was too often in Russia at this time—a tale of frustrations and defeat. Strictly speaking, the comedy interpreted the novel. That is, by exposing the corruption prevalent among public officials and by holding up to ridicule their mismanagement of public affairs, the comedy often revealed the source of the tragedy in Russian life. In a country where universal education did not yet exist, and where the majority of the ruling class could scarcely be called literary-minded, the stage had, potentially at least, a wider audience than the novel. This may partially explain why the censor was more lenient with the novel than with the play and why the novel became the main channel of expression in Russian literature.

In conclusion, for the benefit of the Western reader, the author presents his diagram of the development of a typical Russian novel:

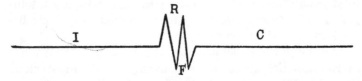

It is immediately apparent from this diagram, that the introduction (I) and the climax (C) are somewhat prolonged. They are practically never abrupt. While, in the typical novel, the plot rises and falls at least twice (R and F), this may occur several times as in Tolstoy's *War and Peace* or Dostoyevsky's *The Idiot*. It is evident, therefore, that there is a marked difference between the technical structure of the typical Russian novel and its standard English or American counterpart.

THE GOLDEN AGE OF RUSSIAN LITERATURE

Denis Ivanovitch Fonvisin

1745-92

ENIS IVANOVITCH FONVISIN, often called the Russian Molière, was born on April 3, 1745, in Moscow, and died on December 1, 1792. He was the descendant of a German prisoner of war, known as Von Visin. After his death, at the suggestion of Pushkin, the writer's name was Russianized into Fonvisin.

Fonvisin's father, a man with only an elementary education, but with a great deal of common sense, instructed him in the rudiments of the Russian and Slavic languages, providing tutors in other fields. In 1755, Denis and his brother, Paul, were enrolled in the gymnasium at Moscow University, established in that year. Although he complained of the teaching personnel, some of whom were addicted to drunkenness and loose living, Denis, nevertheless, admitted that he acquired a considerable fund of knowledge in that institution. In 1760 he entered the university proper, in the department of philosophy, where he remained until 1762.

Fonvisin's literary career began in 1761 with a translation entitled *The Just Jupiter* and a collection of Holberg's *Fables*. These were followed by other translations, including a play by Voltaire. In 1762 he joined the Imperial Guard, only to find that a military career held no appeal for him, whereupon he became a translator in the Russian Foreign Office. In 1764 he began to write plays, the first of which, *Korion,* was performed at the Imperial Theatre in St. Petersburg in the same year. In 1766 his comedy, *The Brigadier,* created a sensation when it was read in the presence of Catherine the Great. In recognition of his many services, the Empress in 1773 presented him with a large estate in the province of Vitebsk, which contained 1180 serfs. The following year he married a widow, Catherine I. Khlopova. During the Pugachev rebellion in 1774, Fonvisin, at the request of Count N. I. Panin (1718-83), Minister for Foreign Affairs under Catherine II, drew up a plan for a constitutional government of Russia. Unfortunately this draft, as well as many other important constitutional documents, was permanently shelved by the Empress and never saw the light of day.

Fonvisin made three trips abroad (1777-78, 1784-85, 1786-87), during which time he visited Poland, Germany, and France. In 1782 his famous comedy, *The Minor,* appeared, but its performance was forbidden by the censor. Thanks to the efforts of Count N. I. Panin, this ban was removed and the play was staged in St. Petersburg on September 24, 1782, where it received a tremendous ovation. In 1790 he published his last play, *The Choice of a Tutor.*

Although Fonvisin wrote many original plays and translated others, his fame in Russian literature rests chiefly on his famous comedy, *The Minor* or *The Young Hopeful* (1782).

THE PLOT OF *THE MINOR* (1782)

The story deals with the affairs of the Prostakov family, ignorant, crude, and avaricious landowners. Mrs. Prostakov is the dominating character in the family. She abuses the servants, treats her husband with scant respect, but lavishes affection upon their son, Mitrofan. The latter is not only stupid, but indolent, and profits not at all from the instruction of the teachers whom his parents have provided, partly because of his dullness, partly because of the incompetency of his tutors.

With the family lives a young relative, Sophia, whom the Prostakovs have forcibly taken under their protection in order to get control of her property. When the play opens, preparations are under way to marry Sophia to Mrs. Prostakov's brother, Skotinin, whose chief enthusiasm in life is pigs. Affairs take a different turn when Sophia receives a letter from her uncle, Starodum, from whom she has not heard for a long time. The letter contains the interesting information that Sophia is to be made heiress to his not inconsiderable fortune.

Mrs. Prostakov forthwith decides that her son, rather than her brother shall marry Sophia. She treats the latter with great consideration and when Starodum arrives, overwhelms him with more or less unwelcome attentions.

Two other guests appear, namely, Milón, who has long been Sophia's sweetheart, and Pravdin, a government official. The latter comes with legal authority to deprive Mrs. Prostakov of the control of her estate if his observations convince him that the tales of her wanton cruelty are true.

Starodum, already aware that Sophia has been detained against her will, discovers that she loves Milón, who is his own choice as a husband for her, and he prepares to take her away with him the following morning. Mrs. Prostakov and Skotinin, seeing a fortune about to slip through their fingers, resolve to detain the heiress, forcibly if necessary, for their advantage.

Sophia is rescued by Milón. Mrs. Prostakov's burst of fury at being thwarted furnishes Pravdin with the occasion he requires to deprive her cf the control of her estate. Starodum leaves with Sophia, sententiously remarking, "Behold the just reward of wickedness!"

The play abounds in characteristic eighteenth-century moralizing and contains an allegorical element, in that the names of some of the characters describe their personalities, e.g. Mrs. Prostakov (Mrs. Simpleton), Skotinin (Mr. Beastly), Starodum (Mr. Oldsense), etc.

FROM *THE MINOR*
ACT V, SCENE VI

Yeremeyevna (showing in the teachers. To Pravdin): Here they are, dear sir, all our rascals.

Vralman: Your Honor? Dit you ask for me?

Kuteykin (to Pravdin): They called unto me, and I came.

Cipherkin: What is your command, your Honor?

Starodum (at the sight of Vralman, looking steadily at him): Why, so it's you, Vralman!

Vralman (recognizing Starodum) : Ay, ay, ay, ay! It eez you, my dear master. (Kissing the skirt of Starodum's kaftan.) Are you feeling vell, my lort?

Pravdin: What? Do you know him?

Starodum: Of course I know him. For three years he was my coachman.

(All are surprised.)

Pravdin: A marvelous teacher!

Starodum: And so you are a teacher here, Vralman! I really thought that you were an honest man and would not attempt anything that you weren't fitted for.

Vralman: Vat can one do, my dear master! I am not the first, I am not the last one! I vandered for tree monts in Moscow vidout a jop; nobody vants a coachman! I had eezer to die of hunger, or be a teacher.

Pravdin (to the teachers) : In the name of the government I have become the guardian of this house and I hereby dismiss you.

Cipherkin: Nothing could be better.

Kuteykin: You dismiss us, your Honor! But we must settle our accounts first.

Pravdin: What is it you want?

Kuteykin: No, my dear sir, my bill is not exceeding short. They owe me for a half-year's tuition, for the shoes which I have worn out in these three years, for my rent, and then again I often made trips here for nothing, and——

Mrs. Prostakov: You greedy soul! Kuteykin! What is this for?

Pravdin: Don't interfere, madam, please.

Mrs. Prostakov: If the truth of the matter be told, what did you teach Mitrofanushka?

Kuteykin: That's his business, not mine.

Pravdin (to Kuteykin) : All right, all right. (To Cipherkin) How much do you receive?

Cipherkin: Me? Nothing.

Mrs. Prostakov: My dear sir, he got ten rubles one year, but he hasn't got a kopek yet for the last year.

Cipherkin: Well then: let those ten rubles cover the shoes I have worn out in two years. We are even now.

Pravdin: And for the tuition?

Cipherkin: Nothing.

Starodum: Why nothing?

Cipherkin: I won't charge anything. He didn't learn anything from me.

Starodum: Just the same—you must be paid.

Cipherkin: No reason for it. I served my tsar for over twenty years. I took money for that service; but for doing nothing I have never received pay, and I won't take any now.

Starodum: Here's an honest man indeed! (Starodum and Milón take money from their purses.)

Pravdin: Aren't you ashamed, Kuteykin?

Kuteykin (bowing his head) : Shame on me, a sinner!

Starodum (to Cipherkin) : This is for you, friend, for your good heart.

Cipherkin: Thank you, your Honor! I am grateful! You may give me a present, if you like. I shall never in my life demand any reward without deserving it.

Milón (handing him money) : Here is some more for you, my man!

Cipherkin: Thank you, too.

Pravdin: It's because you are not like Kuteykin.

Cipherkin: Why, your Honor! I am a soldier!

Pravdin (to Cipherkin) : Well, now go; the Lord be with you!

(Cipherkin goes out.)

Pravdin: And you, Kuteykin, will you come here tomorrow and settle your bill with the mistress herself?

Kuteykin (running away) : With herself! I renounce everything!

Vralman (to Starodum) : Don't desert your olt servant, your Honor! Tak me *mit* you!

Starodum: But Vralman, I imagine you have lost your skill with horses.

Vralman: Ach no, dear master! Leeving with my masters here has alvays seemed to me like leeving among ze horses in ze stable.

Tr. by G. Z. Patrick and G. R. Noyes.

The Minor, as we have already stated, marks the beginning of classical Russian literature. Strictly speaking,

from the age of the *Host of Igor* to the advent of the dilettante Fonvisin, there had been no genuinely Russian
literature. Most literary works during the seventeenth
and eighteenth centuries were imitations, adaptations,
and translations, based upon French schools and authors.
The Minor broke new ground in the field of Russian
letters.

To begin a new epoch two factors at least are necessary—first, an *event*, widely discussed or affecting an interested influential group; and second, a *work*, voicing
the sentiment of the group directly concerned with that
event. With reference to *The Minor*—the Empress Catherine, by her famous Nakaz of 1768, the practical application of which she planned to accelerate through the appointment of a Commission on Public Education in 1782,
excluded from office all sons of the nobility who had not
acquired a certain modicum of education. These Instructions (Nakaz) profoundly disturbed both the higher and
lower nobility throughout Russia. In other words, they
provided the *event*. *The Minor* was the *work* which regis-
tered the sentiment of the interested class, in this case,
the nobility. Hence it marks a new epoch.

The Minor was, moreover, the first genuinely Russian
production to deal with Russian life proper—a natural
outgrowth of Russian environment. The Prostakovs and
the Skotinins were not imported personalities who required interpretation. The reader and the spectator knew
them in flesh and blood. In fact the country was honey-
combed with Mitrofans who created problems in the
home and in the state. Furthermore the treatment of the
serfs, at the hands of the Prostakovs, revealed a situation
which was only too general throughout Russia.

Other Russian authors belittled any attempt to portray in Russian literature the life and the miserable
plight of the lower uncultured classes. Even two contemporaries of Fonvisin, namely, A. P. Sumarokov, 1718-
77, whom Voltaire called the Russian Racine and the
first Russian playwright, and M. B. Lomonosov, 1711-65,

Russia's outstanding scientist and linguist, himself of lower origin, both referred to literature which dealt with the lower classes as ignoble *(podlaya)*. Fonvisin, consciously or unconsciously, elevated this type of writing to an art. Besides its literary value *The Minor* is recognized as an historical document of the utmost importance.

In brief, *The Minor* is the first genuine Russian comedy, not only written in Russian, but faithfully reflecting the seamy side of Russian society. Its author therefore merits the title of forerunner of the classical age in Russian literature. He held up to public ridicule the weak spots in the social institutions of his time. In this respect Fonvisin had no predecessor in Russia. His only successor and superior was Gogol, who began where Fonvisin left off. Mitrofan in *The Minor* has to a certain extent his counterpart in Tony Lumpkin in England.

BIBLIOGRAPHY

Abramovitch, G., and Goloventchenko, F., *Russkaya Literatura (Russian Literature)*, Moscow, 1935.

Bechhofer, C. E., *Five Russian Plays*, E. P. Dutton, 1916.

Mirsky, D. S., *A History of Russian Literature*, 1927.

Noyes, G. R., *Masterpieces of the Russian Drama*, N. Y., 1933.

Spector, Ivar, *Russia: A New History*, "Reign of Empress Catherine II, the Great, 1762-1796," third edition, 1935.

Wiener, Leo, *Anthology of Russian Literature*, Vol. I, N. Y., 1902.

Wiener, Leo, *The Contemporary Drama of Russia*, Boston, 1924.

Alexander Sergeyevitch Pushkin

1799-1837

ALEXANDER SERGEYEVITCH PUSHKIN, often called the Russian Shakespeare, was born on June 6 (May 26, O.S.), 1799, in Moscow, and died as the result of a duel, on February 11 (January 29, O.S.), in St. Petersburg. On his father's side he boasted an aristocratic lineage of six hundred years' duration, while on his mother's side (Nadezhda Osipovna Pushkina, née Hannibal), he traced his origin to Ibrahim Hannibal, an Ethiopian Ras, or "The Negro of Peter the Great."

The young poet Pushkin was one of four children, all of whom were nurtured on the French language and steeped in Russian folklore. The French culture Pushkin owed to his parents and tutors; the folklore to his old nurse, Arina Rodionovna, who filled his impressionable mind with those tales of the Russian past which later formed the warp and the woof of his masterly lyrics.

At the age of twelve Pushkin entered the Lyceum, established in 1810 at Tsarskoe Selo (renamed Detskoe Selo), as an exclusive school for children of the nobility. After six years of mediocre work he was graduated from the Lyceum in June, 1817.

Although he longed to be a Hussar, Pushkin, on receiving his diploma, had to be satisfied with a nominal appointment in the Foreign Office. His liberal leanings and his chequered life in the capital soon led to his banishment to South Russia. Far from the distractions of Petersburg society, Pushkin roamed at will about the then wild south, through the Caucasus and the Crimea, consorting even with the gypsies, and storing up a rich fund of literary data for future use.

After many such exiles, Pushkin was finally pardoned by Nicholas I, 1825-55, and returned to Moscow and St. Petersburg where he promptly became the literary lion of his day. In 1831 he married the young and beautiful Natalie Gontcharova. Evil gossip directed against his young wife's flirtation with a guardsman led Pushkin to challenge Heckeren-Dantes, the son of the Dutch Ambassador, to a duel which resulted in the poet's premature death at the early age of thirty-eight.

In spite of his chequered career, Pushkin was a prolific writer. Much of his work was in prose, as for example, *The Captain's Daughter, The Queen of Spades, Dubrovsky,* and others. As the first writer of Russian tragedies, foreign in form but Russian in content, he also made his contribution to the field of drama. Of these the best example is *Boris Godunov.* But Pushkin's real genius lay in poetry. It was through his verse that the young poet voiced the true sentiment of literary Russia. His greatest achievement, and one which alone would have ensured for him the literary immortality he sought, was the incomparable *Eugene Onegin*—a novel in verse.

THE PLOT OF *EUGENE ONEGIN* (1823-31)

Eugene Onegin, a typical young dandy of the Russian intelligentsia, grows weary of the dissipations of Petersburg society. Recalled to the country by the death of his uncle, whose estate he inherits, he decides to make his home there. He forms a friendship with the romantic young poet, Lensky, the only other educated person in the neighborhood. Lensky is engaged to marry his childhood sweetheart, Olga Larin, a lighthearted but giddy young girl. During a visit to her home, Onegin meets her elder sister, Tatyana, a sensitive idealistic young woman, capable of great loyalty and devotion. A simple country girl, she immediately falls in love with the accomplished and worldly wise Onegin and pours out her passion for him in a letter which has become a literary masterpiece. Onegin, who claims that he is not the marrying kind, delivers a fatherly sermon to Tatyana, and professes to feel for her only a brotherly affection. Suffering from the blow of Onegin's casual rejection of her love, Tatyana pines away, and becomes pale and thin.

Some time later, Eugene's friend, Lensky, induces him to attend Tatyana's name-day party. Onegin, annoyed at the emotion displayed by Tatyana on his arrival, ostentatiously flirts with Lensky's sweetheart, Olga, who thoughtlessly encourages him. The outcome is that Lensky, in a fit of jealous rage, challenges his friend Onegin to a duel in which Lensky, himself, is killed.

After the tragic death of the poet, Onegin, full of remorse, sets out on his travels once again. Olga soon finds consolation in the love of a young army officer whom she marries. Tatyana's mind is, however, still obsessed by thoughts of Onegin. She visits his former home and reads his books. At last her mother, despairing of marrying her off in the country, takes her to Moscow to seek a husband. Tatyana is finally induced by her relatives to marry a distinguished prince from St. Petersburg.

On his subsequent return to the capital Onegin meets Tatyana, no longer the simple country girl who pined for him, but the proud and beautiful queen of St. Petersburg society. Onegin falls madly in love with her, sends her passionate letters, only to find Tatyana totally unresponsive to his ardent but belated advances. During a surprise visit to Tatyana's house, Onegin finds her in tears over his letters. Tatyana confesses her love for him, upbraids him for seeking to dishonor her, and bravely announces her resolution to be true to her husband forever.

TATYANA'S LETTER TO ONEGIN
(CANTO III, STANZA 31)

I write you. If I took an hour
I could not make myself more plain,
And now you have it in your power
To punish me with your disdain.
But if you find you have for me
The smallest drop of sympathy
You will not leave me in such pain.
At first I wanted to keep still;
Indeed, you never would have heard
Of my disgrace a single word
If I had thought, "Perhaps he will
Call on us, if but once a week,

And once more I shall hear him speak,
However rarely." If I might
Answer you just a word and then
Go dreaming of your face again
Till our next meeting, day and night!
They say you are a misanthrope
And find our village life a bore.—
To dazzle you we could not hope,
But you were welcome at our door.

Why did you ever come to call?
For in this far, forgotten spot
We never should have met at all
And all this pain, so burning hot,
I might have missed... And then, why not?
As I grew calm, as people do,
I might have found in later life
A mate and been a faithful wife
And a devoted mother, too.
But no! There is no other man
To whom I could have given my love,
And I am yours by Heaven's plan
Determined in the courts above.
My life so far has been a pledge
Of this sure meeting God would send;
To love you is my privilege,
You are my guardian to the end.
You came to me in dreams at first
And, dimly seen, you still were dear,
Your voice was lovely to my ear,
Your eyes awoke a longing thirst.
That was no dream so long ago!
You came—and instantly I knew!
I was confused but all aglow;
My heart said, "It is he, I know."
Did I not use to talk with you?
You spoke to me when all was still,
When I was out among the poor,
Or when I used to say a prayer
To ease my mind, so sore and ill.
And at those moments, dearest dream,
Was it not you who came to gleam

From out the dark translucency
And bending down so softly, shed
Your love and joy around my bed,
Whispering words of hope to me?
Are you my guardian angel or
A sly, seductive counselor?
Oh, settle all these doubts for me!
It may be vanity and lies
Have cheated my simplicity
And it is destined otherwise...
But be that as it may! For all
My life I give you my affection.
I feel my tears begin to fall
As I beseech you for protection.
For think! I am as if alone;
No one here guesses what I feel;
My senses have begun to reel
And all my love must die unknown.
I write you now: one glance from you
Can kindle hope within my heart
Or tear these dreadful dreams apart
With your reproach, deserved, I know.

I've done. I dare not read it through;
I am half dead with fear and shame,
But I will trust myself to you
With confidence, in honor's name.

                    —Tr. by D. P. RADIN and G. Z. PATRICK.

Whether the English word *poet* is derived from the Greek *poietés,* meaning *maker, creator,* or from the Phoenician hybrid term *ponhis,* signifying the *language of God* or the *language of nobility*—the implication of either derivation is that a poet should speak in a creative, imaginative, and noble language.

Technically speaking, it may be said that true poetry (and that includes to a certain extent also free verse) must possess four essential qualities. First, it must have rhythm—the musical element; it must appeal to the imagination; it must reveal emotional feeling; and finally, and perhaps most important of all, it must have a purpose, *raison d'être*, or express elevated thought (Greek: *spoude*). Lacking these four elements, which are indispensable to true poetry, it cannot be classed as such. It may be a song and the author thereof may be a gifted versifier or singer. A true poet, however, is not solely a bard, but also a co-Creator, in the fullest sense of the word.

A careful study of Pushkin's works in the light of their historical background and development reveals the fact that, with few exceptions, his songs were those of an unusually gifted bard rather than of a poet; or to employ an appropriate Ukrainian term he was a *Kobzar*, albeit of noble rank. A *Kobzar* (bard), broadly speaking, is a national singer, while a poet is universal. In other words, a *Kobzar* is closer to his own people than a poet, who, for the most part, is a citizen of the world. We speak of national poets when we really mean bards *(Kobzars)*. A case in point is Lermontov, known as the Russian Byron, who is a true poet, "poet of eternity," yet he has never occupied the same place as Pushkin in the hearts of the Russian people. For Pushkin, being a *Kobzar par excellence*, has been more intimately related to the Russian people than any other poet in Russian literature. His truth is precisely the truth of the Russians. Pushkin, with his powerful genius, has given us a splendid epitome of the life and art of the Russian people. The real nature of this is best explained in the words of Faust: "Zwei Seelen, ach, wohnen in meiner Brust." On the one hand, his work reveals a passion for all that is new, and on the other, an unswerving devotion to the old, particularly to Russian folklore and ballads.

In this connection it is worthy of note that Pushkin's African extraction was no handicap to him in Russia. Under the tsarist regime a writer might well be persecuted for using his art as a medium for the propagation of liberal ideas, but in spite of this rigid censorship, once he had evinced his ability in a certain line of creative work, and asserted himself as an artist, he was not sub-

ject to discrimination because of color. Pushkin suffered
from political censorship, not from color prejudice.

Pushkin has done more for the Russian language than
Shakespeare for the English. As Peter the Great, in the
span of one short life, sought to bridge the gap created
by the Mongolian invasions, Pushkin cherished the same
dream for Russian literature and the Russian language.
He found it a rough uncut diamond with great potentialities, and he left it a polished medium of expression un-
surpassed by other modern languages. Even into the
foreign words he borrowed, he breathed a new spirit.
In the Russian language he was able to give expression
to the pent-up thoughts and emotions of a previous generation as well as of his own contemporaries. He gave
wings to the Russian language in poetry.

Until Pushkin, Russian writers were for the most
part of the dilettante type—for it was an unwritten tradition that each outstanding noble family should produce
at least one manuscript of merit in each generation.
Pushkin, however, in addition to his other contributions,
made of writing a profession.

Pushkin transmitted to others the inspiration and
ambition to continue that which he himself was not able
to complete in the brief span of his own life. His influence
is clearly discernible throughout the entire period, many
ideas being directly traceable to him. For instance, his
Eugene Onegin, a novel in verse, provided the pattern
for all subsequent novelists in Russia. His *Dubrovsky*
forms an excellent background for Turgenev's *Memoirs
of a Sportsman.* Tolstoy's *War and Peace* was patterned
after Pushkin's *The Captain's Daughter,* while *The Queen
of Spades* by Pushkin may have inspired Dostoyevsky's
Crime and Punishment. To be sure, Dostoyevsky always
acknowledged his indebtedness to Pushkin. For it was
he who made the *Kobzar* famous by evincing his admiration for Pushkin's *The Prophet.* If Belinsky, 1810-48,
the Russian Lessing, was chiefly responsible for discov-
ering Pushkin's talent, it fell to the lot of Dostoyevsky to

proclaim him the greatest poet of the world and the national poet laureate of Russia.

The centenary celebration of Pushkin's death was sponsored in February, 1937, by the exponents of the new as well as of the old regime in Russia. During the early years of the Soviet regime classical Russian literature, including the works of Pushkin, suffered an eclipse. Now, however, because a new nationalism is reasserting itself in Soviet Russia, there has been an unprecedented revival of the Russian classics, interpreted in the light of the Revolution. On the other hand, to the Russian émigrés, the Russia of the Diaspora, Pushkin is a consolation and a comfort, reminding them of the glorious age of accomplishment in the field of Russian culture. Pushkin is the most precious link in the golden chain of this culture. The time has now come when the prophecy of his last lyrical song, the *Exegi monumentum* (1836), has come true:

"The rumor of my fame will sweep through vasty Russia,
And all its peoples speak this name, whose light shall
    reign
Alike for haughty Slav, and Finn, and savage Tungus,
And Kalmuck riders of the plain."

BIBLIOGRAPHY

Baring, Maurice, *An Outline of Russian Literature*, Home University Library.

Cleugh, James, *Prelude to Parnassus*, N. Y., 1937.

Cross, S. H., and Simmons, E. J., *Centennial Essays for Pushkin*, Harvard University Press, 1937.

Elton, Oliver, *Verse from Pushkin and Others*, N. Y., 1935.

Gofman, M. L., and Lifar, Serge, *Pisma Pushkina k N. N. Gontcharovoi (Pushkin's Letters to N. N. Goncharov)*, Paris, 1936.

Graham, Stephen, *Boris Godunof*, Yale University Press, 1933.

Jarintzov, N., *Russian Poets and Poems*, Oxford, 1917.

Krup, Jacob, *Six Poems from the Russian of Pushkin and Lermontov*, N. Y., 1937.

Literaturnoye Nasledstvo (The Literary Heritage). Alexander Pushkin, Moscow, 1936.

Miliukov, P., *Zhivoi Pushkin (The Living Pushkin)*, 1837-1937, Paris, 1937.

Mirsky, D. S., *Pushkin*, E. P. Dutton, 1926.

Noyes, G. R., *Masterpieces of the Russian Drama*, N. Y., 1933.

Olgin, M. J., *Guide to Russian Literature*, N. Y., 1920.

Pushkin—The Man and the Artist (Composite), N. Y., 1937.

Radin, D. P., and Patrick, G. Z., *Eugene Onegin*, University of California Press, 1937.

Simmons, E. J., *Pushkin*, Harvard University Press, 1937.

Tomashevsky, B. (Editor), *A. Pushkin—Sotchinenia (Works)*, Leningrad, 1935.

Wiener, Leo, *Anthology of Russian Literature*, Vol. II, N. Y., 1903.

Wiener, Leo, *Contemporary Drama of Russia*, Boston, 1924.

Yarmolinsky, Avrahm (Editor), *The Works of Alexander Pushkin*, N. Y., 1936.

Alexander Sergeyevitch Griboyedov
1795-1829

ALEXANDER SERGEYEVITCH GRIBOYEDOV was born on January 4, 1795, in Moscow and died on February 11, 1829, in Teheran, Persia. On his father's side he was of Polish descent. Griboyedov was a born linguist as well as a talented musician. His mother gave him the very best education available at that time. At the age of fifteen he entered Moscow University from which he was graduated two years later with a major in Political Ethics. Under excellent teachers he continued his education in other fields, including philosophy, European and Near Eastern languages.

When Napoleon invaded Russia, Griboyedov joined the colors, but his regiment failed to reach the fighting line and he resigned in 1816. From February, 1819, to November, 1821, he was secretary to the Russian embassy in Persia, and subsequently held an office in Georgia. When General Paskevitch, a relative of his, was sent to the Caucasus, Griboyedov joined him and they fought together against Persia. Later Paskevitch commissioned Griboyedov to carry on the peace negotiations with Turkey and Persia. For his services in this connection the Emperor Nicholas I made him Minister Plenipotentiary at Teheran, an appointment productive of unfortunate consequences for the young author. Persian losses were heavy in the treaty negotiated by Griboyedov. As a measure of retaliation against the author of this humiliation Griboyedov and thirty-six others were slain by an infuriated mob at the Teheran embassy on February 11, 1829. Griboyedov's body was removed to Tiflis for burial in the monastery of St. David. His widow, whom he had married but a few months previous, erected a monument there to his memory.

Like Pushkin, Griboyedov began writing at an early

age. In 1815 he translated De Lesser's *Secret du ménage,* followed in 1817 by Barth's *Fausses infidélités.* After writing a comedy, *The Young Spouses,* and other works, he produced his masterpiece and the most widely discussed comedy in Russia at that time, *The Misfortune of Being Clever (Gore ot Uma).* The first draft of this play was made in Tiflis (1822-23), while the final touches were added during Griboyedov's two years' leave of absence in Moscow and St. Petersburg (1823-25). Since the censor vetoed publication, the play was read before Griboyedov's friends in 1824, and hundreds of manuscript copies were circulated. A private theatrical performance in 1825 was the only one which Griboyedov himself ever saw. Its first public performance, at which time the play was sadly mutilated by the censor, took place two years after his death. An expurgated edition appeared in printed form in 1833. The play in its entirety was not presented to the public until 1869, and not until 1903 was the original manuscript discovered and bought by the Historical Museum at Moscow.

THE PLOT OF *THE MISFORTUNE OF BEING CLEVER*
(1823-33)

This drama is pure satire. The scene is laid in the town house of Famusov, a rich landowner and government official. The atmosphere is characterized by artificiality, stupidity, and unadulterated self-interest. The characters are little more than puppets used by the author to portray the weakness and baseness of the society of the time. There is little or no action.

At the beginning of the play we are made aware of the infatuation of Famusov's daughter, Sophia, for Molchalin, his secretary. From motives of self-interest, Molchalin allows Sophia to imagine that he reciprocates her feelings, although he flirts with her maid, Liza, whenever the opportunity occurs. Famusov intrudes unexpectedly upon a rendezvous of his daughter and his secretary, and expresses his displeasure in no uncertain terms. Sophia, with some difficulty, succeeds in mollifying him.

Shortly after, Tchatsky, who has just returned from a lengthy sojourn abroad, calls to pay his respects. He is in love with Sophia, but neither she nor her father approves of him because of his caustic tongue. Tchatsky sees only too clearly the foibles of his countrymen and the prevalence of corruption among Russian officials. He indulges in lengthy tirades upon any and all occasions, although he completely fails to present a constructive remedy for the situation he deplores.

Tchatsky observes Sophia's interest in Molchalin. He is anxious to learn whether her own preference is for Molchalin or for Skalozub, a stupid army officer who has evidently found favor with her father. He is unable to elicit any definite answer from Sophia, who finds him more disagreeable than ever. She resents his severe criticism of her other suitors, which she attributes to spite, and particularly his criticism of Molchalin.

In a spirit of revenge, Sophia circulates a rumor during an evening party at her home, to the effect that Tchatsky has gone mad. The rumor spreads like wildfire among the assembled guests and is accorded general credence, especially when Tchatsky indulges in one of his lengthy tirades upon Russian servility to everything French.

Tchatsky becomes aware that his audience has deserted him for the dance. Disappointed that his homecoming has not proved more successful, he prepares to leave the festivities when he is stopped by Repetilov, who stumbles in drunken fashion up the front steps. Repetilov may be classed among those who are in theory progressive and idealistic, but in reality are garrulous, futile, and intemperate. Tchatsky finds him utterly boring and seizes the first opportunity to slip unseen into a porter's lodge. From this retreat he overhears the departing guests as they discuss his supposed madness.

Tchatsky is completely taken aback, and alarmed in case Sophia may have heard the rumor, which he in no wise suspects her of spreading. As he soliloquizes she suddenly appears and calls Molchalin. Tchatsky resolves to witness their tryst although it may cause him pain.

He hides behind a pillar just as Molchalin comes yawning from his room.

Molchalin proceeds to make love to the maid Liza, who informs him that her mistress is waiting. Both Sophia and Tchatsky overhear this episode, astounded at Molchalin's caddish conduct. Sophia enters and repulses Molchalin, although he grovels at her feet. Her satisfaction in the fact that no one else has witnessed his perfidy is short-lived, when to her consternation, Tchatsky makes his presence known. Molchalin runs away; Tchatsky taunts Sophia, who bursts into tears.

At this moment Famusov enters, accompanied by a crowd of servants, and berates all concerned. He threatens to use all his social and political influence against Tchatsky, but the latter, with cutting sarcasm for father and daughter as well as for Russian society in general, announces his decision to leave Moscow forever. As the play closes, Famusov's chief concern is for what people will say.

FROM *THE MISFORTUNE OF BEING CLEVER*
Translated by Sir Bernard Pares

ACT III, SCENE xxii

Natalya Dmitriyevna: He's here!
Countess Granddaughter: Hush!
All: Hush!
    (They withdraw to the opposite side of the stage from him.)
    Hlestova: See how his eyes he rolls!
He's fixing who to fight; he's itching for a row.
    Famusov (apprehensively): O Lord, have mercy on our sinful souls!
Dear boy, you're rather out of sorts just now;
You're tired and want a rest. Your pulse! You're quite upset!
    Chatsky: Yes, worried and worn out all round,
    My chest from each new shove I get,
My legs with clicking heels, my ears with all this sound,
And most of all my head, from rubbish I'd forget.
    (Goes up to Sophya.)
My spirit is oppressed with some strange misery,

And here, in all this crowd, I am lost. I don't feel right!
    No! Moscow's disabused me quite.
        Hlestova: It's Moscow's fault, you see.
        Famusov (gesticulating to Sophya) : Look, Sophya!
Keep away!
    She doesn't see! What next?
        Sophya (to Chatsky) : Do tell me why you seem so
vexed.
        Chatsky: A trifling incident! Puffed up with pride,
A Frenchy from Bordeaux—in that next room I found
        him—
    Had called a kind of council round him,
    Relating what he felt when forth he hied
To Russia, to the bears, with fear and lamentations.
He came, and what d'you think? They're kind as kind
        can be.
No Russian word you'll hear, no Russian face you'll see:
As if you were at home, your friends and your relations,
Exactly like Bordeaux! Now look: so kind we are,
He's feeling here to-night he's quite a little tsar.
The ladies talk the same, the style of dress no other!
        So pleased—but we aren't, brother!
    He stops—on every side there rise
    Such tender groans, such yearning sighs.
    "Oh, France! Dear France! There's not a country
        like it!"
Say three young princesses: of course at once they strike
        it,
The old refrain that first the childish ear impresses.
    Oh, where's a place with no princesses?
    I breathed a pious supplication
    Aside, though half aloud, that God
Would crush the unclean thing till from our souls he trod
This empty slavish cant of wholesale imitation:
If just a spark he'd throw in any man of spirit,
    Whose words and deeds might sharply school,
    Till we unlearned beneath such wholesome rule
Our sickening desire the strangers' tastes to inherit!
    Declare me reprobate, old-fashioned fool,
But as for me, I find our North is ten times worse,
Since everything was changed for all that's its reverse,

Our manners and our tongue and all we once revered,
Our gracious flowing robes for something new and
        weird—
    A veritable clown's costume,
A monkey's tail behind, a swelling bulge in front,
Against all common sense, to nature an affront,
The movements all constrained, the face without its bloom,
The chin absurd, clean-shaved, with bristles of gray hair,
Short coats, short locks, and wits still shorter than the
        hair.
Though born with the idea that every country's finer,
A little we might take from our good friends in China,
Of their most wise contempt for ways that aren't their
        own.
When shall the foreigner have ceased his endless sermons,
    That even if by our speech alone,
Our good, our clever folk may tell us from the Germans?
"The European style! What is there sounds so well?
    Our home-bred Russian—it's so queer.
Now, how could you translate *Madame, Mademoiselle?*"
"Sudarynya?" "Oh, no!" they drawl into my ear.
    Believe me, at the word, I see,
    They all burst out and laugh at me.
"Sudarynya! Ha! Ha! Ha! What a jawful!
"Sudarynya! Ha! Ha! Ha! How awful."
    I cursed my life and cursed my pride,
    I thought I'd tell them something true,
    But every one had turned aside.
    Well, that's what happened to me—that's not new!
Moscow and Petersburg, if all around we glance,
    Are like this person from Bordeaux in France.
        He opes his mouth—his luck he blesses,
        He wins the hearts of all princesses.
        In Petersburg and Moscow city,
The man who's foe to fake, in face, in manners, speech,
        Whose hapless head—the more's the pity—
    Has half a dozen sound ideas in reach,
If once he has the pluck to bring them all to book—
                                        Look!
    (He looks round: all are waltzing with the greatest
energy: the older folk are all seated at the card tables.)

Although Sir Bernard Pares has provided the best English translation of *The Misfortune of Being Clever,* even his rendition fails to do justice to the author. The play contains innumerable words and expressions which defy translation. For instance, Colonel Skalozub's vocabulary and manner of speech are, in the English version, practically lost to the reader. Molchalin's "psychological Russian" and the dialect used by Madam Hlestova, sister-in-law of Famusov, reveal merely the shadow of their former effectiveness in the original. The play also contains many allusions to Russian proverbs and sayings, while it teems with popular anecdotes and paraphrased aphorisms which cannot be translated satisfactorily. In other words, to begin with, *The Misfortune of Being Clever* should, above all other plays, be read and studied in the original.

The chief characters of the comedy, from an historical standpoint, are Tchatsky, Famusov, and Repetilov. The love theme embracing other persons is of secondary importance. Tchatsky, having a substantial Russian education plus travel and study abroad, represents the elite among the intelligentsia of the Russian Renaissance. On the other hand, Famusov, Sophia's father, is Griboyedov's version of the Prostakovs (Fonvisin)—a man to whom existing abuses and injustices have acquired all the sacred authority of cherished traditions, and who resents any attempt to curb or ameliorate them. He represents the socially dominant influential class in Russia. Opposite him stands Repetilov (the Prattler), a superficial and half-baked intellectual enamored of French culture, who in reality reflects the outlook of a not inconsiderable part of the new generation. From Tchatsky's standpoint, Famusov and Repetilov represent the two extremes in Russian society, both of which are detrimental to the country. Following the *via media,* he seeks a more substantial education along Russian lines, together with freedom of speech and the press on the Western model. He can offer no concrete practical remedy for a world so out of joint, but his criticism contains the elements of the controversy which later developed between the so-called Westernizers and the Slavophiles.

To a Westerner, brought up under a constitutional government where there exists freedom of speech and the press, the tirades in which Tchatsky gives full vent to his pent-up emotions, may well seem verbose and exaggerated—in other words, more like the efforts of the average soapbox orator. In the time of Griboyedov such speeches were well received in Russian literary circles. In a country where rigid censorship was the rule, Griboyedov in this way undertook to perform a daring mission of enlightenment with an altruistic motive. His was an heroic venture, for he had everything to lose and nothing to gain by arousing the animosity of the Russian Famusovs and Repetilovs.

As a typical bona fide Russian intellectual of his time, Tchatsky prefers reform to violent revolution. Like others of his class, his emotional resentment against insufferable conditions led him to subject Russian institutions to a critical analysis and to expose existing abuses to the public gaze. Although Griboyedov did not preach violence against the ruling classes, Tchatsky's "tirades," after a period of crystallization, reached their climax in the abortive Decembrist revolt of 1825—the first Russian revolution.

The influence of this play did not end with the Decembrist revolt. Subsequent Russian writers and leaders studied its verses by heart. Its influence is clearly discernible in Dostoyevsky's work. Tchatsky was undoubtedly a model for Dostoyevsky's Prince Myshkin in *The Idiot*. Prince Myshkin was Dostoyevsky's ideal man, and yet the society of the metropolis made of him an idiot. The same was true of Tchatsky. Griboyedov, in a letter to Katenin, referred to Tchatsky as the only sane person among twenty-five idiots, and yet, thanks to Sophia, the rumor of his madness was accepted as a fact. Rogozhin was apparently Dostoyevsky's version either of Skalozub or Molchalin, for he combines the traits of both.

In brief, *The Misfortune of Being Clever* was written for the elite. It was both a confession of and a protest against the corruption of the official world and the excesses of the younger generation. The shadow of Tchatsky hovered over Russian literature almost to the outbreak of the Russian Revolution of 1917. Its great, although indirect, influence on the latter event can hardly be overestimated.

BIBLIOGRAPHY

Abramovitch, G., and Goloventchenko, F., *Russkaya Literatura (Russian Literature)*, Moscow, 1935.

Mazour, A. G., *The First Russian Revolution, 1825*, University of California Press, 1937.

Mirsky, D. S., *A History of Russian Literature*, 1927.

Noyes, G. R., *Masterpieces of the Russian Drama*, N. Y., 1933.

Olgin, M. J., *Guide to Russian Literature*, N. Y., 1920.

Panayeva, A., *Vospominania (Memoirs)*, Leningrad, 1929.

Piksanov, N., *Tvortcheskaya Istoria "Goria ot Uma" (The Background of "The Misfortune of Being Clever")*, Moscow-Leningrad, 1928. Printed in Germany.

Wiener, Leo, *Anthology of Russian Literature*, Vol. II, N. Y., 1903.

Wiener, Leo, *Contemporary Drama of Russia*, Boston, 1924.

Mikhail Yurevitch Lermontov
1814-41

𝔐IKHAIL YUREVITCH LERMONTOV was born on the 15th of October, 1814, in Moscow, and killed in a duel on the 27th of July, 1841, at Piatigorsk, in the Caucasus. He was descended from a Scotchman by the name of George Lermont (Learmont), who was in the Polish service during the Time of Trouble in Russia (1598-1613), and was imprisoned by the Russians. In 1613 Lermont entered the Russian military service, and was given an estate in the province of Kostroma. Lermont traced his genealogy to Thomas the Rhymer, an ancient Scottish king and poet whose fame has been sung by Sir Walter Scott.

The father of the poet Lermontov was a poor captain in the infantry who possessed a small estate in the province of Tula. He married a wealthy girl in opposition to her mother's wishes. The marriage was not a happy one, and his wife died in 1817 leaving one son—the future poet. The young boy's grandmother took possession of the child and brought him up on her estate in the province of Pinza. He had French and English tutors and studied other European languages, including Greek.

In 1828, after a two-year sojourn in the Caucasus, which left a lasting impression, Lermontov was placed in the Boarding School for Young Nobles in Moscow, which was affiliated with Moscow University. In 1830 he entered the university but was expelled two years later for some trifling escapade. He then entered the School for Guards' Cadets in St. Petersburg, being graduated in 1834 as an officer of the Imperial Hussars. During his school career he had already learned to enjoy Pushkin and Schiller, but his favorite poet was Byron, whose life he chose as an example for himself to follow. It was during his career in the army, when he led the life common to officers of that time, that he produced his earliest poems—*The Peterhof Fête, The Lancer's Wife, Mongo,* and others.

Lermontov first attracted general attention with his *Ballad of the Tsar Ivan Vasilyevitch* (1832), and his prose novel *The Hero of Our Times* (1839-41). His rapid rise to fame really began when in 1837 he published *On the Death of a Poet,* a poem in which he openly reproached the courtiers for Pushkin's death. For this Nicholas I banished him to his favorite resort, the Caucasus, to serve as an ensign. In 1838 he was pardoned and returned to St. Petersburg. Two years later, after a duel with Barante, the son of the French Ambassador, he was again exiled to the Caucasus. Here, in 1841, he was killed in a duel by a fellow-officer, Major Martinov, at the early age of twenty-seven.

In addition to his longer poems, such as *The Demon* and *Mtsyri,* Lermontov wrote many short lyrics, such as *The Angel, The Prayer,* and *The Sail.*

THE PLOT OF *THE HERO OF OUR TIMES* (1839-41)

The most important of Lermontov's novels is *The Hero of Our Times,* which appeared with a preface in 1841, but which was originally published by installments in a Russian periodical, 1839-40. This autobiographical prose novel consists of a series of four parts, each complete in itself, although the hero is the same throughout.

Petchorin, the hero, is a man who has drained the cup of pleasure in civilized society to its dregs, and who, as a result, no longer cherishes any sentimental illusions concerning men, women, or life in general. In the cynical frame of mind engendered by disillusionment he can find no happiness and is overcome by ennui. Yet Petchorin possesses some admirable qualities: reckless courage and willingness to sacrifice himself—perhaps not so much from altruistic motives as on account of his contempt for life. After a series of adventures, he comes to his logical end in a duel.

FROM *THE DEMON*

And over the Caucasian ranges
Flew the exile from Paradise;
Beneath, Kazbek, like diamond's edges,
Flashed its eternal snow and ice;
Black as a creviced den confining
A serpent, deep below ran twining
The narrow chasm of Daryal;
And down its way, like lion roaring,
There leapt the stream of Terek, foaming,
With a frayed main along its back.
Both mountain beast and soaring eagle
Circling against the azure sky
Harked to the calling of the waters;
And golden clouds, due north, all day
Flew rapidly along its way
From far-off southern countries roaming.
And closely crowding gloomy rocks,
Mysteriously still and pensive,
Inclined their heads with snowy locks,
Watching the flickering waves, attentive.
And castle-towers on the cliffs
Scowled with dark menace through the hazes—
The giants, there to dominate
Where Caucasus its gateway raises!
Both wild and glorious was the world
Around him; but the haughty ghost
Contemptuously cast a glance
On the creations of his Lord,
And naught of what he saw or thought
Reflected in his countenance.

—Tr. by N. JARINTZOV

FROM *ON THE DEATH OF A POET*

And you, the proud and shameless progeny
Of fathers famous for their infamy,
You, who with servile heel have trampled down
The fragments of great names laid low by chance,
You, hungry crowd that swarms about the throne,
Butchers of freedom, and genius, and glory,

You hide behind the shelter of the law,
Before you, right and justice must be dumb!
But, parasites of vice, there's God's assize;
There is an awful court of law that waits.
You cannot reach it with the sound of gold;
It knows your thoughts beforehand and your deeds;
And vainly you shall call the lying witness;
That shall not help you any more;
And not with all the filth of all your gore
Shall you wash out the poet's righteous blood.

—Tr. by M. BARING

THE ANGEL

At midnight an angel was floating on high
    And softly he sang through the sky.
The crescent, the stars and the clouds in a throng
    All listened to his holy song.

He sang of the Spirits by sin undismayed
    In the bliss of green Paradise shade.
God's greatness he sang, and the praise of his Lord
    Rang true with deep heartfelt accord.

He carried a soul in his arms, to this life
    Of tears and of sorrowful strife,
And the tune of that lay, although wordless, sank deep
    For the soul through its lifetime to keep.

And here in this world, through the long, weary time,
    It pined with a longing sublime,
And the dull songs of earth could not ever replace
    The tunes of the Heavenly space.

—Tr. by N. JARINTZOV

THE PRAYER

In life's hard, trying moments,
    With sorrow in my breast,
I breathe a prayer most wonderful,
    Which ever brings me rest.

There is a power of blessedness
  In those sweet words enshrined,
Thought cannot grasp their sacred charm
  That calms the anxious mind.

Doubt stays no more, the soul is free,
  Her burden rolls away,
Her faith renewed, tears bring relief,
  When this sweet prayer I pray.

                        —Tr. by F. P. MARCHANT

Lermontov and Pushkin have a great deal in common. Both were of remote foreign extraction. One of Pushkin's ancestors was an Ethiopian Ras, while Lermontov's progenitor was a Scotchman. Pushkin was reared by an old nurse, Lermontov by his grandmother (Arseniev, born Stolypin). Both matured early, physically as well as mentally. Both began to write at an early age—about twelve—and in the French language. Each poet lived a chequered life, and thereby acquired the reputation of a Don Juan. Both died prematurely—Pushkin was barely thirty-eight, while Lermontov was only twenty-seven. Each met death tragically in a duel after indirectly predicting his fate: Pushkin in *Eugene Onegin*, Lermontov in *The Hero of Our Times*. Finally, both were essentially lyric poets, each called the Byron of Russia, although it seems evident now that in reality they emulated Byron rather than imitated him.

Although Lermontov as a poet is much superior to Pushkin, he is normally ranked as the second greatest poet of Russia. Unlike Pushkin, whose writings reflect the past and present of Russia and afford a glimpse into her future, Lermontov is primarily the poet of the Caucasus. He first visited this region as a lad, and was twice banished there—a punishment which proved to be a blessing in disguise. The prerequisite for a full appreciation of Lermontov's poetry is a knowledge of the Caucasus region as it was in the early nineteenth century. The Caucasus made of Lermontov more than a mere successor to Pushkin. It was due to the scenic grandeur of that environment that he inaugurated the age of romanticism in Russian literature.

The Caucasus has inspired many other Russian writers besides Lermontov. Its great natural beauty and the picturesque customs of the various nationalities living there seem to have served as a source of inspiration for all who visited the region. It will suffice to mention Pushkin, Tolstoy, and even Gorky, the last of the classical writers, whose first story, *Makar Chudra* (1892) was published in a local newspaper, *Kavkaz (The Caucasus),* when he worked in a railway depot in Tiflis. But Lermontov was the real exponent of the Caucasus. Without his influence, Tolstoy might never have written *The Cossacks,* which is in reality a new version of *The Hero of Our Times.* Moreover, Lermontov's *The Demon* may have inspired Andreyev's *Anathema.* Although much has been written about the Caucasus, and of late collections of Georgian stories and poems have been published, there is still room for a first-class analysis of the rôle of the Caucasus in Russian literature and politics.

It is in part due to Lermontov that Russian literature —a literature in which the East and the West meet—has such a fascination. Pushkin primarily interpreted western Russia to the Eastern world, whereas Lermontov, through the Caucasus, interpreted the East to western Russia and the world.

In spite of the fact that he claimed to possess "a Russian soul," Lermontov is a poet of eternity. The message of the poet of the Caucasus was universal, and from their snow-capped peaks he revealed the whole universe. Take away from Pushkin his Russian ballads, legends, and folklore and there would remain but a shadow. Not so with Lermontov. As long as there exist lofty, snow-capped mountains, beautiful valleys, blue or black seas, rivers, bright days, and starry nights, Lermontov will always be read and understood as a poet of nature.

Amidst the scenic splendor of the Caucasus, Lermontov matured early. If we did not know his age we could never guess that in some respects he was as mature at fifteen when he began *The Demon* as when he was killed at the age of twenty-seven. Only a mature mind could have produced the first Russian psychological novel, *The Hero of Our Times*, at the early age of twenty-five. The maturity of Lermontov is a subject which might well form the basis for a good dissertation.

After a careful study of Lermontov's life and literary career, and after visualizing that cliff in the Caucasus where he was fatally wounded in a duel, one is unconsciously reminded of the words of King David on the death of his faithful friend Jonathan (II Samuel 1:25): "How are the mighty fallen in the midst of the battle! Jonathan is slain upon thy high places." There could be no more fitting epitaph for the poet Lermontov.

BIBLIOGRAPHY

Abramovitch, G., and Goloventchenko, F., *Russkaya Literatura (Russian Literature)*, Moscow, 1935.

Baring, Maurice, *An Outline of Russian Literature*, Home University Library.

Essad-Bey, *The Twelve Secrets of the Caucasus*, N. Y., 1931.

Halle, Fannina W., *Women in the Soviet East*, N. Y., 1938.

Jarintzov, N., *Russian Poets and Poems*, Oxford, 1917.

Krup, Jacob, *Six Poems from the Russian of Pushkin and Lermontov*, N. Y., 1937.

Olgin, M. J., *Guide to Russian Literature*, N. Y., 1920.

Wiener, Leo, *Anthology of Russian Literature*, Vol. II, N. Y., 1903.

Nikolai Vasilyevitch Gogol
1809-52

NIKOLAI VASILYEVITCH GOGOL, often called the Russian Mark Twain, was born on March 31, 1809, at Sorotchintsy, in the Province of Poltava (Ukraine), and died on March 3, 1852, in Moscow. His ancestry may be traced to the Ukrainian Cossacks and clergy. By implication we are led to infer that his priestly forebear was a member of the Polish nobility.

Gogol's father, Vasily Afanasyevitch Gogol-Yanovsky, 1780-1825, passed most of his days in the secluded patriarchal environment of the farm where he was born. His life was that of a typical provincial nobleman of his time in Russia. Although listed as a government employee, his service was nominal rather than actual. In 1805 he retired with the lowest civilian rank conferred upon noblemen in pre-revolutionary Russia, that of Collegiate Assessor. Gogol-Yanovsky was a patron of the theatre, wrote verse, produced comedies, and asumed the rôle of an actor. Gardening was his hobby. Had he not confined his talent solely to his birthplace, he might have made a name for himself in the field of fine arts. In 1808 he married Masha (Mashenka) Kosiarovsky, daughter of a landowner, reared like himself in a devout patriarchal Orthodox family. Within a year Masha gave birth to a son called "Nicky."

Nikolai Vasilyevitch Gogol (Yanovsky was dropped), the father of modern Russian realism, was thus born to a family of moderately well-to-do "old world proprietors." He was a sickly child, and as a man he was frail and far from robust. His early environment and the vivid tales he heard in his father's home of the life and exploits of the Cossacks left an indelible imprint upon the lad's imagination.

Gogol's first tutor was a divinity student (seminarist). In 1819, however, he and his younger brother were taken to Poltava, capital of the province of that name, where they attended grade school for the better part of a year. After his brother's death, Gogol was sent to the Nyezhin Gymnasium in the province of Tchernigov, erected by Count Bezborodok for the children of privileged nobility. This institution was later renamed the Lyceum after its predecessor at Tsarskoe Selo, which Pushkin attended. Although Gogol's early scholastic record at the Lyceum was poor, he was unusually successful in his extracurricular activities, especially in journalism and drama. For *The Star*, a school periodical issued in longhand, he wrote "The Brothers Tverislavitch," but unfortunately this story was lost. Other stories and poems produced at the Gymnasium shared the same fate. Gogol entered heart and soul into the school theatrical activities, and his talent for the stage was acknowledged by all.

After his graduation from the Nyezhin Gymnasium in 1828, Gogol, accompanied by a schoolmate, Danilevsky, and a serf, Yakim, went to St. Petersburg. After an unsuccessful attempt to become an actor, he turned to literature, publishing his poem, "Italy," in the journal *A Son of the Fatherland*. In 1829 he published privately his *Hans Kuchelgarten*, an idyl in verse, under the signature of V. Alov, with an introduction by the "publisher." A series of unfavorable reviews led him to collect all the unsold copies of the idyl and consign them to the flames. After a fruitless search for a position in St. Petersburg, he decided to seek his fortune abroad. To finance the trip he availed himself of money provided by his mother for the payment of the interest on their mortgaged estate.

On his return from western Europe, Gogol finally obtained a part-time position in one of the chancelleries, and later secured a post in the Department of Appanages (Udely), where he remained from 1830-32. During these years he published a series of sketches, *Evenings at the*

Farmhouse near Dikanka. In these he exploited his grandfather's tales of Cossack life. The sketches attracted immediate attention, and served to introduce their author to the elite literary circle of Pushkin and Zhukovsky, who obtained for him an instructorship in history at St. Petersburg University in 1834. Although his first lecture was brilliantly delivered, he soon discovered that in the historical field he did not measure up to academic standards, and resigned to devote himself exclusively to literature.

From 1832-34 appeared Gogol's second series of Ukranian sketches, *Mirgorod* (collected in 1835), including among others, *Taras Bulba, Old World Proprietors,* and *How the Two Ivans Quarrelled. Taras Bulba,* rewritten and enlarged in 1842, presented a vivid picture of Cossack struggles with the Catholic Poles and Mohammedan Tartars in the sixteenth century. It was an epic in poetic prose and the best historical novel of its time. The other two sketches were detailed studies of the picturesque life of the villages of Little Russia (Ukraine). Later Gogol wrote a series of sketches in romantic vein, among which was *Arabesque* (1834), dealing with the life of Great Russia, and in particular with St. Petersburg. His best as well as the most epoch-making story in the history of Russian literature was *The Cloak* (1834).

In 1836 Gogol published his immortal comedy, *The Revizor (The Inspector-General),* in which the ignorance, corruption, trickery, and arbitrariness of provincial bureaucracy were held up to ridicule. This mordant satire elicited an outburst of rage from the incapable provincial officials at whom it was directed, and its representation would certainly have been banned, but for the Emperor Nicholas I who appeared rather to enjoy the situation thus created. Gogol's intense mortification at the general protest against his play undermined his health. For the next twelve years (1836-48), he spent most of his time abroad, principally in Rome.

In 1842 Gogol produced the first genuine Russian

novel, *Dead Souls*. It was a novel without a plot in which the author again satirized public abuses and the barbarism of provincial manners. Laughter with tears in the background and a note of irony are the dominant notes in this remarkable novel, in which Gogol introduced a succession of types from all classes of Russian society. The second volume of *Dead Souls* was practically finished in 1845, when the author, in a fit of hypochondria, a disease which had made of him a religious mystic and a champion of autocracy, consigned the precious manuscript to the flames. A rough draft and detached scraps of it discovered after his death were pieced together and published by his friends. These survivals clearly reflect Gogol's declining intellectual powers. To cap the climax he published in 1847 *Excerpts from Correspondence with My Friends* which marked the nadir of his artistic work.

In 1848 Gogol made a pilgrimage to the Holy Land. He died in Russia on March 3 (February 21, O.S.), 1852, at eight o'clock in the morning.

THE PLOT OF *THE CLOAK* (1834)

Akaky Akakiyevitch holds a humble position as a letter-copying clerk in one of the government departments. His life has been devoted to the copying of letters for so long that he is incapable of any other employment even in leisure moments. The other clerks constantly make him the butt of their jests. Akaky Akakiyevitch wears a rusty metal-colored uniform which has been patched and re-patched until it can be mended no more. Petrovitch the tailor insists that his patron must have a new cloak. From now on the poor clerk's thoughts are focussed upon one objective—the future cloak. At length, after months of self-denial, during which time Akaky Akakiyevitch deprives himself of tea and candles and half-starves himself to secure the necessary money, the cloak, his one pride and joy, is obtained. The clerks of his department decide that the occasion merits a special celebration, and Akaky Akakiyevitch is persuaded to attend a party at the home of one of their number. On the way home from this party his new cloak is stolen by robbers to the utter despair of its owner, who in vain seeks redress from the police and from a prominent official recommended by the clerks. In the cold winter storms Akaky Akakiyevitch contracts a fever and dies of exposure. After his death the rumor prevails that his ghost haunts the Kalinkin Bridge and other parts of the city, dragging cloaks from the shoulders of terrified persons, until at last he seizes the cloak of the prominent official who refused to help him in his dire need.

THE PLOT OF *THE REVIZOR (THE INSPECTOR-GENERAL)* (1836-42)

The leading character in this five-act comedy is a half-starved chancery scribe by the name of Khlestakov, who has been marooned in a provincial town after losing his money at cards. The mayor and his corrupt subordinates mistake the young gambler for the Inspector-General whose arrival, incognito, is expected hourly. For the news of the Inspector's unannounced visit has been revealed in a private letter opened and read by the prying postmaster. Khlestakov is invited to accept the mayor's hospitality, and there follows a tale of corruption, jealousy, and brutality in which Khlestakov so far forgets the bounds of propriety as to make love to the mayor's wife and daughter. After accepting bribes under the guise of loans from various officials he escapes from the town, leaving behind him a sarcastic letter which the postmaster reads to a perplexed assembly of provincial notables. At this inauspicious moment the door opens and a policeman announces the arrival of the real Revizor.

THE PLOT OF *DEAD SOULS* (1842)

Paul Ivanovitch Tchitchikov is a plausible, ambitious, and entertaining impostor who travels about provincial Russia on a curious mission, accompanied by his valet Petrushka and his coachman Selifan. Tchitchikov has already been involved in several shady enterprises, all undertaken for the love of gain, and all ending disastrously for him. As chief clerk in a government department, as a member of the Building Commission, and again as head of the Customs, Tchitchikov has suffered dismissal for the misappropriation of funds. After these unfortunate experiences he conceives the unique idea of retrieving his fortunes through the purchase of the dead souls of Russian serfs. With serfdom still in vogue in Russia, each landowner paid a poll tax to the Government for every soul, dead or alive, listed as his property in the last census returns. Tchitchikov's ambitious program is to buy these dead souls for little or nothing from willing landowners only too pleased to be freed from the responsibility of the poll tax, mortgage them at a bank, and with the money secured to purchase an estate and live souls, thereby procuring a comfortable income and a respectable source of livelihood for the heirs he anticipates.

With this purpose in view, Tchitchikov arrives in the provincial town of N. Posing as a Collegiate Councillor and landowner, he hastens to pay his respects to the Governor, the Vice-Governor, the Public Prosecutor, the President of the Local Council, the Chief of Police, and other local officials, making such an excellent impression upon one and all that he is deluged with invitations to evening parties and dinners.

After this auspicious beginning, and with his reputation securely established, Tchitchikov sets about his business of acquiring dead souls from the neighboring landowners. The amiable Manilov donates all of his free of charge. The widow Korobotchka, an obstinate old woman, sells hers at fifteen rubles per soul. The boorish Sobakevitch, after stating his price at one hundred rubles, contents himself with two and a half rubles per soul. The miserly Plushkin surrenders one hundred and twenty dead souls on Tchitchikov's guarantee to take over the poll tax. Only with the rascally Nozdrev does Tchitchikov fail to reach a satisfactory agreement, having at last met his match in the art of roguery. He hastens to town to secure the proper registration of his purchases, a step greatly facilitated by his previous contacts with the local officials. His extensive purchases now ensure for Tchitchikov his reputation as a wealthy landowner and a highly eligible bachelor, since the officials concerned have no idea that the souls he purchased were dead. He is lionized by the entire community, and particularly by the ladies.

With his scheme well on the way to a successful fruition, Tchitchikov suddenly meets with frustration. He has not reckoned with the tongue of the garrulous widow Korobotchka and with the angry Nozdrev. The widow spreads wild rumors about his visit to her estate which eventually reach the ear of the Vice-Governor. The drunken Nozdrev makes a public declaration at the Governor's ball of Tchitchikov's nefarious scheme. As these rumors spread from house to house, they become more and more extravagant, until at length Tchitchikov himself is forced to flee, before the local officials who now show him the cold shoulder can contrive to bring him to justice.

FROM *DEAD SOULS*

... Tchitchikov smiled with gratification at the sensation of driving fast. For what Russian does not love to drive fast? Which of us does not at times yearn to give his horses their head, and to let them go, and to cry, "To the devil with the world!"? At such moments a great force seems to uplift one as on wings; and one flies, and everything else flies, but contrariwise—both the *verst* stones, and traders riding on the shafts of their waggons, and the forest with dark lines of spruce and fir amid which may be heard the axe of the woodcutter and the croaking of the raven. Yes, out of a dim, remote distance the road comes toward one, and while nothing save the sky and the light clouds through which the moon is cleaving her way seem halted, the brief glimpses wherein one can discern nothing clearly have in them a pervading touch of mystery. Ah, *troika, troika,* swift as a bird, who was it first invented you? Only among a hardy race of folk can you have come to birth—only in a land which, though poor and rough, lies spread over half the world, and spans *versts* the counting whereof would leave one with aching eyes. Nor are you a modishly-fashioned vehicle of the road—a thing of clamps and iron. Rather, you are a vehicle but shapen and fitted with the axe or chisel of some handy peasant of Yaroslav. Nor are you driven by a coachman clothed in German livery, but by a man bearded and mittened. See him as he mounts, and flourishes his whip, and breaks into a long-drawn song! Away like the wind go the horses, and the wheels, with their spokes, become transparent circles, and the road seems to quiver beneath them, and a pedestrian, with a cry of astonishment, halts to watch the vehicle as it flies, flies, flies on its way until it becomes lost on the ultimate horizon—a speck amid a cloud of dust!

And you, Russia of mine—are not you also speeding like a *troika* which nought can overtake? Is not the road smoking beneath your wheels, and the bridges thundering as you cross them, and everything being left in the rear, and the spectators, struck with the portent, halting to wonder whether you be not a thunderbolt launched from heaven? What does that awe-inspiring progress of yours foretell? What is the unknown force which lies within your mysterious steeds? Surely the winds themselves must abide in their manes, and every vein in their bodies be an ear stretched to catch the celestial message which bids them, with iron-girded breasts, and hooves which barely touch the earth as they gallop, fly forward on a mission of God? Whither, then, are you speeding, O Russia of mine? Whither? Answer me! But no answer comes—only the weird sound of your collar-bells. Rent into a thousand shreds, the air roars past you, for you are overtaking the whole world, and shall one day force all nations, all empires to stand aside, to give you way!

In the the brief span of ten years, from 1832 to 1842, years of constructive and prolific work, Gogol gave to the world the best he had to offer. Prior to 1832 his works bore the mark of immaturity, and those produced subsequent to 1842 were in the nature of an anticlimax to the zenith of his literary career. It would almost seem that in these ten years of voluminous production the fire of his genius had been reduced to ashes, and the fuel to replenish it was lacking.

In the history of Russian literature, 1842 should be hailed as a red-letter year. For the publication of *Dead Souls* in that year marked the birth of the genuinely realistic Russian novel, thereby inaugurating the age of prose in Russian literature. Gogol was the father of the Russian novel, and as previously stated, it was the novel which occupied the most prominent place in the field of Russian letters.

Although Gogol's work reflected Russian life as a whole, we immediately associate it with South Russia. Just as when we speak of Lermontov we visualize the Caucasus, when we turn to Gogol we think chiefly in terms of the Ukraine. Gogol first attained popularity by his sketches of Ukrainian life. These sketches were widely read, not because of their rich content, but chiefly because they revealed a new world to the people of Great Russia. The North Russians of the period in question looked upon Southern Russia as the Americans for many years regarded the West. Just as the stories of the wild West, real or fictitious, made a tremendous appeal to men in the more settled parts of the United States, so Gogol's early sketches of Ukrainian life, present or past, stirred the imagination of Russians elsewhere. His historical novel, *Taras Bulba,* referred to above, became the first and foremost classic on the Russian Cossacks. The sixteenth-century Cossacks depicted in this novel held the same appeal for the Russian reader as the exploits of the Western cowboys for Americans. These tales hold the key to Gogol's widespread popularity.

The Cloak. Gogol's famous story *The Cloak* also broke new ground in Russian letters. *The Cloak* is not the best story in Russian literature, as some critics claim, but it was the most epoch-making literary production. Here for the first time, the sad plight of the low-salaried chancery clerk attracted the attention of Russian society. Prior to this, the Akaky Akakiyevitches, if they were ever mentioned, received only incidental recognition, and never captured a leading rôle. There were thousands of them in Russia, toiling for a mere pittance, yet striving to maintain the standard of living and of dressing demanded of them. In *The Cloak* they received for the first time a new deal when Gogol relegated the titled bureaucracy to the background in a story which was essentially economic and social. He therefore gave a new tone to Russian literature. That note of sympathy for the oppressed, so characteristic of later Russian writers, who selected now one group, now another as the object of their concern, reached its zenith under Dostoyevsky. Gogol, in addition to arousing the public conscience, laid the foundations for a new literary school in which many of his successors were trained. It is hardly an exaggeration to say in the words of one great Russian author, Dostoyevsky, that all Russian literature emanated from that cloak! So great was its influence that Russian literary critics have enumerated about two hundred stories written in the same vein.

While *The Cloak* is essentially a sociological story, later critics have sometimes read into it a religious significance. It is a well-known fact that Gogol was a theological student, steeped in church folklore, particularly in the lives of the saints. Bearing this in mind, some of his critics have regarded the story as a kind of parable, in which the "cloak" in reality stood for the "devil," or for any material object with which man might become obsessed, thereby bringing upon himself untold suffering not only in this world but in the hereafter. If this, too, was Gogol's purpose, we are confronted with the anomaly of a religious mystic who became the founder of a sociological, materialistic literature. Just as Tolstoy, the moralist, was responsible for introducing the sex novel into Russian literature *(Kreutzer Sonata)*, so Gogol, to whom in later life all mundane things were totally insignificant, laid the foundation in *The Cloak* for materialism in classical Russian fiction.

The Revizor. As we have already stated, Gogol evinced his talent for drama at an early age. He wrote many plays, but the best of all was *The Revizor (The Inspector-General)*. *The Revizor* is the national comedy of Russia, and ever since its initial performance it has retained its crown of popularity. Because it holds up corruption and inefficient bureaucracy to ridicule, it is a play that will endure under any regime. Although some Western critics who approach the analysis of Russian plays with Western tools have maintained that there is no such thing as Russian drama, they have failed to realize that the Russian playwright, consciously or unconsciously, stresses character portrayal at the expense of action and other technicalities that loom so large to the Western mind. In the typical Russian play the plot evolves from and is an outgrowth of character portrayal. The same is true, not only of Russian drama, but of Russian literature in general. Russians emphasize the *who* not the *what*. With reference to *The Revizor*, however, it is universally conceded that even technically speaking the play measures up to the standards of a Western drama.

The Revizor has done more to effect a bureaucratic housecleaning than any number of serious articles directed against a corrupt officialdom. The fact that the Emperor Nicholas I himself overruled the censor and granted permission to stage the play was sufficient to stir up some activity in the various chancelleries of autocratic Russia. The Emperor's position in this matter was obvious. He wanted to show a corrupt officialdom that he was aware of what was going on in Russia.

Upon closer analysis of *The Revizor*, we see that Gogol, in spite of his merciless exposure of the bureaucracy, did not attack the institution of autocracy. He merely pointed out the incongruity between the office and the behavior of its incumbent, between duty and abuse of power or privilege. Gogol's criticism was constructive rather than destructive. Constructive criticism is indispensable in every field of human endeavor, particularly in the state. For this reason Nicholas I, the most autocratic tsar of the nineteenth century, permitted the staging of *The Revizor*.

While the scene of *The Revizor* was laid in a small locality, its message was national. Encouraged by the Emperor's support and by the elite of Russian society—in spite of the bitter criticism of officials at whom the play was aimed—Gogol conceived a new work, almost a sequel to *The Revizor*, which was destined to play a greater rôle in the history of Russia, and which dealt a severe blow to the institution of serfdom. The work in question, which has come to be of the utmost historical importance, was later called *Dead Souls*.

Dead Souls. Whereas the action of *The Revizor* took place in a single town, and was confined to one restricted group of people among whom there was not a single redeeming feature—worse than Sodom and Gomorrah—the setting for *Dead Souls* was Russia in miniature. It embraced various classes and social strata, officials and civilians, landowners and serfs, who pass before the reader as on a literary screen. These characters had their prototypes in real life. *Dead Souls* may therefore be termed the first genuinely realistic Russian novel, because it dealt with Russian life *per se*, with a burning issue which occupied the best minds of Russia throughout the nineteenth century—the problem of serfdom—a parallel to which, against a different background, may be found in the United States. The chief difference is that the Russian serfs, unlike the American negroes, were of the same stock and the same religion as their masters.

If it is true that Pushkin suggested the theme of the novel in question, the title and message are certainly Gogol's. Originally he intended to write a trilogy, entitled "The Adventures of Tchitchikov," but all that remains to posterity is the first part and pieces of the second. In the second part Gogol intended to work out the moral regeneration of Tchitchikov—an idea which provided a pattern for subsequent Russian writers, particularly for Dostoyevsky *(Crime and Punishment)* and

Tolstoy *(Resurrection)*. The moral is the same, for Tchitchikov, Raskolnikov, and Nekhludov were victims of their environment and ruling passions. But Gogol, by the regeneration of Tchitchikov, would have delivered an indirect attack on the political and social structure of autocratic Russia, and that was not his purpose. To understand Gogol, one must remember that his criticism was constructive. He aimed at individuals—not at the body politic. He held up corruption to ridicule but did not question the divine authority of autocracy. He rather aimed at those who by their very abuse of power undermined it, as subsequent events were to show.

The change in title from "The Adventures of Tchitchikov" to *Dead Souls* was not, therefore, accidental. In the light of his constructive criticism and profound knowledge of Russian institutions *Dead Souls* represented the accurate diagnosis of a competent physician. For the appellation *Dead Souls* can be attributed not only to the deceased serfs in the novel, but to Russia as a whole. A combination of ignorance, superstition, corruption, inefficiency, graft, and abuse of power produced an environment in Russia only for dead souls—not for the living. Gogol called the child by its name. Small wonder that when Pushkin first heard the book read he cried: "God, what a sad country Russia is!"

Dead Souls was the most mature and the most profound work that Gogol produced—the crown of his creative imagination. As in the case of *The Brothers Karamazov* by Dostoyevsky, Gogol's masterpiece remained unfinished. Although, technically speaking, *Dead Souls* is a novel without a plot, the character of Tchitchikov binds all its separate parts together. The various chapters are like distinct sections of one big department store.

Before Gogol only individual protests were voiced against existing corruption and the misery of the unprivileged classes. Gogol not only summed these up, but diagnosed the disease. His successors suggested remedies —remedies which fell into two main categories—Westernization and Slavophilism.

BIBLIOGRAPHY

Abramovitch, G., and Goloventchenko, F., *Russkaya Literatura (Russian Literature)*, Moscow, 1935.

Baring, Maurice, *An Outline of Russian Literature*, Home University Library.

Kropotkin, Peter, *Russian Literature*, N. Y., 1905.

Lavrin, Janko, *Gogol*, London, 1926.

Mirsky, D. S., *A History of Russian Literature*, N. Y., 1927.

Niva (periodical), No. 11, Vol. XL, Russia, 1909.

Noyes, G. R., *Masterpieces of the Russian Drama*, N. Y., 1933.

Olgin, M. J., *Guide to Russian Literature*, N. Y., 1920.

Phelps, W. L., *Essays on Russian Novelists*, N. Y., 1916.

Tchizhevsky, Dm., *"Gogol's Cloak"* (in Russian), *Annales Contemporaines*, LXXII, Paris, 1938.

Tsanoff, R. A., *The Problem of Life in the Russian Novel*, Rice Institute, 1917.

Wiener, Leo, *Anthology of Russian Literature*, Vol. II, N. Y., 1903.

Wiener, Leo, *The Contemporary Drama of Russia*, Boston, 1924.

Yarmolinsky, Avrahm, *Russian Literature*, Chicago, 1931.

Ivan Alexandrovitch Gontcharov

1812-91

*I*VAN ALEXANDROVITCH GONTCHAROV was born on July 18, 1812, in Simbirsk, on the banks of the Volga and the Sviyagi, and died on September 27, 1891, in St. Petersburg. He is one of the few Russian authors whose ancestry cannot be traced to foreign extraction. Gontcharov's father was a wealthy merchant, and since the educational facilities of Simbirsk proved entirely inadequate, he sent his son at the age of ten to a private school for children of the nobility, from which he returned home only for his vacations. Later young Gontcharov matriculated at the Moscow School of Commerce and attended Moscow University, where he majored in literature. After his graduation from the University in 1836 he entered the civil service, where he occupied several positions, first as secretary to the Governor of Simbirsk, then in the Ministry of Finance, and finally in the Department of Censorship. For a time he was also editor of the official organ, *The Northern Post*.

The lust for adventure seized Gontcharov in the middle of the century, and between 1852 and 1854 he made a world tour, even visiting Japan as secretary to Admiral Putiatin, to negotiate a commercial treaty. On his return to Russia he published a collection of stories describing his voyage around the world under the title *Frigate Pallas* (1856-57). He retired with a pension in 1873.

Gontcharov began his literary career by publishing translations from Schiller, Goethe, and the English novelists. He also translated one of the novels of Eugène Sue. His first original work was *A Common Story*, a novel which appeared in 1847 and received immediate recognition. This was followed by *Frigate Pallas*, mentioned above, which was also a great success because the descriptions of his voyage to Japan and elsewhere were the choicest of their kind in Russian literature. In 1859 Gontcharov's immortal novel, *Oblomov*, was published, followed by *Precipice* ten years later. Of his three novels *Oblomov* is much the best.

THE PLOT OF *OBLOMOV* (1859)

The story concerns Ilya Ilyitch Oblomov, a typical well-to-do landowner, who faces spiritual, if not actual physical, death from a life of inactivity, and whose inertia is so great that he can scarcely take the trouble to rise from his bed. Oblomov has lived in St. Petersburg for twelve years on the income of an estate near the Asiatic border which he never visits, but which he continually plans to modernize. Because life seems too arduous and exacting he has given up his career in the government service, and, little by little his social activities, for dressing gown and slippers. He now rarely leaves his unkempt apartments, where he is cared for by an old family serf, Zahar, whose grouchiness is only exceeded by his laziness. A few friends continue to visit and dine with him, among them Tarantyev, an unscrupulous parasite, who serves as a clerk in a government office, and who is more adept in solving other people's problems than his own.

On the morning when the story opens Oblomov receives a triple dose of bad news—a notice from the landlord that he must move, a letter from his bailiff to the effect that all is not well with his estate and that his income from it will be reduced considerably, and a warning from his doctor that a continuation of his present mode of existence—rich food plus inactivity—will soon kill him. Oblomov finds it impossible to cope with one of these problems, much less all of them.

At this critical juncture Oblomov's one tried and trusted friend, Andrey Stolz, a successful but well-educated and much-traveled businessman of German extraction, returns to St. Petersburg. Stolz resolves that "now or never" he must save his friend from Oblomovism

—this dreaming of dreams which are never realized because their practical achievement requires an exertion which would disturb Oblomov's unruffled existence.

Stolz introduces Oblomov to his young friend Olga Sergeyevna, an attractive girl of rare beauty of character with a talent for music. Her singing temporarily arouses Oblomov from his lethargy, and his love for Olga reawakens his youthful ambition to live a useful life. Oblomov dreams of a home, a wife and children, a life of peaceful serenity. But the summer months pass by and he takes none of the practical steps necessary to put his affairs in order at Oblomovka. Consequently he postpones time and again any formal request for Olga's hand.

Through the efforts of Tarantyev, Oblomov meanwhile moves to the Vyborg side of St. Petersburg, to the home of the buxom widow Agafya Matveyevna Pshenitsyn and her rascally brother Ivan Matveyevitch. The widow, although uncultured and unintelligent, is a good-hearted and capable housewife. When the obstacles to his marriage with Olga begin to depress Oblomov, he makes fewer and fewer trips to her home. Finally Olga recognizes that not even she can save him from himself, and with a sick heart, she breaks their secret engagement. Oblomov rapidly lapses into the state of inertia in which we found him at the beginning of the novel. His landlady and her children become the center of his little world beyond which he does not stir.

Olga, in her efforts to forget, travels with her aunt to Paris, where she again meets Stolz. He discovers that he loves her, and in spite of her love for Oblomov, he soon succeeds in making her his wife. A year later Stolz visits Oblomov, only to find that he has become the victim of the fraudulent greed of Tarantyev and Ivan Matveyevitch, the landlady's brother. Once more he sets his friend's affairs in order, but he cannot pry him loose from his environment. On a subsequent visit, several years later, Stolz makes a final effort, for Olga's sake, to carry Oblomov off to the country. He finds too late that his friend has married the stupid but well-meaning widow, has had a stroke, and that there is no longer any hope for his regeneration. Two years later Oblomov dies of inactivity and overeating. Stolz adopts his young son, Andrey, to educate him in his own home and to save him from an uncultured environment. The widow Agafya Matveyevna continues to grieve for Oblomov, whose life for seven years was the focal point of her existence. Zahar becomes a beggar.

FROM *OBLOMOV*

Ilya Ilyitch's complexion was neither rosy nor dark nor pale, but indefinite, or perhaps it seemed so because there was a certain slackness about the muscles of his face, unusual at his age; this may have been due to lack of fresh air or exercise, or to some other reason. The smooth and excessively white skin of his neck, his small soft hands and plump shoulders, suggested a certain physical effeminacy. His movements were restrained and gentle; there was a certain lazy gracefulness about them even if he were alarmed. If his mind was troubled, his eyes were clouded, his forehead wrinkled, and an interplay of hesitation, sadness, and fear was reflected in his face; but the disturbance seldom took the form of a definite idea and still more seldom reached the point of a decision. It merely found expression in a sigh and died down in apathy or drowsiness.

How well Oblomov's dress suited his calm features and soft body! He wore a dressing-gown of Persian material, a regular Eastern dressing-gown without anything European about it—no tassels, no velvet, no waist, and so roomy that he could wrap it round him twice. The sleeves, in true Asiatic fashion, gradually widened from the wrists to the shoulders. Although the dressing-gown had lost its original freshness and was shiny in places with an acquired and not a natural lustre, it still preserved its brilliant Eastern coloring, and the stuff was as strong as ever.

The dressing-gown had a number of invaluable qualities in Oblomov's eyes: it was soft and pliable; it did not get in his way; it obeyed the least movement of his body, like a docile slave.

Oblomov never wore a tie or a waistcoat at home because he liked comfort and freedom. He wore long, soft, wide slippers; when he got up from bed he put his feet straight into them without looking.

Lying down was not for Ilya Ilyitch either a necessity as it is for a sick or a sleepy man, or an occasional need as it is for a person who is tired, or a pleasure as it is for a sluggard: it was his normal state. When he was at home—and he was almost always at home—he was lying down, and invariably in the same room, the one in which we have found him and which served him as bedroom, study, and reception-room. He had three more rooms, but he seldom looked into them, only, perhaps, in the morning when his servant swept his study—which did not happen every day. In those other rooms the furniture was covered and the curtains were drawn.

The room in which Ilya Ilyitch was lying at the first glance seemed splendid. It had a mahogany bureau, two silk-upholstered sofas, a handsome screen embroidered with fruit and flowers never to be seen in nature. It had silk curtains, carpets, several pictures, bronze, and china, and a number of pretty knick-knacks. But the experienced eye of a person of good taste would detect at once that all these things were put there merely to comply with unavoidable conventions. This was all Oblomov had in mind when he furnished his study. A refined taste could not have been content with these heavy, clumsy mahogany chairs and shaky chiffoniers. The back of one of the sofas had sunk in, the inlaid wood had come unstuck in places.

The pictures, the vases, and the knick-knacks were no better.

The owner himself, however, looked at the furniture of his study coldly and unconcernedly, as though wondering who could have brought all this stuff there. It was because of Oblomov's indifference towards his property, and perhaps because of the still greater indifference of his servant, Zahar, that the study struck one, at a more careful inspection, by its neglected and untidy condition. Dusty cobwebs hung in festoons round the pictures on the walls; mirrors, instead of reflecting objects, might have served as tablets for writing memoranda in the dust; there were stains on the carpets; a towel had been left on the sofa. Almost every morning a dirty plate, with a salt-cellar and a bone from the previous night's supper, was to be seen on the crumb-covered table.

If it had not been for this plate and for a freshly smoked pipe by the bed, and for the owner himself lying in it, one might have thought that the room was uninhabited—everything was so dusty and faded and devoid of all traces of human presence. It is true there were two or three open books and a newspaper on the chiffoniers, an inkstand and pens on the bureau; but the open pages had turned yellow and were covered with dust—evidently they had been left so for weeks; the newspaper dated from last year, and if one dipped a pen into the inkstand a startled fly might perhaps come buzzing out of it.

. . . .

. . . "It's—" Stolz broke off, trying to think of a word to describe this kind of existence—"it's a sort of . . . Oblomovism," he said at last.

"Ob-lo-movism!" Ilya Ilyitch pronounced slowly, marveling at the strange word and dividing it into syllables, "Ob-lo-movism!"

He looked at Stolz with a strange fixity.

"What, then, is the ideal life, you think? What is not Oblomovism?" he asked timidly and without enthusiasm. "Doesn't everyone strive for the very same things that I dream of? Why," he added more confidently, "isn't it the purpose of all your running about, your passions, wars, trade, politics—to secure rest, to attain this ideal of a lost paradise?"

"Your very Utopia is that of an Oblomov," Stolz retorted.

"Everyone seeks peace and rest," Oblomov defended himself.

"No, not everyone, and ten years ago you, too, sought something very different."

"What was it?" Oblomov asked in perplexity, turning his thoughts on the past.

"Think, try to remember. Where are your books, your translations?"

"Zahar put them away," Oblomov answered. "I expect they are in a corner somewhere."

"In a corner!" Stolz said reproachfully. "In the same corner as your plans 'to work so long as you have any strength left, because Russia needs hands and brains to make use of her inexhaustible wealth' (these were your words); to work in order to rest more happily, and to rest meant to live in another artistic, beautiful aspect of life, the life of poets and artists. Has Zahar put all these plans of yours in a corner too? Do you remember how after you had finished with books you wanted to visit foreign countries so as to know and to love your own the better? 'The whole of life is work and thought,' you used to repeat then; 'obscure, unrecognized but unremitting work'; 'to die knowing that you have done your share'—in what corner have you put that?"

. . . .

"You will stop working some day," Oblomov remarked.

"Never. Why should I?"

"When you have doubled your capital," Oblomov said.

"I won't stop when I have squared it."

"Then why do you work so hard," Oblomov began after a pause, "if it isn't for the sake of providing for your future and then retiring to the country?"

"Oblomovism in the country!" Stolz said.

"Or to attain a high rank and social position and then enjoy in honorable inactivity a well-earned rest?..."

"Oblomovism in Petersburg," Stolz answered.

"When, then, are you going to live?" Oblomov asked, annoyed at his remarks. "Why slave all your life?"

"For the sake of the work itself and nothing else. Work gives form, and completeness, and a purpose to life, at any rate for me. Here, now, you have banished work from your life, and what is the result? I shall try to raise you up, perhaps for the last time. If after this you will still go on sitting here with the Tarantyevs and Alexeyevs you will be done for, you will be a burden to yourself. Now or never!" he concluded.

Oblomov listened, looking at him with anxious eyes. It was as though his friend were holding a mirror before him and he was frightened when he recognized himself.

"Don't scold me, Andrey, better help me!" he began with a sigh. "I suffer from it myself; had you seen me earlier in the day and heard the way I was bewailing my fate and digging my own grave you would not have had the heart to reproach me. I know and understand it all, but I have no strength, no will. Give me some of your will and intelligence and lead me where you like. I may perhaps follow you, but alone I shall not stir from the spot. You are quite right, it is now or never. In another year it will be too late!"

Oblomov, the classical Russian novel produced by Gontcharov, was an elongation of, if not a sequel to, *Dead Souls.* In abridged form it might have served as an additional chapter in that plotless novel. Both Gogol and Gontcharov diagnosed the national distemper—one labeled it *dead souls,* the other *Oblomovism.* However, in spite of Gontcharov's emphasis upon the negative side of human nature, *Oblomov* is not so gloomy as *Dead Souls,* and the atmosphere is fresher. When his novel first appeared it made a tremendous impression, for the Oblomovs were more familiar to the reading public than the Tchitchikovs, and many a Russian recognized himself in Oblomov as in a mirror. As Turgenev once said, "As long as there remains one Russian, Oblomov will be remembered."

At the same time *Oblomov* paved the way for practically all of Turgenev's novels. All Turgenev's negative masculine types found their prototype in Ilya Oblomov, while Olga, Gontcharov's heroine, became the pattern for all the active feminine characters of Turgenev. It occasioned no surprise to many Russians when Gontcharov hurled the accusation of plagiarism against the great novelist of the century—Ivan Turgenev. But instead of being condemned, Turgenev was completely exonerated from this literary heresy—and justly so. The similarity of their ideas was a mere coincidence, for both novelists belonged to the same class, were confronted with similar problems, and in the course of everyday life came into actual contact with the types whom they portrayed.

In the classical novel *Oblomov*, Gontcharov depicted the life of the idle-rich nobility of the middle of the nineteenth century from the cradle to the grave. No other author in Russian literature known to us has ever given such a vivid and faithful portrait of Russia's Oblomovs. Oblomov spent the better part of his life in dressing gown and slippers—the outward symbols of the mental and physical stagnation of the wearer—and it took Gontcharov an entire chapter to get him out of bed! It is very difficult to give in English the exact connotation of the Russian word *pokoy*, which implies *repose, seclusion,* and *unruffled peace*. Oblomov sacrificed everything to gain *pokoy*. This word supplies the key to Oblomov's character and to Oblomovism. *Pokoy* occupies the same prominent place in *Oblomov* as *smirenie* in the work of Dostoyevsky. *Smirenie* was a sublimation of *pokoy*. Both were distinctly Slavic traits, particularly characteristic of those directly or indirectly attached to the land. It was natural, therefore, that Oblomov and Oblomovism should become household words throughout Russia, just as Tartuffe in France, Pecksniff in England, and Babbitt in America. From this time on the idle-rich nobility became a legitimate target for attack, and many Russian authors were not slow to avail themselves of this opportunity.

In *Oblomov*, Gontcharov depicts the clash between tradition and innovation in the nineteenth-century Russia —between the old patriarchal landowners and the new industrial bourgeoisie represented by the successful and enterprising businessman; between rural life and urbanization; between culture and civilization. In this respect Gontcharov may be considered a forerunner of Tchekhov, whose own version of Oblomovism is to be found in all his plays. Throughout Tchekhov's works—and this is particularly true of *The Cherry Orchard*—there runs like a scarlet thread, the same clash between the old and the new in Russia. Ranevsky in *The Cherry Orchard* was Tchekhov's version of Oblomov, and Lopakhin his version of Stolz. Tchekhov skilfully wove the problem of ruralism versus urbanization into the texture of this play.

Oblomov at his best was, as we have seen, a true representative of a declining patriarchal society whose roots were fixed firmly in the past. It took many generations to achieve the society of which Oblomov was, perhaps, the last representative. Gontcharov's novel was therefore in a sense a monument to that past. Until the dawn of the "practical age" Oblomovism represented an ideal devoutly to be wished. When Gontcharov wrote, *pokoy*, the *summum bonum* of life to every Oblomov, was rapidly becoming a lost horizon. When the age of industry began to encroach upon patriarchal society, in protest against the hustle-bustle of the practical businessman, the Oblomovs turned their backs upon it all, and defied the world in dressing gown and slippers. They clung till the last ditch to what they believed to be the Russian heritage.

Gontcharov, himself a *barin* (nobleman), dealt with Oblomov sympathetically. He did not condemn everything in Oblomovism, and upon Oblomov himself he bestowed more positive than negative traits. It was not even Gontcharov's purpose to deprive the Oblomovs entirely of *pokoy*, for he was never an enemy of the existing order—but rather to place a price upon it. He wanted to purge Oblomovism of its less desirable attributes, laziness and neglect, and to add to it a new meaning. *Pokoy* as the reward of labor and the exercise of practical ability was his ideal.

In Stolz, Gontcharov attempted to portray the practical and enterprising businessman—the antithesis of Oblomov—whom he prophetically recognized as the leader of the new age. Gontcharov seems to have realized that it would take many Stolzes under Russian names to change the inherent characteristics of the Oblomovs. He would like to have seen Oblomov co-operate with Stolz.

But Oblomov could not bring himself to adopt a mode of life which necessitated work and action, as well as everyday contact with the seamy side of life from which he held himself aloof, and he turned a deaf ear to Stolz's dreams of the approaching age of industrialism. There remained, therefore, only a choice between Oblomovism and Stolzism, and, as we have seen, Gontcharov predicted the triumph of the latter. He could only hope that victory would not come at the expense of the strong points of Oblomov's generation. In these two characters, Oblomov and Stolz, we find the forerunners of the nation-wide controversy between the Slavophiles and the Westernizers. Oblomov's better traits were the source of Slavophilism. Stolz's ideas were echoed again and again by the Westernizers.

In the person of Olga, Gontcharov has drawn a portrait of the new woman in Russia who began to wrestle with Oblomovism. Herself a member of the St. Petersburg nobility, she was, nevertheless, ahead of her contemporaries. She was active and persistent, with a fine mind, yet deep and tender feelings. She was also honest, decent, and sincere. As yet she had not acquired an established outlook on life or settled convictions but she was in search of them. Because of her love for Oblomov, she tried to expose his weak traits, to arouse him from his inertia, and to induce him to assume his responsibilities. She did not dwell at length upon his positive features, but it was because of these that she loved him. Like Gontcharov, she believed that if Oblomov could be cured of these negative qualities, he could continue to play a leading rôle in Russian society without resigning his place to the Stolzes. Unfortunately Olga failed. Turgenev's heroines met the same fate of frustration when they sought to eradicate the Oblomovism of their time in their lovers. Next to Pushkin's Tatyana, Olga represented the best in Russian womanhood, until she was partially eclipsed by the appearance of Turgenev's Liza.

In the person of Zahar, Gontcharov represented the

eternal serf, loyal as a dog to his master, yet dishonest in trifles, inefficient, and incurably lazy. Although he does not contribute a great deal to the novel, he was, nevertheless, an indispensable fixture in the structure of the society of his time. The portrayal of his entire career as a serf, from the time when he began to put on his young master's stockings to his end as a beggar, reveals Gontcharov's intimate knowledge of the life of the masses to whom Zahar belonged.

All in all we may say that *Oblomov* from an historical standpoint, and more especially as a sociological study of Russia in the middle of the nineteenth century, is almost indispensable. Without *Oblomov* one cannot understand Turgenev and Tchekhov.

BIBLIOGRAPHY

Abramovitch, G., and Goloventchenko, F., *Russkaya Literatura (Russian Literature)*, Moscow, 1935.

Baring, Maurice, *An Outline of Russian Literature*, Home University Library.

Kropotkin, Peter, *Russian Literature*, N. Y., 1905.

Mirsky, D. S., *A History of Russian Literature*, N. Y., 1927.

Olgin, M. J., *Guide to Russian Literature*, N. Y., 1920.

Phelps, W. L., *Essays on Russian Novelists*, N. Y., 1916.

Tsanoff, R. A., *The Problem of Life in the Russian Novel*, Rice Institute, 1917.

Wiener, Leo, *Anthology of Russian Literature*, Vol. II, N. Y., 1903.

Yarmolinsky, Avrahm, *Russian Literature*, Chicago, 1931.

Ivan Sergeyevitch Turgenev
1818-83

*I*VAN SERGEYEVITCH TURGENEV was born on November 10, 1818, at Orel, midway between Moscow and Kiev, and died on September 3, 1883, at his Bougival villa near Paris. On October 9, 1883, he was buried in the Volkov cemetery in St. Petersburg.

Various family heirlooms and insignia point to the fact that one of Turgenev's ancestors was a Tartar nobleman by the name of Turga. Another, Yakov Turgenev, a court jester of Peter the Great, was supposed to have assisted that monarch in his reforms. The author's cousin, Nikolai Turgenev, was implicated in the Decembrist revolt of 1825 and banished, together with his associates, to Siberia.

Ivan Turgenev was the son of a wealthy landowner and retired cavalry colonel. His childhood was spent on the family estate at Spask (Spask-Lutovinov) in the province of Orel, surrounded by governesses, tutors, nurses, seamstresses, and serfs of various ranks and appellations. He received his elementary education and his knowledge of other languages from foreign tutors, while a self-taught serf imbued him with a love for the Russian language and Russian poetry. The entire household was dominated by the iron hand of his mother, Varvara Petrovna.

In 1827 the Turgenev family moved to Moscow, and young Turgenev, at the age of nine, was placed in a private pension, the Veidengammer. Later he spent two and a half years in another pension at the Armenian Institute (subsequently called Lazarevsky). In 1833, when he was barely fifteen years of age, Turgenev entered Moscow University, only to be transferred a year later, because of his father's change of residence, to St. Petersburg

University. He was graduated in 1836 with majors in literature, philosophy, and philology, and with the title of "regular student."

Because of his early training with its stress upon foreign languages, Turgenev read French and German with native facility and acquired a speaking acquaintance with English. Turgenev was one of the few Russian writers to understand English.

It is also important to note that Turgenev's mother, Varvara Petrovna (whose relations with her son were often strained to the breaking point, chiefly because of their divergent views on the treatment of serfs), was herself passionately fond of reading. Although she in general preferred foreign works to Russian, she was also conversant with outstanding Russian authors of the time like Sumarokov, Lomonosov, Derzhavin, Karamzin, Zhukovsky, Pushkin, Gogol, and even Lermontov.

In the spring of 1838, Turgenev, accompanied by a valet-serf, set out for Germany to complete his education by auditing lectures at the University of Berlin, the fount of Hegelian philosophy. The two years, 1838-39 and 1840-41, spent intermittently abroad, were of the utmost importance in the life of the great novelist.

In order to qualify for a chair in philosophy, Turgenev obtained his Master's degree in 1842. The following year he accepted an office in the Ministry for Internal Affairs, which he resigned in 1845 to devote himself exclusively to literature.

No biographical sketch of Turgenev would be complete without reference to his relations with Madame Viardot (Pauline Garcia), a great French singer whom he met in 1843 in St. Petersburg when she made her first appearance there. Their friendship lasted forty years. It helps to explain why, aside from political reasons, Turgenev spent so much of his time abroad. Turgenev was Madame Viardot's senior by three years. She came from a Spanish family of great musical talent. A. Panayeva in her *Memoirs* testifies that she was of Jewish descent. Her father, Manuel Garcia, was a renowned tenor, an artist, and a professor of voice (1775-1832). In 1841 Pauline Garcia married Louis Viardot, who was then director of the Italian theater in Paris where she was a debutante. He was twenty years older than his talented wife, well educated, and known as the translator of *Don Quixote,* as well as many of Turgenev's works, into French.

Turgenev's literary career began with the writing of verse. *Parasha* was his first work, written in 1843, the year of his father's death. This was followed by *A Conversation* (1844), *A Landowner* (1845), *Andrei* (1845), and about twoscore shorter poems. In other words, until 1847 Turgenev figured predominantly as a poet. After 1847 he turned exclusively to prose. In that year he published *Khor and Kalinitch,* the first of a series of twenty-five sketches produced in book form in 1852, and later called *Memoirs of a Sportsman.*

Although Turgenev wrote a number of plays, novelettes, and short stories, in addition to the *Memoirs,* his fame rests chiefly upon seven novels, written over a period of twenty years. These are *Rudin* (1856), *A House of Gentlefolk* (1859), *On the Eve* (1860), *Fathers and Children* (1862), *Smoke* (1867), *Spring Freshets* (1873), and *Virgin Soil* (1876). By virtue of these and the *Memoirs* he was recognized by his contemporaries as the greatest living Russian writer.

I. *THE MEMOIRS OF A SPORTSMAN* (1847-52)

The literary career of Turgenev may then be divided into three main periods: 1. verse (1843-47); 2. short sketches (1847-52); and 3. the novel (1856-76). His plays, novelettes, and short stories were supplementary and subordinate to these three main groups.

Turgenev began to write his *Memoirs of a Sportsman* in an age of great unrest. The seething discontent among the peoples of Western Europe found expression in 1848 in revolution in France, the Germanic Confederation, Austria-Hungary, and Italy. In the United States the problem of slavery—one of the major causes of the Civil War—occupied a prominent place in American political and social life. This world turmoil could not but influence and agitate public opinion in Russia. As in our time the advocates of Bolshevism and their opponents the Fascists align themselves in two separate camps—in those days in Russia there were both advocates and opponents of the reform and revolutionary movements abroad. In Russia sympathy and opposition were expressed in two main movements, the origins of which may be traced much earlier, but which crystallized in these years— Westernism and Slavophilism.

Slavophilism was not a political movement, but a natural outgrowth of the Russian temperament. It stood for no striking reforms, but rather for a reassertion of the inherent good qualities in the Russian character. Its orientation was strictly national. Westernism, on the other hand, was an imported product which found many sponsors in Russia. In fact, the greatest liberals were almost automatically classified as Westernizers, although there were actually as many in the opposite camp. The Westernizers stood for a western orientation, that is, they wanted their institutions, political, economic, and social, modeled upon those of Western Europe, particularly upon those of France and England. "Philosophically speaking," says Masaryk, "the difference between the Westernizers and the Slavophiles is tantamount to the difference between Hegel and Schelling. Cherishing Hegel, the Westernizers cherished the rationalism condemned by the Slavophiles, and Schelling's belief in the absolutes was replaced by relativism." (Spirit of Russia, p. 339.)

The literary exponents of Westernism and Slavophilism in the period under consideration were Turgenev and Dostoyevsky. Turgenev was the most articulate mouthpiece of the Westernizers and around him this whole movement centered. Dostoyevsky filled a similar rôle for the Slavophiles. Only in this light can we understand the novels of these two leaders. Each of Turgenev's novels has its counterpart in a work by Dostoyevsky—the one expressing the point of view of the Westernizers, the other of the Slavophiles.

The Memoirs of a Sportsman affords what may be termed a preview of Turgenev's novels. Outwardly speaking a series of harmless sketches, the *Memoirs* were, if indirectly, at least partially responsible for the abolition of serfdom in Russia, as Alexander II himself admitted on one occasion. These sketches, more than any other work in Russian literature, elicited sympathy for the plight of four fifths of Russian humanity. While in *Dead Souls*, Gogol dealt indirectly with the institution of serfdom, describing for the most part its physical status, in *The Memoirs of a Sportsman*, Turgenev most artistically depicted, for the first time, the life of the serf at its best. In this work he revealed the soul of the serf—a soul which was not so different from his master's, at times even superior. The sketches displayed so much objectivity that they immediately won universal approbation and established Turgenev's reputation as an author.

Inasmuch as Turgenev read *Uncle Tom's Cabin* by Harriet Beecher Stowe, an allusion to which is found in his novel *Smoke*, some comparison between the American classic and *The Memoirs of a Sportsman* may be of interest to American readers.

The institution of slavery dawned in America in 1619 when the first slave ship landed at Jamestown, Virginia, with slaves for the pioneer planters. Russian serfdom dates to 1581, in the reign of Ivan the Terrible, when the serfs were "affixed" to the soil for a period of years, and later for life. By the time of Catherine the Great (1762-96) they had for all practical purposes become the personal property of Russian landed proprietors or of the Russian state. Thus in the nineteenth century America and Russia alike were faced with the problem of a subject people—in America a black people, but in Russia a people of the same race and religion as their masters. By the year 1852 slavery in America threatened to divide the Union, serfdom in Russia to upset the monarchy. In this year the two books mentioned above, both destined to play an important rôle in the abolitionist movement in their respective countries, were published.

These books were an "open sesame" to literary fame for both Turgenev and Mrs. Stowe. Turgenev was lifted from obscurity to the very first rank of Russian writers. For a time he had the distinction of being the only Russian novelist of international reputation. Through him Russian literature was introduced to France and the Western world.

In personality no two authors could be more unlike than Turgenev and Harriet Beecher Stowe. Mrs. Stowe was deeply religious and highly emotional—just the type to produce a piece of literature appealing to sentiment rather than to reason. In her heart she nourished a violent hatred for the institution of slavery. Both her father and her husband were strong abolitionists, and the horrors of slavery were topics for daily conversation in her home. Living in the border state of Ohio, she had every opportunity to witness firsthand the terrible plight of fugitives trying to escape to freedom. More than once Professor Stowe's home was a place of refuge for fleeing slaves. The passing of the Fugitive Slave Law finally aroused her to action. It is said that a member of Mrs. Stowe's family suggested in a letter that she "write something that would make the whole nation feel what an accursed thing slavery is." Acting upon this suggestion, she produced some unrivaled anti-slavery propaganda in the form of a novel which has outlived the era in which it was written. The book was first published as a serial in the abolitionist periodical *The National Era*.

Ivan Turgenev lacked Mrs. Stowe's religious faith; neither was he a propagandist. Being a highly cultured man with a sympathetic nature, he too hated slavery, or serfdom, as it is usually called in Russia. In his mother's home he had ample opportunity to witness at close range the master's cruel treatment of the serf. While roaming about Russia with his dog and his gun on hunting expeditions, he stored up material for his *Memoirs*. It was then that he learned to know and appreciate the serf as a human being with a soul. However, Turgenev did not write *The Memoirs of a Sportsman* with the object of arousing pity for the serf. He did so unwittingly, and the book became a social document without the connivance of the author.

Of the two writers, Turgenev was by far the greater realist. He wrote of the peasants as he found them, with simplicity and directness and without embroidery. His sketches fall naturally into four groups. Some were purely descriptive of the scenery of forest and steppe; some like "Khor and Kalinitch" were character sketches; while others consisted entirely of conversation addressed to the narrator as in "A Hamlet of Shchegry" or of conversation overheard, as in "Byezhin Prairie." Each sketch was complete—almost a novel in itself.

The *Memoirs* revealed Turgenev's skill and delicacy in character analysis both of men and dogs. He depicted the peasants more sympathetically than the upper classes. His squires were invariably vulgar, cruel, or ineffective, whereas he took pains to emphasize the humanity, imaginativeness, intelligence, and dignity, as well as the poetic and artistic gifts of the peasants. Yet his characters were not overdrawn. Turgenev did not dwell on atrocities which were the exception rather than the rule, nor did he try to idealize his serfs. By painting life-portraits of sensible, reasoning, and affectionate human beings bowed down by the yoke of serfdom, side by side with life-portraits of their mean and shallow masters, the landed proprietors, he, in a wholly unobtrusive manner, awakened in his readers a consciousness of the injustice and ineptitude of serfdom.

Harriet Beecher Stowe did not owe her success to the

literary merits of her novel. From an artistic point of view there is little to admire in *Uncle Tom's Cabin*. On the other hand, Turgenev's *Memoirs* represent artistic perfection. Turgenev was a poet in essence, and his early apprenticeship in poetic discipline lent elegance and finish to his prose style. If the *Memoirs* had been launched at another time, it is doubtful if their readers would have been conscious of their social significance. Their literary excellence would have won renown for Turgenev under any regime. Some critics feel that in artistry of presentation Turgenev never surpassed or even equaled *The Memoirs of a Sportsman*.

Nor, as we have said, can Mrs. Stowe compete with Turgenev as a realist. In spite of the "Key" she provided to prove that *Uncle Tom's Cabin* was based upon actual facts, her novel did not give a true picture of life on a Southern plantation. It was realistic only in spots. The plot was rambling and disconnected. Mrs. Stowe did excel as a storyteller and had the power to picture scenes vividly. She admirably relieved the gloom of her novel with choice bits of humor, but she placed undue stress upon the piety, suffering, and despair of the slave. Consequently, the pathos of her story was overdone and her characters were overdrawn, especially Uncle Tom and Eva. She made of the former a saint rather than a human being and of the latter an angel rather than a child. Turgenev lacked the temperament of Mrs. Stowe, but his innate truthfulness, his artistry, and his calmness made a more lasting impression than a mere display of sentiment and emotion could have secured. In spite of their differences, however, *Uncle Tom's Cabin* and *The Memoirs of a Sportsman* played a significant rôle at a critical time in their respective countries.

II. *TURGENEV'S NOVELS* (1856-76)
1. THE PLOT OF *RUDIN* (1856)

Rudin, the hero of Turgenev's novel by that name, is a man of ideals, education, and oratorical talent, but not a practical man of action. We first meet him in the conventional society of the period in the home of Darya Mikhailovna, where his personality arouses the most intense likes and dislikes. The mistress of the home is very much taken with him, and he continues to enjoy her patronage until he has the temerity to fall in love with her young daughter, Natalya. The young girl herself, with the enthusiasm of youth, is quite ready to sacrifice present comfort and future security for the man she loves, but she is bitterly disillusioned when she finds that his love has no heroic qualities.

Compelled to withdraw from the protection of Darya Mikhailovna in consequence of this love affair, Rudin leads a wandering, unsuccessful life, strongly suggestive of the roamings of a picaresque hero. He is killed in the July insurrection of 1848 in Paris, almost the last survivor of a lost and foreign cause. As he falls, a fleeing insurgent refers to him as a "Polonais."

2. THE PLOT OF *A HOUSE OF GENTLEFOLK* (1859)

Fyodor Ivanitch Lavretsky is the son of a peasant mother and an aristocratic father. His childhood was not especially happy, nor was his education particularly profitable. For his higher education he had to wait until after the death of his father, who ended his days in mental and physical infirmity.

At the age of twenty-three Lavretsky begins his university career in Moscow. Already he is mature in appearance, but in reality completely naïve in his knowledge of the world and of mankind. For this reason he becomes infatuated with Varvara Pavlovna, without having any comprehension of her true character and personality. They are married, and the wife at once becomes absorbed in the frivolities of social life which make no particular appeal to her studious husband. He raises no objection, however, but withdraws more and more to his studies. Eventually he discovers quite by accident that his wife is unfaithful to him and leaves her immediately.

Lavretsky returns to his former home with the intention of devoting himself to the improvement of his

estate. He endeavors to pick up the threads of his former life. While visiting relatives in the neighborhood, he
meets and is attracted by Liza Kalitin, a young girl of
nineteen. Liza has no special talents or physical charms,
but she is deeply religious and maintains high ideals of
conduct. She has a suitor by the name of Panshin, a
man of the world, of whom her mother enthusiastically
approves, and whom she might have married out of
obedience had not Lavretsky urged her to obey solely the
dictates of her own heart. A sympathetic understanding
develops between the middle-aged man and the young
girl.

At this psychological moment, Lavretsky sees in a
foreign paper a notice of the death of his wife. Deeming
himself free, he no longer imposes any restraint upon his
feelings. He reveals to Liza his love for her, and finds to
his deep joy that it is reciprocated. As Lavretsky's complete happiness seems about to be realized his wife unexpectedly reappears. With demonstrations which he recognizes as hypocritical, but which he is powerless to
combat, she forces him to acknowledge her and live with
her as his wife once more.

Although crushed by the ruination of all their hopes,
both Lavretsky and Liza exhibit strength of character.
The girl enters a convent, and he devotes himself to the
management of his estate, which at that time constituted
a humanitarian rather than a business proposition. The
author portrays him in later years as a man who is not
embittered by his sorrow, but who can feel sincere satisfaction in the happiness of others.

3. THE PLOT OF *ON THE EVE* (1860)

Bersenev, a student and philosopher, invites his
friend Insarov to share his home during the summer.
He secures Insarov's entry into the society of the neighborhood, and is particularly enthusiastic in praise of
him to Elena Nikolayevna, with whom he is in love although he does not fully realize it.

Insarov is not a Russian but a Bulgarian, whose sole
passion is service to his country. He believes that love,

especially "Russian" love, can have no place in his life,
and seeks to avoid any entanglements. In spite of himself, however, he falls in love with Elena, who is already
in love with him, her interest having been first aroused
by Bersenev's praise.

Insarov departs for Moscow, in which city Elena's
family also maintains a residence. Knowing that their
engagement would meet with the most violent opposition
on the part of Elena's parents, their communications and
meetings are conducted with the utmost secrecy. Insarov
becomes dangerously ill, which brings matters to a crisis.
When he has partially recovered they secretly marry. It
is not long, however, before Elena's family learns of her
marriage. Her father in fury threatens legal action. Her
mother, although heartbroken over the whole affair, is
determined that her daughter shall not be disgraced and
succeeds, at no small cost, in calming his wrath and al-
tering his purpose.

Insarov has long been chafing under the delay which
keeps him from his country where war is threatening.
Although he is still far from well, he resolves to wait no
longer but to join his compatriots, who are eager for his
support. Naturally his wife will accompany him as she
has long affirmed that she has no life apart from him.
They leave amid demonstrations of grief on the part of
her family and friends. But Insarov is fated never to
reach his destination nor to attain his purpose. He dies
in Venice while awaiting transportation for the last lap
of his journey. Elena buries him in his native land.
From that time she vanishes completely, and no efforts of
her family provide any clue to what has become of her.

4. THE PLOT OF FATHERS AND CHILDREN (1862)

As the story opens, Nikolai Petrovitch Kirsanov is
awaiting with impatience the return of his son, Arkady,
from the University of St. Petersburg, where he has just
taken his degree. When the young man finally arrives,
the father greets him with delight and affection not un-
mixed with embarrassment. Arkady introduces his friend
Bazarov who is to spend part of the vacation with them.

Nikolai Petrovitch welcomes the visitor, and all set out for the family estate.

This estate, which is called Maryino in memory of the wife of Nikolai Petrovitch, is causing the latter much anxiety and financial difficulty because of the laziness and maliciousness of the peasants living upon it. His family consists of an unmarried older brother, his mistress Fenitchka, and her infant son. Nikolai Petrovitch explains to Arkady with much confusion that Fenitchka is installed in the house and suggests her removal, but he is considerably relieved when the young man takes a decidedly broad-minded view of the matter.

Arkady has become acquainted with Bazarov at the University, where the latter was engaged in the study of medicine in preparation to become a district doctor. Arkady admires his friend intensely and tries to emulate him. Bazarov, however, does not fit in very well with Arkady's family. He despises their mode of thought and their ideals, making little effort to conceal either his boredom or contempt. In reply to questions he announces that in principle he is a Nihilist. In particular he arouses the animosity of Nikolai Petrovitch's elder brother, Pavel Petrovitch, who prides himself upon the perfection of his dress and manners and the correctness of his views.

Arkady and Bazarov avail themselves of an invitation to attend a diplomatic function in the town of X. The older members of the family are considerably relieved by the departure of Bazarov, although some of the younger persons about the estate regret his absence.

The most important event of the ensuing festivities for Arkady and Bazarov is their meeting with a wealthy, fascinating young widow, Madame Odintsov, with whom they both fall in love. They readily accept an invitation to visit her estate. Here Bazarov seems to have considerable advantage over his friend in winning the lady's favor, Arkady being forced to put up with the companionship of her young sister, Katya, which at the time, wounds his vanity. When Bazarov finally makes a declaration of love to Madame Odintsov, he meets with a distinctly cool response, although his personality has in-

terested her to the extent that she is loath to give up
his companionship.

On the following day Bazarov and Arkady take their
departure. The former decides to pay a long-deferred
visit to his aged parents, who have been awaiting his
arrival with pathetic eagerness. When he reaches home,
he is curt and abrupt with the old people, and to their
bitter disappointment, remains only three days.

The young men now return to Maryino, stopping en
route at Madame Odintsov's estate, where they do not
seem to be especially welcome. Upon arriving at Maryino,
Bazarov plunges into experimental work, which he began
upon the occasion of his first visit. Arkady, finding that
he has less and less in common with his friend, departs
again for Madame Odintsov's estate, influenced by his
growing fondness for the young sister Katya. Bazarov's
stay at Maryino is brought to an abrupt conclusion by a
rather absurd duel with Pavel Petrovitch, who objects
to Bazarov's attitude toward Fenitchka.

Bazarov returns home, although he cannot avoid
breaking his journey in order to visit Madame Odintsov.
He makes no headway with the young widow, but learns
that Arkady is to marry Katya. Upon reaching home,
Bazarov announces to his delighted parents that he intends to spend six weeks with them, but that he wishes
to work and must not be disturbed. The pathetic old
people keep out of his way and seek with anxious solicitude to further his comfort. Bazarov acquires an infec-
tion while dissecting the body of a typhus victim. Realizing the hopelessness of his situation, he sends word to
Madame Odintsov that he is dying. She comes to him,
bringing a doctor who, however, is able to do nothing.
She herself realizes that her feeling for the dying man is
not that of love. Bazarov dies, and the author gives a
touching picture of the old parents' grief and despair.

5. THE PLOT OF *SMOKE* (1867)

Grigory Mihailovitch Litvinov, a young student in
Moscow, becomes acquainted with the Osinins, a noble
but impoverished family. He soon falls deeply in love

with the eldest daughter, Irina, a girl of seventeen. For some time Irina remains entirely indifferent to his advances. At last, when he has given up all hope of winning her affections, her attitude changes, and she consents to an engagement. Irina's parents raise no objections although they are rather disappointed that their daughter has not made a more brilliant match.

After a great deal of persuasion on the part of her parents, and with the consent of Litvinov, Irina agrees to attend a court ball in Moscow. After the ball, however, she refuses to see Litvinov again. He learns from her father that she has been a sensation at the court, and from Irina, that she wishes to terminate the engagement.

Years pass, and Litvinov has in a measure outlived the suffering which this separation cost him. He is engaged to his cousin, Tatyana, whom he expects to meet in Baden-Baden. Unexpectedly Irina comes into his life again. She is married and moves in a society which she affects to despise. She will not permit Litvinov to avoid her, and presently his former love has revived in all its intensity. Irina proposes to leave her husband for Litvinov. As a result he abruptly changes his plans and breaks his engagement with Tatyana upon her arrival in Baden-Baden. When, after all this confusion and unhappiness, Irina cannot bring herself to take the final step toward separation from her husband, Litvinov is left once more to his own devices.

Wretchedly unhappy, he returns to his estate in Russia. As the train rushes along, he watches the clouds of smoke which whirl past the window, and "suddenly it all seemed as smoke to him, everything, his own life, Russian life—everything human, especially everything Russian."

For two years Litvinov devotes himself exclusively to the task of putting his estate in order. News of his former betrothed, Tatyana, reaches him from time to time, and at length he seeks to renew their acquaintance. She invites him cordially to visit her and her aunt. Litvinov responds with alacrity, and upon his arrival at her home, falls on his knees before her.

6. THE PLOT OF *SPRING FRESHETS* (1873)

Sanin, a young man of twenty-three, stops in Frankfurt on his way home to Russia from Italy. By chance he steps into a small confectionery shop just in time to render assistance to a young boy in a swoon. The boy's mother, who is mistress of the shop, and his sister, are extremely grateful to Sanin and show their appreciation by entertaining him as an honored guest. The sister Gemma is very beautiful, and though of Italian birth and sympathies, she is engaged to a prosperous young German head clerk by the name of Herr Klüber.

Sanin accompanies Gemma, her betrothed, and her brother on a Sunday excursion. During the day Gemma is the recipient of unpleasant attentions from a drunken German officer. Herr Klüber does not take active exception to this, but Sanin resents it so strongly that a duel takes place. The duel comes to nothing, for the officer refuses to do other than fire in the air. Gemma, however, is so much impressed by the whole affair that she breaks her engagement with Herr Klüber, much to her mother's distress. Her mother is even less pleased, when, shortly after this incident, Gemma announces that Klüber has been replaced by Sanin. After family harmony has been restored, Gemma and Sanin discuss their marriage plans. Sanin plans to raise funds by the sale of his estate, if and when he can dispose of it.

While Sanin racks his brain for a solution to this problem, he unexpectedly runs across a former schoolmate by the name of Poltsov. The latter, though quite unprepossessing both mentally and physically, has married a wealthy and beautiful woman. It occurs to Sanin that this woman might consider the purchase of his estate. With this purpose in view, he accompanies Poltsov to Wiesbaden, where she is staying.

Madame Poltsov proves to be a beautiful but very sensuous woman. She is favorably disposed toward the purchase of Sanin's estate, but defers her decision until he is fully within her power. Her skill in fascinating and subordinating men is so great that she soon accomplishes her purpose. In an incredibly short time, Sanin is her absolute slave. He forsakes Gemma and departs with the Poltsovs to Italy.

Sanin pays dearly for his weakness of character, for late middle age finds him alone, weary, bitter, and disillusioned. Acting upon impulse, he goes to Frankfurt to find some trace of Gemma. Eventually, in the Frankfurt directory, he comes upon the name of the very German officer with whom he fought the duel so many years before. With the assistance of this officer, Sanin soon learns that Gemma has long since emigrated to America and is married to a merchant. He writes to her. In reply, she expresses no animosity toward him for his shabby treatment of her, since he has indirectly contributed to her present happiness. She sends him a portrait of her eighteen-year-old daughter, who is a replica of Gemma herself at that age, and who is about to be married. Sanin sends the girl a magnificent pearl necklace, to which is attached a little garnet cross which Gemma had given him at the time of their engagement.

7. THE PLOT OF *VIRGIN SOIL* (1876)

Alexey Dimitrovitch Nezhdanov is the natural son of a nobleman. Unable to assume any position in society, he associates with revolutionists, whose ideas he believes he shares. A wealthy gentleman by the name of Sipiagin offers him a post as tutor to his son, and being in great need of funds, Nezhdanov accepts.

In his capacity as tutor, Nezhdanov at first finds favor, but later alienates Sipiagin, not so much because of his radical views as by the manner in which he expresses them. On the other hand, he arouses the interest and affection of Marianne, Sipiagin's young niece, who is chafing against her position of dependence in her uncle's home.

Marianne also cherishes revolutionary views, and the two young people soon become attached to one another. They declare their mutual love and resolve to go away together. Since they are both rather impractical, they consult one of Nezhdanov's friends, Solomin, who is manager of a factory not far from the Sipiagin estate. Solomin is a man of great ability and unusual good sense. While he believes that a social readjustment is necessary, and has aligned himself with the revolutionists, he does not look for a sudden change, and takes an exceedingly practical view of affairs in general.

At Solomin's suggestion, Marianne and Nezhdanov take up their residence with him and prepare themselves for service to the people, pending the coming of the revolution and their own marriage. Marianne adapts herself easily and happily, and her belief in the cause to which she has devoted herself never wavers. Nezhdanov, on the contrary, finds himself increasingly out of sympathy with the work he is trying to do. He postpones his marriage to Marianne, who, while she still loves him, turns more and more to Solomin for advice and direction.

The Government, meanwhile, learns of the revolutionary movement with which they are connected. Nezhdanov's arrest is imminent. It is essential that he and Marianne marry at once and seek another refuge. Nezhdanov, however, realizing that he is utterly incapable of carrying to its logical conclusion the course of procedure upon which he has embarked, commits suicide by shooting himself.

Solomin, who must flee because he, too, is the object of Government suspicion, takes Marianne away from the factory and marries her to protect her reputation. They do not appear again, but it is implied that they live happily.

In addition to these characters, Turgenev presents others who are gay, pleasing, pathetic, or tragic, and who contribute their part to the development of the story. Among them are the beautiful Madame Sipiagin and the pompous Kallomeitsev; the quaint Fimoushka and Fomoushka; the cripple, Paklin, who suffers bitterly because of his deformity and the contempt in which he is generally held; and Mashurina, who loves Nezhdanov deeply despite the fact that she is ugly and his senior in age. Particularly tragic is the fate of Markelov, who, notwithstanding his fine qualities, is uniformly unsuccessful in all that he undertakes, and who, after he has been beaten and delivered to the authorities by the peasants he tried to help, suffers only because he was betrayed by the man whom he trusted the most.

FROM *FATHERS AND CHILDREN*

"... What sort of person is Bazarov?"—Arkady laughed.—"Would you like me to tell you, my dear uncle, what sort of person he really is?"

"Pray do, my dear nephew."

"He is a nihilist."

"What?"—asked Nikolai Petrovitch; and Pavel Petrovitch lifted his knife, with a bit of butter sticking to the blade, in the air, and remained motionless.

"He is a nihilist,"—repeated Arkady.

"A nihilist," said Nikolai Petrovitch.—"That's derived from the Latin *nihil, nothing*, so far as I can judge; consequently, that word denotes a man who ... who recognizes nothing."

"Say: 'who respects nothing,' "—put in Pavel Petrovitch, and turned his attention once more to his butter.

"Who approaches everything from a critical point of view,"—remarked Arkady.

"And isn't that exactly the same thing?"—inquired Pavel Petrovitch.

"No, it is not exactly the same thing. A nihilist is a man who does not bow before any authority whatever, who does not accept a single principle on faith, with whatever respect that principle may be environed."

"And do you think that's a good thing?"—interrupted Pavel Petrovitch.

"That depends on who it is, dear uncle. It's all right for some, and very bad for others."

"You don't say so. Well, I see that's not in our line. We old timers assume that, without princíples" (Pavel Petrovitch pronounced this word softly, in the French style. Arkady, on the contrary, pronounced it "prínciples," throwing the accent on the first syllable), "without princíples, taken as you say on faith, it is impossible to take a step, or to breathe. *Vous avez changé tout cela.* God grant you health and the rank of a general, but we'll

be content to admire the Messrs. . . . what do you call
them?"

"Nihilists,"—said Arkady distinctly.

"Yes. They used to be Hegelists, and now they are
nihilists. We shall see whether you can exist in a void,
in a vacuum; but now, be so good as to ring the bell,
brother Nikolai Petrovitch, it is time for me to drink my
cocoa."   . . . .

"And that is called nihilism?"

"And that is called nihilism,"—repeated Bazarov
again, this time with peculiar insolence.

Pavel Petrovitch narrowed his eyes slightly.

"So that's it!" said he, in a strangely quiet voice.—
"Nihilism is to cure all our woes, and you, you are our
deliverers and heroes. But why do you abuse others,—
even those same reformers, for example? Don't you prate
like all the rest?"

"Whatever our faults, we don't err in that respect,"
muttered Bazarov between his teeth.

"What, then? Do you do anything, pray? Are you
preparing to act?"

Bazarov made no reply. Pavel Petrovitch suddenly
began to tremble, but he immediately regained control
of himself.

"H'm! . . . To act, to destroy . . . " he continued.—"But
why demolish without even knowing the reason?"

"We destroy because we are a force,"—remarked
Arkady.

Pavel Petrovitch looked at his nephew, and laughed.

"Yes, a force,—and a force is not accountable to anyone,"—said Arkady, and straightened himself up.

"Unfortunate young man," groaned Pavel Petrovitch;
he was positively unable to restrain himself any longer:
—"if you could only realize what you are upholding in
Russia by your worthless *isms!* No, that would try the
patience of an angel! Force! There is force in the savage
Kalmyk, and in the Mongolian also, but what is that to
us?—What is precious to us—is civilization,—yes, yes,
my dear sir, its fruits are dear to us. And don't tell me
that those fruits are worthless: the poorest dauber, *un*

barbouilleur, the fellow who drums a tune on the piano for five kopeks an evening,—all of them are more useful than you, because they are representatives of civilization, and not of crude Mongolian force! You imagine that you are progressive, but in reality you are only fit for a Kalmyk hovel; A force! But pray recollect, you forceful gentlemen, that after all you are only four men and a half, but there are others—millions, who will not permit you to trample under foot their most sacred beliefs, who will crush you!"

"If we are crushed, it will serve us right,"—said Bazarov.—"Only, that remains to be seen. We are not so few in number as you suppose."

"What? Jesting aside, do you think you can cope, cope with the whole people?"

"Moscow was burned to the ground by a farthing candle, you know,"—replied Bazarov.

—Tr. by I. Spector

FROM *VIRGIN SOIL*

" . . . And what is Solomin doing?" Mashurina asked. She had suddenly ceased wishing to hear Paklin talk about *him.*

"Solomin!" Paklin exclaimed. "He's a clever chap! turned out well too. He's left the old factory and taken all the best men with him. There was one fellow there called Pavel—could do anything; he's taken him along too. They say he has a small factory of his own now, somewhere near Perm, run on co-operative lines. He's all right! he'll stick to anything he undertakes. Got some grit in him! His strength lies in the fact that he doesn't attempt to cure all the social ills with one blow. What a rum set we are to be sure, we Russians! We sit down quietly and wait for something or some one to come along and cure us all at once; heal all our wounds, pull out all our diseases, like a bad tooth. But who or what is to work this magic spell, Darwinism, the land, the Archbishop Perepentiev, a foreign war, we don't know and don't care, but we must have our tooth pulled out for us!

It's nothing but mere idleness, sluggishness, want of thinking. Solomin, on the other hand, is different; he doesn't go in for pulling teeth—he knows what he's about!"

. . . .

"Bravo!" Paklin exclaimed. "Well, countess, have another cup. There is just one other thing I wanted to say to you. It seemed to me that you expressed yourself rather contemptuously of Solomin. But I tell you that people like him are the real men! It's difficult to understand them at first, but, believe me, they're the real men. The future is in their hands. They are not heroes, not even 'heroes of labour' as some crank of an American, or Englishman, called them in a book he wrote for the edification of us heathens, but they are robust, strong, dull men of the people. They are exactly what we want just now. You have only to look at Solomin. A head as clear as the day and a body as strong as an ox. Isn't that a wonder in itself? Why, any man with us in Russia who had had any brains, or feelings, or a conscience, has always been a physical wreck. Solomin's heart aches just as ours does; he hates the same things that we hate, but his nerves are of iron and his body is under his full control. He's a splendid man, I tell you! Why, think of it! here is a man with ideals, and no nonsense about him; educated and from the people, simple, yet all there. . . . What more do you want?

"It's of no consequence," Paklin continued, working himself up more and more, without noticing that Mashurina had long ago ceased listening to him and was looking away somewhere, "it's of no consequence that Russia is now full of all sorts of queer people, fanatics, officials, generals plain and decorated, Epicureans, imitators, all manner of cranks. I once knew a lady, a certain Havrona Prishtekov, who, one fine day, suddenly turned a legitimist and assured everybody that when she died they had only to open her body and the name of Henry V. would be found engraven on her heart! All these people do not count, my dear lady; our true salvation lies with the Solomins, the dull, plain, but wise Solomins!"

Turgenev's novels may be regarded as sketches on a larger scale than those which composed the *Memoirs of a Sportsman,* and they dealt with different problems. The novels span a period of twenty years, from 1856 to 1876, a period which practically coincided with the reign of Alexander II. The era was one of relative freedom in Russia, during which serfdom was abolished, *zemstvos* were established, trial by jury introduced, the term of military service reduced, and many unpopular laws repealed or mitigated.

The reign of Alexander II may be called Russia's Victorian Age—an age in which liberalism kept pace with industrialism and in which the rights of the individual were respected and guaranteed. It was, moreover, the zenith of the golden age of Russian literature and art. To offset England's rostrum of famous writers, her Tennyson and Browning, Carlyle, Dickens, and Thackeray, the Alexandrian age produced Turgenev, Dostoyevsky, Tolstoy, and many other poets and thinkers of the first rank. But behind superficial resemblances there is a profound difference between the relative positions of Russia and Great Britain. In the England of Tennyson freedom had broadened slowly from precedent to precedent. Culture was the mellow fruit of a literary heritage based upon Chaucerian, Elizabethan, and eighteenth-century traditions. Russia bridged the gap from barbarism to culture within the brief span of a few decades. In England's golden age the loyalty of the masses to the throne reached its climax. In Russia the relaxation of the censorship let loose forces directed toward the destruction of the Romanov dynasty, among them Nihilism, which later amalgamated with the more positive but equally destructive Marxism.

Turgenev was chiefly responsible for making the novel of the Alexandrian age the vehicle for the expression of opinions on and criticism of the foremost political, social, and economic issues of the day. Each of his novels had its thesis, relevant to one or more of the specific problems which faced his contemporaries. When Turgenev became a convinced Westernizer he realized that simply to diagnose Russia's ills in the manner of Gogol or Gontcharov would never provide an adequate solution of her problems. He must go beyond constructive criticism and suggest a remedy. The remedy which he believed would solve all Russia's problems for generations to come was the substitution of constitutional for autocratic government. In his novels beginning with *Rudin* and ending with *Virgin Soil*, Turgenev carried on his search for a leader capable of achieving that aim. Only in this light can we understand the trend of thought revealed in these works. They form the best background for the history of the Russian Revolution, for, in his search for a leader, Turgenev parades before us in review his various candidates for the task, most of whom are failures. It took him twenty years to locate his leader, who emerged from his last novel, *Virgin Soil*, not in the rôle of the leading character, Nezhdanov, but in the person of Solomin, a representative of the middle class. Turgenev's remedy for Russian political, economic, and social problems was a strong middle class.

It was not until 1906 that the Russian Government began to take cognizance of this class and to sponsor it. Under the premiership of Stolypin, 1906-11, several million peasants were given the opportunity to form the nucleus of a middle class in Russia. Although Turgenev intended this class to champion reform—to aid in the creation of a liberal constitutional government in Russia—the Tsarist Government used it to strengthen the position of the monarchy. As a result the majority of this group was dispossessed by the Soviet Government during the first years of the Five Year Plan.

Rudin. When Turgenev looked about for a leader he naturally turned first in *Rudin* (originally *A Natural Genius*), to the student body. Many of his contemporaries thought that in the person of Dmitri Rudin, he described his friend and classmate at Berlin University, Michael

Bakunin, the political anarchist. Others held that Rudin was a projection of Turgenev himself during his student days. But Rudin did not measure up to Turgenev's expectations. By nature he was more of an Oblomov than a man of action. When he finally decided to act he met death in a foreign cause, somewhere in France, and even for that he received no credit, for those who located his dead body believed him to be a Pole. In brief, in the person of Rudin, Turgenev has given us a most faithful and vivid portrait of the "superfluous" or "undesirable" man, who "speaks like a giant" but "acts like a pigmy."

A House of Gentlefolk. Turgenev, after this denouement, was advised to abandon his search for a leader among the student youth, and to seek him instead among the nobility proper. This he did in *A House of Gentlefolk* (also *A Nobleman's Nest*), which established his reputation as a novelist. Although the heroine, Liza Kalitin, stole the show in this novel, Turgenev's interest centered in Fyodor Lavretsky, a character who combined traits favorable both to the Westernizers and the Slavophiles, and who, therefore, had no enemies in Russia. But Lavretsky in practice symbolized the decadence of the landed aristocracy, as, with a sigh of resignation, he abandoned his task and passed the torch to the new generation in which he had great faith.

On the Eve. After this second frustration, Turgenev either lost faith in Russian characters, or, more likely, he wished to delegate ideas, which would not have been popular with the authorities if uttered by a Russian, to a Bulgarian. For this purpose he chose the Bulgarian Insarov, who became the hero of his third novel *On the Eve*. Turgenev acknowledged that he owed the theme of this novel to V. Karatayev, a friend who was killed in the Crimean War. In *On the Eve* it was Turgenev's purpose to encourage all Russian liberals to emulate Insarov. Although Insarov's cause was, on the surface, national, in that he dreamed of the liberation of Bulgaria from the Turkish yoke, Turgenev's contemporaries were expected to read between the lines, and by substituting liberalism or constitutionalism for nationalism, to discover the real cause—the liberation of Russia from autocracy.

Turgenev's ruse calls to mind a similar expedient of the author of the Book of Job, who, when he wished to voice a protest against the world order of Jehovah, and the plight of the people of Israel, selected a non-Jewish spokesman in the person of Job, and permitted him to express statements which, from a Jew, would never have been tolerated. Turgenev's purpose was essentially the same, only the setting was different. Very few understood that purpose, and because Insarov was the only positive male character among Turgenev's heroes, Turgenev himself was condemned by many critics for conferring such an honor upon a foreigner whom he had dragged from the Bulgarian marshes.

Fathers and Children. When Insarov was rejected, Turgenev set out to prove that a Russian character was even more capable of assuming leadership than a Bulgarian. Bazarov, the hero of *Fathers and Children*, was supposed to be Turgenev's ideal type, stronger even than Insarov. Strange as it may seem, however, no sooner did he select a Russian character than that character proved a weakling whose every project met with frustration. Bazarov came to be known as a Nihilist. By setting forth the tenets of Nihilism, Turgenev, like Gogol and Gontcharov, assumed the rôle of diagnostician instead of supplying the remedy. Nihilism joined dead souls and Oblomovism in the list of Russian household words.

Strictly speaking, if we are to judge by the spirit of the work, Turgenev did not preach Nihilism in this novel. Nor did he create Bazarov—he discovered him. It was Turgenev's purpose to direct the attention of the authorities to this new movement which was rapidly taking root in Russian soil. Far from preaching violence or Nihilism through Bazarov, Turgenev sounded a warning against this dangerous newcomer, as if he would say—"Your

type of government gave birth to this type of man. Mend
your ways by introducing more and better reforms before it is too late. Do you not hear the threats of Bazarov?" Instead of heeding the warning, however, most
of the authorities and conservative society in general,
were displeased with Bazarov and condemned Turgenev
accordingly. Many members of higher Russian society
chose to regard his novel as a serious attempt to negate
the "culture of the nobility." On the other hand, the
liberals, particularly the Westernizers, thought that in
Bazarov, Turgenev defeated his own purpose. *Fathers
and Children* became, therefore, the most controversial
and the most widely discussed novel in Russia and has
remained so. The impression was given that Turgenev
became frightened of his own creation: that he gave
Bazarov a chance to expound his ideas, but when he
reached the point where he was ready to translate those
ideas into action, Turgenev, the *deus ex machina*, fearing
that his hero might become a Frankenstein or a Golem,
stepped into the arena in person and brought Bazarov's
life to a premature end.

One of the few to understand the message of *Fathers
and Children* was Dostoyevsky, who wrote what we might
call its sequel from the Slavophile point of view in his
novel *The Possessed*. Dostoyevsky began where Turgenev
left off, by depicting the Bazarovs in action, with startling
results. After reading *The Possessed* we are less likely to
condemn Turgenev for the annihilation of his own
creature.

Smoke. When the furore over *Fathers and Children*
died down Turgenev produced *Smoke*. This novel, strictly speaking, was a rebuttal to the criticisms of those
authorities and conservatives who misconstrued his message in *Fathers and Children*. He held up many of their
ideas to ridicule, and indirectly implied that they were
incapable of grasping this message or the liberal recom-
mendations of the Westernizers, because they wasted

their time on trivialities, or as he said, in trying to hypnotize a turtle.

Spring Freshets. *Smoke* was followed by *Spring Freshets,* in which, although it does not deal with the background of current events in Russia proper, Turgenev produced another negative type in the person of Sanin, who met with frustration in both love and business. In 1880 Turgenev omitted *Spring Freshets* from a volume containing his other six novels, because he considered that he had not been sufficiently objective in his treatment of Sanin and the other characters. To Turgenev, objectivity was one of the most indispensable elements in any novel, and since this one did not measure up to his own standards, he classified it as a separate story. Nevertheless *Spring Freshets* is an important link in the chain of Turgenev's novels. In the first place, many critics regarded Sanin as a self-portrait of Turgenev. In the second place, the novel caused some international repercussions. The German press, in Germany as well as in Russia, began a campaign against Turgenev because of his portrayal of the German character, Klüber, and the German officers, Baron von Dongof and Von Richter. After the publication of *Fathers and Children* and *Smoke,* Turgenev lost many Russian friends and followers; *Spring Freshets* likewise deprived him of his German friends and sympathizers.

Virgin Soil. As we have indicated in the beginning, it was not until his last novel, *Virgin Soil,* the most mature of all, that Turgenev finally reached his goal. Moreover, it was not his leading character, Nezhdanov, who measured up to the author's requirements for leadership, but Solomin, the practical factory manager and highly respected representative of the new industrial age. It was during this period that industry started to develop rapidly in Russia, and the businessman began to assert himself as in any industrial country. The practical man who talked seldom but acted often and with decision came into vogue. Solomin was Turgenev's version of Stolz in *Oblomov*.

We must remember that Turgenev was seeking political change rather than social revolution. Solomin, too, hoped that the new era could be inaugurated by evolutionary means rather than by violent revolution. Although, as we have seen heretofore, Turgenev was at times inclined to side even with the revolutionists to effect the downfall of autocracy, either his aristocratic lineage or his native sagacity finally led him to distrust the leadership of the Bazarovs. Solomin was a man of different caliber—one who appealed to the majority of constructive liberals in Russia.

Virgin Soil is based chiefly on the "Narodniki" Movement ("Go to the People"), which came into vogue among the radicals at this time. Instead of working longer in the dark among small groups of adherents, the young revolutionists determined to popularize their message by carrying it directly to the people at large. They wanted to get a firsthand knowledge of the people whose conditions they hoped to ameliorate. As a result they discovered that they had overestimated the "People's" intelligence and maturity, or "consciousness." The soil must be prepared for revolution. Turgenev diagnosed the situation by calling his novel *Virgin Soil,* and he recommended through his mouthpiece, Solomin, a slower but a surer and more practical method of reform, by painstaking education of the people and by gradual evolution, rather than by sudden and violent revolution. History proves that both his diagnosis and his remedy were correct.

The study of Turgenev's novels, therefore, clearly indicates how closely interwoven Russian literature is with current events. His novels faithfully reflected Russian life and the controversial issues of the day. If we had no history whatever of the period in question we could still reproduce it in part from Turgenev's novels.

BIBLIOGRAPHY

Abramovitch, G., and Goloventchenko, F., *Russkaya Literatura (Russian Literature)*, Moscow, 1935.

Berdyaev, Nicholas, *The Origin of Russian Communism*, N. Y., 1937.

Baring, Maurice, *An Outline of Russian Literature*, Home University Library.

Carr, E. H., *Michael Bakunin*, London, 1937.

Graham, Stephen, *Tsar of Freedom: Alexander II*, Yale University Press, 1935.

Grevs, I. M., *Istoria Odnoi Luibvi (A History of One Love)*, Moscow, 1928. Printed in Germany.

Kropotkin, Peter, *Russian Literature*, N. Y., 1905.

Mirsky, D. S., *A History of Russian Literature*, N. Y., 1927.

Nelson, John H., *The Negro Character in American Literature*, Kansas University Bulletin, Vol. 27, No. 15, 1926.

Noyes, G. R., *Masterpieces of the Russian Drama*, N. Y., 1933.

Olgin, M. J., *Guide to Russian Literature*, N. Y., 1920.

Panayeva, Avdotya, *Vospominania (Memoirs)*, Leningrad, 1929.

Phelps, W. L., *Essays on Russian Novelists*, N. Y., 1916.

Reed, John C., *The Brothers' War*, Boston, 1905.

Stowe, Harriet B., *Uncle Tom's Cabin*.

Tsanoff, R. A., *The Problem of Life in the Russian Novel*, Rice Institute, 1917.

Wiener, Leo, *Anthology of Russian Literature*, Vol. II, N. Y., 1903.

Yarmolinsky, Avrahm, *Turgenev the Man, His Art and His Age*, N. Y., 1926.

Fyodor Mikhailovitch Dostoyevsky

1821-81

FYODOR MIKHAILOVITCH DOSTOYEVSKY was born on November 11, 1821, in Moscow, and died on February 9, 1881, in St. Petersburg. He was the second son in a family of seven children. Through his father, Mikhail Andreyevitch Dostoyevsky, a retired military physician, he belonged to the nobility (gentry); through his mother, Marie Netchayeva, to the respectable well-to-do middle class.

The entire family resided in a tiny official flat of two or three rooms. Later, however, they bought two estates in the province of Tula, about one hundred and ten miles from Moscow. It became the custom of the Dostoyevsky family to visit the Darovoye estate for the summer season, and this periodic change of scene supplied the children with new impressions of country life. The Dostoyevskys never petted or indulged their children, but, in accordance with the precepts of the time, made them conform to an exemplary system of discipline and a discreet mode of life. Fyodor was not permitted to walk unaccompanied until he was sixteen years of age.

The education of the children began at an early age. Their mother taught them the Russian alphabet. Their father instructed the two eldest boys, Mikhail and Fyodor, in Latin. Visiting tutors did the rest—one of whom, a certain Father Deacon, expounded the Holy Scriptures in such a way that they made a lasting impression on the mind of the young Fyodor. At the age of ten Fyodor read Schiller's *Die Räuber*, followed by Dickens, Sir Walter Scott, George Sand, Shakespeare, Victor Hugo, Pushkin, and Zhukovsky. When he was thirteen he was sent to the Tchermak boarding school, reputedly the best private school in Moscow. In 1837, when his mother died, his father took the two eldest boys to St. Petersburg to place them in the School for Military Engineers. By some inadvertence, no doubt, the robust Mikhail was rejected as physically unfit, whereas the sickly Fyodor was given a certificate of perfect health. Mikhail left for the Engineers' School in Revel, and Fyodor remained alone in St. Petersburg for the next three years. After being graduated as an ensign in 1841, Fyodor remained another year in order to secure the rank of sub-lieutenant. In 1843 he was employed in the draughting department of the School of Military Service. The following year his father died, and Fyodor resigned his commission in order to devote his life to literature.

At first Dostoyevsky tried his hand at translations, in which he eagerly invited the co-operation of his brother Mikhail. His first independent work, and the one which established his reputation as an author, was the novelette, *Poor People,* completed at the age of twenty-four, and published in 1846.

Being in dire financial straits at the time, a state of affairs which soon became chronic, Dostoyevsky threatened to hang himself if the novel was rejected. It seems likely that he was completely unprepared for the burst of enthusiasm with which it was received by the leading critics of the day. The poet Nekrasov, to whom the manuscript was submitted, stayed up all night to read it, rang Dostoyevsky's bell at four in the morning, and embraced him with joy. He at once hailed Dostoyevsky as a new Gogol. Even Belinsky, the Russian Lessing, who could make or break the career of a budding writer, received him with enthusiasm and encouragement. Dostoyevsky's name shot up like a meteor in literary circles, and he became convinced that he had reached the peak of his fame.

Dostoyevsky's promising literary career soon came to an abrupt termination. On April 5, 1849, he, together with his associates, was arrested for participation in a secret society with headquarters at the home of Mikhail Vasilyevitch Petrashevsky (1821-66), where Fourier and other sociologists were expounded and discussed. Dostoyevsky's particular crime consisted of his having read to the group Belinsky's famous letter to Gogol, of 1847, in which he accused the latter of reactionary and dogmatic leanings. For this Dostoyevsky, whose socialist principles were already weakening under pressure from the Slavophile theories so characteristic of his later years, was condemned to death. After eight months in prison, he and his comrades were led out to be shot. As the soldiers were taking aim a messenger from Tsar Nicholas I announced the commutation of the death penalty. Dostoyevsky was sentenced to four years at hard labor in a Siberian prison camp, followed by lifelong service as a common soldier in the Siberian army. In 1859 he was pardoned by Alexander II and returned to St. Petersburg. It was during his Siberian exile that Dostoyevsky conceived the idea of writing *Memoirs from a Dead House,* which was published shortly after his return, 1861-62, and which, as a chronicle of his experiences under the frightful regime of the prison camp, was received with loud acclaim even by Tolstoy. The Siberian ordeal served to aggravate an epileptic condition to which Dostoyevsky was subject for the rest of his life, and which he has described so vividly in *The Idiot* (1869).

While serving as a soldier in Siberia, Dostoyevsky met the widow Marya Isayeva, whom he married on February 6, 1857. This marriage, which proved unhappy, was terminated in 1864 when his wife died of consumption in Moscow. Later, in order to fulfill a literary contract, Dostoyevsky hired as a stenographer, Anna Grigorevna Snitkina, many years his junior, and married her on February 27, 1867, after a courtship of only a few months. The next four years he spent abroad in order to avoid imprisonment for debt. His second wife proved to be of great assistance to him in the management of his finances. Four children were born to them.

At a meeting of the Society of Lovers of Russian Literature on the occasion of the unveiling of Pushkin's monument in Moscow on June 20, 1880, Dostoyevsky delivered a remarkable address, which drew thunderous applause from the Westernizers as well as from the Slavophiles, and which promoted him to the rank of a national hero. He died on February 9, 1881, at 8:38 o'clock in the evening, and was buried on February 15 in the cemetery of the Alexander Nevsky monastery in St. Petersburg. His funeral was a pageant in which all classes of Russian society were represented.

Dostoyevsky's literary career may be divided roughly into three periods: the first, from 1846, when *Poor People* was published, to 1849, the year of his arrest; the second, from 1859, the date of his pardon, to 1864, when he lost his first wife and brother; the third, from 1864, a year marked by the publication of his *Letters from the Underworld*, to 1880, when he delivered his famous speech on Pushkin. Dostoyevsky's fame rests largely on his four major novels, *Crime and Punishment* (1866), *The Idiot* (1869), *The Possessed* (1873), and *The Brothers Karamazov* (1880).

THE PLOT OF *POOR PEOPLE* (1846)

This short novel consists exclusively of an exchange of letters between Makar Dievushkin, a poverty-stricken copyist in one of the government offices of St. Petersburg, and Barbara Dobroselova, a frail and destitute orphan who makes a precarious living as a seamstress. Makar loves the unhappy girl, who lives across the courtyard from him in dingy surroundings, as if she were his daughter. He denies himself even the necessities of life in order to supply her with a cloak, bonbons, grapes, and roses, or to treat her to a trip to the theatre. His generosity forces him to pawn his only respectable uniform, to wear his shoes until the toes stick out, and to leave his room rent unpaid. In desperation he seeks to borrow money, and when that fails he takes to drink to drown his sorrows. Only the generosity of his superior in office saves him from absolute penury by a gift of one hundred rubles.

Barbara accepts Makar's gifts, while protesting

against his extravagance. She is unable, owing to her
precarious health, to obtain sufficient work to pay her
expenses. Weary of the struggle, she longs to return to
the country, where in her childhood under better financial
conditions, she spent her happiest days. While she is
viewing the future with fear and uncertainty, since there
seems to be no hope of Makar's improved financial position, Monsieur Bwikov, a man of considerable property,
makes Barbara an offer of marriage, and proposes to
remove her from her drab surroundings to his estate on
the Russian steppes of which she will be mistress. In
great distress of mind and spirit Barbara consents, for
she can see no other way of escape from a mode of life
which becomes increasingly difficult for her to bear. She
feverishly prepares for her wedding with the short-tem-
pered Bwikov and for her departure from St. Petersburg. Makar, who has lived only for her, although he has
been content for the most part to confine their relations
to correspondence, is now broken hearted.

THE PLOT OF *CRIME AND PUNISHMENT* (1866)

The hero of *Crime and Punishment* is a poverty-
stricken student by the name of Rodion Romanovitch
Raskolnikov, who is forced by circumstances to live in
the worst slums of St. Petersburg. The slender income
of his mother and sister, whom he dearly loves, cannot
provide the funds necesary for the completion of the university career on which his future depends. In desperate
financial straits, Raskolnikov pawns a ring given to him
by his sister and his dead father's gold watch to a disagreeable old woman, Alena Ivanovna, who makes a profitable living out of the misfortunes of her clients. Haunted by the need of securing money for the completion of
his studies, as well as for the support of his mother and
sister, Raskolnikov conceives the idea of killing and
robbing the old moneylender "who preys on other lives."

Raskolnikov begins to associate with Sonya, the
daughter of a confirmed drunkard, who has become a
prostitute in order to save her family from starvation.
He becomes more than ever aware of the depths of pov-

erty and misery around him. In the moody and unbalanced frame of mind engendered by these conditions, the murder of the old woman seems justifiable, and the idea takes complete possession of him. His sensitive nature revolts, however, at the thought of killing her with a hatchet, his only weapon. Only when he learns that his sister, Dunya, is about to marry a well-to-do but despicable old man, in order that he, Raskolnikov, may secure funds for his education—only then can he bring himself to the point of committing the crime. He determines at all costs to prevent a marriage which would ruin his sister's life.

Raskolnikov therefore perpetrates his dastardly deed in the hope of devoting the profits of a useless old woman to a useful purpose. In doing so, however, he is forced to commit a second—this time an unpremeditated crime —by killing the pious sister of the moneylender, who inadvertently becomes a witness to his first murder. In the excitement he entirely neglects to secure the money for the sake of which he became a criminal.

Raskolnikov successfully evades apprehension by the authorities, but only at a tremendous cost. Perpetually haunted by the fear of being caught, his crime becomes an obsession with him, and he endures the tortures of the damned. At length, in desperation, he confesses everything to Sonya, the prostitute, whose misery is as profound as his own, although of a different origin. She persuades him, in the hope of his regeneration, to confess his crime to the authorities and pay the penalty. The penalty is seven years in Siberia; but he does not face it alone. Sonya goes with him and becomes the good angel of his wretched fellow prisoners in their hour of need. Raskolnikov and Sonya look forward eagerly to the end of the seven years when he will be released and can begin life anew.

THE PLOT OF *THE IDIOT* (1869)

The idiot is Prince Myshkin, a simple childlike man of ancient Russian lineage, whose soul is so transparent that he can live in a den of iniquity without besmirching his own character. Because of his sincere humility and his habit of turning the other cheek, his companions regard him as a fool, although they fall victims in spite of themselves to the magnetic charm of his saintly personality.

From early youth Prince Myshkin has suffered from epilepsy—a disease which has seriously affected his physical and mental faculties. When he returns to Russia to assume the responsibilities of a rich inheritance, two women, Aglia Epantchin, the daughter of a general, and Nastasya Filipovna, the discarded mistress of a wealthy merchant, fall in love with him. Out of sheer pity for her wretchedness, Prince Myshkin, who in his mild way returns the affection of both women, prepares to marry Nastasya. She, however, refuses to accept the sacrifice, and surrenders herself to the tender mercies of another suitor, Rogozhin. The latter, a man of ungovernable passions, mad with jealousy because he cannot monopolize the love of Nastasya, gives way to primitive impulses and murders her. There follows the memorable vigil of Rogozhin and Myshkin by the corpse of the unhappy woman.

For his crime Rogozhin is exiled to Siberia. Aglia marries a dishonest adventurer, who later deserts her. Prince Myshkin leaves for Switzerland in a state of physical disability and mental derangement.

THE PLOT OF *THE POSSESSED* (1873)

The hero of this story is Nikolai Stavrogin, a handsome, outwardly polished, brilliant young man with a heart as cold as steel. He is the son of Varvara Petrovna, a wealthy and domineering widow, who lives at her Skvoryeshniki estate on the outskirts of a provincial capital, in the vicinity of which the entire narrative takes place. Nikolai Stavrogin is a man with a past—a past which includes degradation from his rank in the army, several questionable moral escapades, and a secret marriage with a feeble-minded cripple, Marya Timofyevna. In St. Petersburg he has associated with the lower depths of society. There is much in his personality which repels his fellow townsmen, and his extraordinary behavior at times gives rise to rumors about his sanity. The powerful influence of this strange man, who is more often in the background than in the foreground, directs the lives of many of the characters in this novel.

Stavrogin's chief tool is Pyotr Verkhovensky, a totally unscrupulous, garrulous, and insolent knave, who poses as an organizer for the revolutionary Nihilists. He claims to represent a central revolutionary committee, whose object is to effect a network of local committees throughout Russia. He insinuates himself, with comparative ease, into the graces of honest but dull-witted people of responsible position in the province, wilfully misleads them with the object of producing disorder and of making revolutionary capital out of that disorder. Murder, suicide, and incendiarism are, in his opinion, legitimate weapons to further the cause of Nihilism. Verkhovensky practically idolizes Stavrogin, on whom he focuses all his hopes for the success of revolutionary Nihilism.

Verkhovensky finds the nucleus of his committee among the local radicals of the provincial capital. These include Kirillov, a madman in search of the superman, who by committing suicide to end fear and pain, will become a Man-God, and thereby emancipate humanity. To substantiate his beliefs Kirillov has offered to sacrifice his own life for the revolutionary cause whenever it shall be demanded of him. Another member of the group is the student Shatov, an ex-serf from Varvara Petrovna's estate, who has renounced Socialism for Slavophilism, and who would gladly cut loose from his radical associates, if they would only let him. He looks to Stavrogin as the hope of the Christian Slavophile movement, but his associates fear that if he is permitted to abandon Nihilism he will betray them to the authorities. Among the other members of the organization are Virginsky, a self-taught government clerk, poverty-stricken, but full of vague hopes for the future; Shigalov, Virginsky's brother-in-law; and Lyamshin, a Jew with some musical talent, who serves the government in the humble capacity of post-office clerk. These men, organized by Verkhovensky and directed by Stavrogin, are the "Possessed" or "Devils."

Verkhovensky has won favor with the new Governor's wife, Yulia Mikhailovna von Lembke, a vain but ambitious woman who seeks recognition as a person of the most fashionable liberal and democratic views. He inspires her to put on a fête for the benefit of the poor governesses of the province. The fête is ruined by the disorderly tactics of Verkhovensky's committee; the Governor and his wife are disgraced, and the former loses his mind.

Meanwhile the same committee, with the knowledge if not with the consent of Stavrogin, sets fire to a section of the provincial capital in order to conceal the murder of Stavrogin's crippled wife and her brother, whose timely removal leaves him free to marry a young girl of good family, Lizavetta Drozdov, who is madly in love with him. Lizavetta, after sacrificing her honor to the merciless Stavrogin, finds that he does not love her. She leaves him, only to be killed by a vindictive mob outside the house where the crippled wife of Stavrogin lies murdered.

No mercy is shown and no quarter granted in the methods pursued by the Nihilists. Verkhovensky feels that to bind his revolutionary rascals to secrecy, they must all be implicated in the murder of Shatov, who as a renegade to the cause, is too dangerous alive. Shatov's murder is planned and executed in spite of the feeble protests of some members of the group, at the very time that his wife's return and the birth of her son have opened up a new horizon for him. Kirillov is persuaded to assume the guilt of the murder and to commit suicide for the good of the cause.

Verkhovensky's plans are totally upset, however, by Stavrogin's sudden departure for St. Petersburg in order to evade possible trial for the murder of his wife, and the betrayal of the group by the deranged Lyamshin. Scenting trouble, Verkhovensky likewise deserts his associates and escapes abroad, leaving the others to face the music. Stavrogin returns secretly to Skvoryeshniki, but realizing that his life has been a total failure, he proceeds to hang himself in the attic.

THE PLOT OF *THE BROTHERS KARAMAZOV* (1880)

The central figures in this unfinished novel are Fyodor Karamazov, his three sons, Dimitri, Ivan, and Alyosha, and his illegitimate son Smerdyakov. The father is a sensual brute who abandoned his sons in their infancy for women and drink, and who has appropriated for his own use the property left to Dimitri by his unfortunate mother. The three sons have inherited the forceful personality of their father, but in other respects they are remarkably unlike. Dimitri (Mitya) is a wayward and passionate but lovable young man, in spite of his shortcomings, who harbors in his heart a bitter hatred for his father. Ivan, the second brother and the most intellectual of the three, is a skeptic and a materialist. Alyosha, the monk, is a saintly character, who devotes his boundless energy to the service of God and his fellow man. Smerdyakov is an epileptic idiot.

Dimitri is in love with Katerina Ivanovna, whose father, a superior officer, has embezzled funds and threatens to commit suicide. Dimitri offers to pay her father's debt if she will visit him secretly and alone at night. Katerina reluctantly submits to save her father from dishonor. Dimitri's better nature triumphs at the interview, and he dismisses Katerina in silence. She is fascinated by the nobility of his action, and henceforth her sole aim in life is to save Dimitri from following in his father's footsteps. Ivan Karamazov, who acts as an intermediary between Dimitri and his sweetheart, falls in love with Katerina himself. Meanwhile Dimitri, in spite of the solicitude of Katerina, begins to reveal the violent, sensual nature of the Karamazovs. He becomes infatuated with the beautiful Grushenka, former mistress of a Polish officer, using for her pleasure a considerable sum of money entrusted to him by Katerina for a relative in Moscow. Unfortunately for Dimitri, his father also covets Grushenka and promises her three thousand rubles if she will come to him. The rivalry of Dimitri and Fyodor for the favor of Grushenka intensifies Dimitri's hatred for his father, whom he threatens to kill if he finds him with her.

Smerdyakov, the natural son of Fyodor, and his father's confidant on the subject of his relations with Grushenka, betrays him to both Dimitri and Ivan. He warns Ivan to leave the village, predicting that Dimitri will kill his father because of Grushenka and because he needs the money his father has promised her. Smerdyakov points out that their father's death will bring each of the sons four thousand rubles, and that, if he, Smerdyakov, should suffer an attack of epilepsy during Ivan's absence, there will be no one to protect Fyodor from Dimitri. In spite of his better judgment, Ivan follows the advice of Smerdyakov, aware that his departure may facilitate his father's murder.

During the absence of Ivan, Dimitri, in search of Grushenka, proceeds with a pistol to his father's room. He is only prevented from killing Fyodor by Grigory, a watchman on the estate. Dimitri's failure does not save Fyodor. He is killed by Smerdyakov, who is found suffering from an epileptic fit near his father's body. All the circumstantial evidence is against Dimitri, who is found guilty of patricide. Ivan, conscious that as an accomplice he is really responsible for the murder, broods over his guilt until he loses his mind. Smerdyakov, the actual perpetrator of the crime, hangs himself. Dimitri is exiled to Siberia, where Grushenka accompanies him.

FROM *THE POSSESSED*

. . . Shatov interrupted, waving his hand.

"Do you remember your expression that 'an atheist can't be a Russian,' that 'an atheist at once ceases to be a Russian'? Do you remember saying that?"

"Did I?" Nikolay Vsyevolodovitch (Stavrogin) questioned him back.

"You ask? You've forgotten? And yet that was one of the truest statements of the leading peculiarity of the Russian soul, which you divined. You can't have forgotten it! I will remind you of something else: you said then that 'a man who was not orthodox could not be a Russian.'"

"I imagine that's a Slavophil idea."

"The Slavophils of to-day disown it. Nowadays, people have grown cleverer. But you went further: you believed that Roman Catholicism was not Christianity; you asserted that Rome proclaimed Christ subject to the third temptation of the devil. Announcing to all the world that

Christ without an earthly kingdom cannot hold his ground upon earth, Catholicism by so doing proclaimed Antichrist and ruined the whole Western world. You pointed out that if France is in agonies now it's simply the fault of Catholicism, for she has rejected the iniquitous God of Rome and has not found a new one. That's what you could say then! I remember our conversations."

"If I believed, no doubt I should repeat it even now. I wasn't lying when I spoke as though I had faith," Nikolay Vsyevolodovitch pronounced very earnestly. "But I must tell you, this repetition of my ideas in the past makes a very disagreeable impression on me. Can't you leave off?"

"If you believe it?" repeated Shatov, paying not the slightest attention to this request. "But didn't you tell me that if it were mathematically proved to you that the truth excludes Christ, you'd prefer to stick to Christ rather than to the truth? Did you say that? Did you?" . . .

Shatov bent forward in his chair again and again held up his finger for a moment.

"Not a single nation," he went on, as though reading it line by line, still gazing menacingly at Stavrogin, "not a single nation has ever been founded on principles of science or reason. There has never been an example of it, except for a brief moment, through folly. Socialism is from its very nature bound to be atheism, seeing that it has from the very first proclaimed that it is an atheistic organization of society, and that it intends to establish itself exclusively on the elements of science and reason. Science and reason have, from the beginning of time, played a secondary and subordinate part in the life of nations; so it will be till the end of time. Nations are built up and moved by another force which sways and dominates them, the origin of which is unknown and inexplicable: that force is the force of an insatiable desire to go on to the end, though at the same time it denies that end. It is the force of the persistent spirit of life, as the Scriptures call it, 'the river of living water,' the drying up of which is threatened in the Apocalypse. It's the aesthetic principle, as the philosophers call it, the ethical principle with which they identify it, 'the seeking for God,' as I call it more simply. The object of every

national movement, in every people and at every period
of its existence is only the seeking for its god, who must
be its own god, and the faith in him as the only true one.
God is the synthetic personality of the whole people, taken
from its beginning to its end. It has never happened that
all, or even many, peoples have had one common god, but
each has always had its own. It's a sign of the decay of
nations when they begin to have gods in common. When
gods begin to be common to several nations the gods are
dying and the faith in them, together with the nations
themselves. The stronger a people, the more individual
their god. There never has been a nation without a religion, that is, without an idea of good and evil. Every
people has its own conception of good and evil, and its
own good and evil. When the same conceptions of good
and evil become prevalent in several nations, then these
nations are dying, and then the very distinction between
good and evil is beginning to disappear. . . .

"If a great people does not believe that the truth is
only to be found in itself alone (in itself alone and in it
exclusively) ; if it does not believe that it alone is fit and
destined to raise up and save all the rest by its truth, it
would at once sink into being ethnographical material,
and not a great people. A really great people can never
accept a secondary part in the history of Humanity, nor
even one of the first, but will have the first part. A nation
which loses this belief ceases to be a nation. But there is
only one truth, and therefore only a single one out of the
nations can have the true God, even though other nations
may have great gods of their own. Only one nation is
'god-bearing,' that's the Russian people, and . . . and . . .
can you think me such a fool, Stavrogin," he yelled fran-
tically all at once, "that I can't distinguish whether my
words at this moment are the rotten old commonplaces
that have been ground out in all the Slavophil mills in
Moscow, or a perfectly new saying, the last word, the
sole word of renewal and resurrection, and . . . and what
do I care for your laughter at this minute! What do I
care that you utterly, utterly fail to understand me, not a
word, not a sound! Oh, how I despise your haughty
laughter and your look at this minute!"

As we have already stated, each of Turgenev's novels has its counterpart in a work by Dostoyevsky. We shall begin our discussion of Dostoyevsky with a further comparison of these two authors. To understand the difference between Turgenev and Dostoyevsky is to comprehend the sharp distinction between culture and civilization. By culture is meant something organic and inherent. By civilization is understood something mechanical and artificial. Culture depends upon a certain locality, and is therefore, the natural outgrowth of a particular soil or environment. Civilization, on the other hand, does not necessarily depend upon geographical phenomena. It may appear everywhere or anywhere. Culture implies birth and growth; civilization calls to mind inventions and material betterment. For instance, if a person wishes to fly, he invents an aeroplane. That represents civilization. But, if the same person could grow wings on his body, that would denote culture. Character is culture; manners— civilization. If a person lacks character, nobody can give it to him. A character cannot be acquired, but good manners can be taught to anyone, even to an animal. To illustrate further, music is culture, the science of music is civilization. Anyone can study music, but not everyone can be a musician. Emerson represents American culture; Edison and Ford—American civilization. Culture is static; civilization, dynamic. Culture is feeling or emotion; civilization, rationalism and analysis. Culture is lyric; civilization—epic. We can tame or civilize practically every living thing, but we can cultivate only certain of them. We cultivate plants, but we do not civilize them. Thus a person may be highly cultured and possess little civilization, or *vice versa*. The East stressed culture —the West emphasized civilization. Civilization is the more objective, while culture is subjective. Culture stresses the heart; civilization the mind. The ancient Hebrews, for instance, were primarily a cultured people —the Romans predominantly a civilized nation; whereas the Greeks were fortunate in possessing both culture and civilization.

The novels of Dostoyevsky faithfully represent Russian character at its best and at its worst. In the works of Turgenev civilization predominates. In other words, the Slavophiles, whose most outstanding literary exponent was Dostoyevsky, consciously or unconsciously voiced the sentiment of Russian culture; while the Westernizers, whose principal champion was Turgenev, represented civilization—more specifically Western civilization. Only in this light can we grasp the underlying motives of these two great novelists.

Although he refrained from calling the child by its real name, Dostoyevsky always vigorously opposed the importation of foreign culture at the expense of Russian culture. In his own words, "No nation on earth, no society with a certain measure of stability, has been developed to order, on the lines of a program imported from abroad." This does not mean that Dostoyevsky blindly opposed everything foreign merely because it was alien. He was against foreign ideas when they threatened to supplant native influences. He had no objection to the introduction of foreign technique, mechanical equipment, inventions, and so forth. In other words, he was not antagonistic to the importation of civilization because that is transferable and changeable and does not depend on local environment. What he valiantly and consistently condemned was the importation of foreign "isms," that is, foreign culture, for he believed that culture could only be transplanted at the expense of native characteristics. Culture must grow like a tree.

Two terms of Chinese origin are commonly used in Japan for patriotism. These are *aikoku* and *yukoku*. Both terms are expressions of love for one's country, the difference being that the former, *aikoku*, signifies positive love of country, whereas the latter, *yukoku*, denotes negative love for the fatherland. In Japan at present the *aikoku* has superseded the *yukoku* patriot. In Russian literature, we may designate Turgenev and his followers as *yukoku* patriots, whereas Dostoyevsky and his disciples may be classified as *aikoku* patriots. For there is no doubt but that most of the Westernizers were as good Russian patriots as the staunchest of Slavophiles, the difference being that the Westernizers for the most part exposed the shortcomings of the Russian character and the backwardness of their country in contrast to the rapid material progress and advanced ideas of the West. They presented the negative side of the picture, while the Slavophiles expressed their patriotism, rightly or wrongly, by advancing the strong points of Russian character and Russian culture in general—the positive side of the picture.

Dostoyevsky's method of characterization was the exact opposite of Turgenev's. Where Turgenev discovered his characters, Dostoyevsky for the most part created them. Turgenev's artistry stopped when the individual was completely drawn; Dostoyevsky's artistry began when the individual, having been almost scientifically portrayed, began to act, and although beset by seemingly insuperable obstacles, moved sincerely and artistically through a lifetime of climax. This incidentally throws an interesting light on the fact that Dostoyevsky's short stories were never so successful as his novels; while Turgenev's short sketches were greater works of art than his novels.

Turgenev was not great enough to control the characters he portrayed, and to follow them through to their logical end. Hence, the frustrations. In this respect Dostoyevsky proved himself the greater genius. Turgenev's characters differ from Dostoyevsky's principally in the degree of their individuality and stature. Turgenev's characters formed the loom on which Dostoyevsky's were woven. The latter are potentially similar to the former, but Dostoyevsky begins where Turgenev left off. He intensifies what conflict there is already, and adds so much more that the proportion of adversity to normality becomes contorted to a degree which is invariably responsible for the insanity of the character in question. At this point Dostoyevsky is ready to begin the significant portion of his novel.

A few of Turgenev's characters might have been used to advantage and even with great profit by Dostoyevsky. He could have incorporated Lavretsky into his novels, after intensification to the point of abnormality. Bazarov, before his death, would have been an interesting figure for Dostoyevsky to begin with, and Bazarov's parents would have fitted admirably into one of his novels. "For such people as they are not to be found in your grand society even in the daytime with a light." (Bazarov.) Of them all, perhaps Fenitchka, the mistress of the elder Kirsanov, came closer than the rest to being a creation of Dostoyevsky. Bazarov once said of her: "She'll go to destruction probably. Well, she'll extricate herself somehow or other." This was the nearest that Turgenev ever came to Dostoyevsky in the field of characterization.

Turgenev considered foreigners superior to most Russians (Insarov), and his more or less positive Russian types spoke at least a foreign tongue (Solomin). On the other hand, Dostoyevsky considered most Russians superior to most foreigners. Every one of his admirable characters was of pure Russian descent. In fact, according to Dostoyevsky, there were no bad Russians. They became so only when they came into contact with alien "isms." Even Sonya, the prostitute, he implies, was better than all the foreigners. In other words, according to Dostoyevsky, Russians are essentially good, if they remain Russians.

In brief, Dostoyevsky was a genius, while Turgenev was an artist. Turgenev achieved his mark through restraint—Dostoyevsky through the absence of restraint. Turgenev was vivid through expression, Dostoyevsky through passion. Turgenev was a man of the world, Dostoyevsky an innocent. Turgenev wrote like an innocent and Dostoyevsky like a man of the world.

Poor People. In the light of the above explanation, Dostoyevsky's major novels may seem more intelligible to Western readers. Let us consider briefly his first short novelette, *Poor People*. An outsider on reading this novel in letters, may well wonder why it created such a sensation in the Russian literary world, even prior to its publication in 1846. Why did leading critics predict the rise of a new Gogol? In the first place, Dostoyevsky revealed in this novel a remarkable maturity of thought for a young man barely twenty-four years of age. Moreover, his literary style was both powerful and polished, not by any means inferior to the work of the best writers of his generation. Finally, and most important of all, without detracting from the originality of *Poor People*, Dostoyevsky enlarged upon Gogol's *Cloak*, which had already become a classic, and which had been extensively imitated. The literary exponents of the Russian poor enjoyed great popularity, and in consequence, their books were bestsellers, although this was not their purpose. The title of Dostoyevsky's small novel might be applied to an entire library of works produced by his contemporaries on the plight of the Russian poor. Later critics discovered in *Poor People* the germs of philosophy which permeated all Dostoyevsky's subsequent novels—just as *Sevastopol* supplied a preview to the rest of Tolstoy's works.

Crime and Punishment. Although this, the most popular of Dostoyevsky's novels among foreigners in general, has a gruesome plot, it was never meant to be a glorified detective story. Russian literature was not written for the entertainment of its readers, and the plot of *Crime and Punishment* is of secondary importance. The main idea, which runs like a scarlet thread through this and through his three subsequent novels, is the clash between the Slavophiles and the Westernizers. With *Crime and Punishment*, the controversy between these two camps began in earnest. The novel served both as a rebuttal to Turgenev and as an exposition of the Slavophile point of view on political, economic, and social matters. The reader must be warned again not to approach Dostoyevsky's major novels with Western tools. If Dostoyevsky had written his novels in the West he would never have secured a publisher.

Crime and Punishment marks the breach between Dostoyevsky and the radicals. Like Turgenev he was in search of a leader, and like him, he turned first to the student body. Raskolnikov is a much more interesting person, however, than Turgenev's Rudin or even Bazarov. Even the choice of his name served a particular purpose. The etymological derivation of Raskolnikov is *raskol*, meaning schism, rift, break, or detachment. It is another name for *bezpotchvenik*, a word coined by the Russian critic Grigorovitch, and extensively employed by the Slavophiles when they referred to the Westernizers. In free translation a *bezpotchvenik* is one who is detached from the soil, in contrast to one who is rooted in the soil. The name of Raskolnikov thus supplies the key to the entire novel. Before he was captivated by the rationalism of the West, our hero was decent and led a useful life. From the time he became a "Raskolnikov," he entered upon the path which led to crime.

Raskolnikov may be regarded as Turgenev's Rudin or Nezhdanov in action, presented from the Slavophile standpoint. His crime was the result of rationalism and cold logic, no feelings being involved. Not that Raskolnikov had no heart or emotions. But, according to Dostoyevsky, the science of the West, which was based on facts and laws, obliterated all human feeling. In *Crime and Punishment,* as in his three subsequent novels, Dostoyevsky emphasizes the struggle for supremacy between the heart and the mind. When the mind takes the upper hand, the result is crime; but when the heart prevails resurrection follows. As long as Raskolnikov remained under the influence of Western intellectualism, his life was miserable, and he became a detriment to society. When his Russian heart (soul) reasserted itself, he became a new man.

In other words, it was Dostoyevsky's conviction that the mind without the heart was like a body without a soul.

Greek culture included both; Plato stressed the mind, Aristotle the heart. Greek culture would have been less interesting if either had dominated to the exclusion of the other. This, too, was the genius of Christianity— that it appealed both to the heart and to the mind, although the former predominated.

What was true of Raskolnikov may be applied to Sonya. She was not as well educated as he, but, according to Dostoyevsky, her thinking reflected the rationalism of the West. She became a prostitute, not from preference, but to save her family from starvation. The result was that she saved neither her family nor herself. When her Russian heart reasserted itself, she experienced a resurrection, breathed new life into Raskolnikov, and became a source of comfort and consolation to others. By way of digression, Dostoyevsky was the first author in Russian literature to lift a prostitute from degradation and contempt and to place her on a par with the most virtuous heroines of world literature. She became the moral force in the tragedy, and she served as a warning against a social order which was the product of Western rationalism. Dostoyevsky gave Sonya a new deal.

It may be of interest to observe that Dostoyevsky dealt with his criminals as the prophet of the Old Testament dealt with the erring members of his flock. They passed through four stages: sin (crime), punishment (suffering), repentance (resurrection), and forgiveness (love). It may seem strange that Dostoyevsky, who was imbued with the teachings of the New Testament, where forgiveness is not necessarily dependent upon punishment, should subject his heroes to this purge. This becomes clear when the reader bears in mind that to Dostoyevsky, Love, the greatest thing in the world, evolved only from suffering. It would be erroneous to accept the dictum of many critics who maintain that he made a religion or a fetish of suffering. He did not advocate suffering for the sake of suffering, but rather as a price which the individual, society, or nation must pay in life for the *summum bonum*.

Although Western Christianity and the literature influenced by it have paid a great deal of homage to the element of suffering, the West lacks the depth of experience in this field which Eastern European Christianity has acquired. A striking example of this is to be found in Emerson, the American Dostoyevsky. Both Emerson and Dostoyevsky were mystics; both believed in truth from within, as the superiority of the heart over the mind. Both men were deeply religious, and each was accepted as a prophet by his own people. In his essay, *The Over-Soul*, Emerson, like Dostoyevsky, expressed his belief that the most divine attribute of man is Love. But here the paths of the two philosophers, who have so much in common, began to diverge. Emerson did not believe this Love to be the outcome of suffering. Emerson was a Westerner, Dostoyevsky an Easterner. Therein lies the difference.

Although the main issue in *Crime and Punishment* is political, there exists also an ethical problem. Was it ethical for Raskolnikov to murder the wretched pawnbroker, whom he regarded as a social parasite, so that he might use the blood money to complete his education and thereby become a useful member of society? Furthermore, was it ethical for his sister, Dunya, to marry a man she despised in order to finance her brother's education and assure his future? Finally, was it ethical on the part of Sonya to subject herself to humiliation, suffering, disgrace, and danger in order to feed a drunken father and a starving family? In Western Europe at that time many writers condoned as well as commended such a sacrifice of self. The individual thinking of the age might be transferred to the class. Was it ethical for one class or group, by implication the Westernizers, to destroy another in order to produce what they thought would be a better world?

In brief, Dostoyevsky's main purpose in *Crime and Punishment* was to show that Raskolnikov and his followers, when they fell victims to the imported "isms" of the West, became criminals; but after going through certain processes which restored them to their own culture and soil, they reasserted themselves and became useful members of society. All Dostoyevsky's criminals needed was a new start in life, and for this he felt that they required no assistance or enlightenment from the West. All that was necessary was for them to rediscover the potentialities of Russian culture, and to develop them accordingly.

Although Dostoyevsky did not kill Raskolnikov as Turgenev did Rudin, he was through with him, once his resurrection was assured. In his next novel, he sought a more ideal type—one far removed from the poverty-stricken student. Like Turgenev he went to his "house of gentlefolk" for Prince Myshkin, the hero of *The Idiot*.

The Idiot. Prince Myshkin, Dostoyevsky's new candidate for leadership, differed materially from Turgenev's Lavretsky. He had a magnetic personality which immediately commanded attention. People who agreed or disagreed with him, whether wise or flippant, adults or children, of whatever rank or station, listened to what the Prince had to say. No one hated him. It seemed as if he were about to assume leadership and settle all their problems by Peace. But like the Christ, whom Myshkin in certain scenes distinctly resembles, he was crucified by the mob who termed him an idiot. The action of the mob abruptly terminated Myshkin's career, although it was apparent that he was much wiser than they. At times it almost seems that the idiot is a projection of the author himself, for it is a well-established fact that the Westernizers not infrequently hurled the epithet of idiot or that of epileptic at Dostoyevsky. In this novel he takes pains to prove that the idiot is wiser and saner than all of them, that, in fact, they themselves are the idiots, and it is he who suffers for their transgressions.

Psychopathologists and criminologists have paid homage to the remarkable contribution of Dostoyevsky in *The Idiot*, in which he anticipated with a great degree of accuracy many modern scientific developments in these fields. Far from being distressed by his epileptic condition, Prince Myshkin, voicing the sentiment of Dostoyevsky, regarded this disease as an asset rather than a liability. In fact, he implied that his talent or genius was directly attributable to his infirmity. It is interesting to note that a number of historical figures have been victims of epilepsy. Theologians or scholars, as the case may be, have advanced the theory that the prophet Ezekiel, St. Paul, Mohammed, Caesar, Constantine the Great, Catherine the Great, Alexander I of Russia, Napoleon, and Dostoyevsky all suffered from this disease.

The Possessed. While the controversy still raged over *Fathers and Children,* Dostoyevsky, instead of continuing his hitherto fruitless search for a leader, wrote a sequel to Turgenev's novel, which he called *The Possessed (The Devils).* Strictly speaking, in *The Possessed* Dostoyevsky portrayed the Bazarovs in action. When the novel appeared in 1873 it shook Russian society profoundly, particularly the Western camp. Many of Dostoyevsky's adversaries branded him again as an idiot and an epileptic who exaggerated and defamed the liberal and socialist movements. Even as late as 1913 Maxim Gorky published a protest against the production of *The Possessed* by the Moscow Art Theatre. In spite of the anger of the Westernizers, this novel crowned Dostoyevsky as the prophet of Russia. Within a few years of its completion the violence of the anarchists afforded convincing proof of the validity of his contentions.

The following statement by Nicholas Berdyaev in his *Freedom and the Spirit* admirably reflects Dostoyevsky's philosophy regarding revolutionists in general and the radicals of *The Possessed* in particular:

" ... Revolutionaries (and counter-revolutionaries too) never begin by overcoming and getting rid of the evil in themselves; they prefer to exterminate it in others in its secondary and outward manifestations. A revolutionary attitude towards life is a superficial one and lacks depth. There is nothing radical about revolutions; they are to a big extent simply masquerades in which nothing is changed but the outward dress of the performers. Revolutions do not so much overcome evil as give new birth to it by provoking fresh evil.

"It is true that revolutions have certain positive results besides and that they determine new epochs in history, but the good which they do is the result not of revolutionary but of post-revolutionary activity." (pp. 186-87).

Dostoyevsky implies that the characters of *The Possessed,* even the notorious Pyotr Verkhovensky, were essentially good, but for the fact that their energies have been directed into improper channels. Using Shatov as his mouthpiece, he maintained that they could only be redeemed by driving out the devils and making room for the healing properties of the Orthodox faith. By Orthodoxy, Dostoyevsky meant the ideal church, the church as conceived by Solovyov, Berdyaev, and Bulgakov—a church of freedom of the spirit and high religious devotion. No matter what "ism" people professed, no matter what cause they espoused even to the extent of self-sacrifice, without religious faith Dostoyevsky believed that they built their foundation upon the sand. In other words, the foundation of all foundations, the philosophy of all philosophies, the cause of all causes, was religion—the Orthodox faith, without which people became "possessed."

Arriving at this conclusion, Dostoyevsky ventured another prophecy—that Russia would eventually become the savior of Christian civilization. Since the Russian Church was dogmatically nearer to the Protestant Church and ritualistically closer to the Roman Catholic, he believed that it was destined to become the bridge which would eventually unite the three. In his opinion the Russian Orthodox Church was the only one which had retained its purity, since in the West, science had practically

eclipsed Protestantism, and the merits of Roman Catholicism were obscured by too much organization and tem-
poral power. Although at times Dostoyevsky virulently
attacked the Roman Catholic Church, especially in the
chapter of *The Brothers Karamazov* entitled "The Great
Inquisitor," on the other hand, he paid great homage to
certain virtues which are distinctly characteristic of Roman Catholicism. For this reason many Catholic critics
have found him inconsistent and consider that he defeated
his own purpose.

The Brothers Karamazov. Since he believed Russia
would be saved by a spiritual leader rather than by a
statesman or revolutionist, Dostoyevsky sought the fulfilment of his dream in the person of Alyosha, one of
the Brothers Karamazov. Unfortunately this, his final
novel, remained unfinished, and his ideal hero, Alyosha,
undeveloped. Whether or not Dostoyevsky planned to
write four or five volumes on *The Brothers Karamazov*
cannot be established with certainty in spite of certain
allusions to the contrary. Whether, on the spur of the
moment, he was tempted to change the nature of Alyosha,
and to transform him into a villain, remains equally obscure. Following the spirit of the novel, it would seem
that Dostoyevsky wished to make of Alyosha a Redeemer
and a Russian leader. At times it appears that he lost
faith even in Alyosha, believing that only a miracle could
save Russia. Alyosha, coming as he did from the family
of the Karamazovs, might well be considered a miracle.

The story of *The Brothers Karamazov* is, in many respects, an epic of Russian life. Each member of the
family represented a slice of Russian society. Dimitri
was an uncultured and unconscious Slavophile, whereas
Ivan, the brain of the trio, directly or indirectly represented the Westernizers. Smerdyakov, the illegitimate
son, stood for the imitative mob which follows the leader
and becomes a tool in the hands of the theoreticians. His
father, Fyodor Karamazov, belonged to the sensuous,
indifferent, reactionary group of the old generation.

Alyosha was destined to reconcile the classes represented by Dimitri and Ivan. If, as some critics maintain, Dostoyevsky possessed in turn the traits of each of the Karamazovs, this would merely tend to substantiate the fact that he more than any other Russian author truthfully reflected the Russian people at their best and at their worst.

It seems clear from the very outset that Dostoyevsky felt more sympathy for Dimitri than for Ivan. Dimitri, in spite of his shortcomings, was essentially good at heart. Purged by suffering for a crime which he did not commit, he might have been redeemed, might have become a normal being—an eventuality which was hardly possible in the case of Ivan. With his desire to dominate it was very difficult for Ivan to bow even to circumstances. When he was forced to do so he became mentally unbalanced. Although the actual murder of Fyodor Karamazov must be laid at Smerdyakov's door, it was Ivan's brain that engineered the crime. Dostoyevsky clearly suggests that Smerdyakov had Ivan's sanction to murder his father. Since Dostoyevsky's philosophy of life was almost identical with that of the Near East, where the motive of the sinner or criminal as a rule receives greater consideration than the actual deed, he therefore blamed Ivan for the crime and labeled Smerdyakov his blind tool.

In this novel, even more than in *The Possessed*, Dostoyevsky asserted the necessity of religion and faith in the Christ. In spite of his conviction that the Christian Church would eventually save Russia, and make of it a model nation, whose light would radiate to the four corners of the earth, in this work he did not shut his eyes to the abuses and superstitions within the Church. Through churchmen of the caliber of Father Zosima and Alyosha he hoped to remedy its faults.

In *The Brothers Karamazov*, Dostoyevsky made the most earnest attempt ever made in Russian literature to iron out the various controversial issues which confronted his countrymen. For this reason it is surprising to find that in this first volume he devoted more space to the arguments of his opponents than to his own rebuttal. No Westernizer ever presented his case more convincingly than Ivan in *The Brothers Karamazov*. No Westernizer has provided an equally clear analysis of the fundamental principles of Slavophilism. In fact, the Westernizers seem to have tacitly agreed to maintain a sort of censorship against Slavophilism in their writings, while Dostoyevsky, whom they termed a dogmatic Slavophile, was broad-minded enough to open his columns to his adversaries and to present the case of the Westernizers on the social order and on religion in a most articulate manner. No wonder Pobiedonostsev and his fellow-reactionaries were both frightened and shocked by the religious discussions between Ivan and Alyosha! They were only pacified when Dostoyevsky assured them of a rebuttal in the second volume. Death intervened before he could fulfil that promise, and Dostoyevsky died like a true Christian, turning the other cheek. Perhaps, for this reason, his message was all the more powerful.

To sum up, Dostoyevsky's novels are the noblest expression of nineteenth-century Slavophilism. Placing the heart above the intellect, he opposed all manifestations of foreign "isms" whose purpose was to supplant or eclipse Russian virtues, which were the product of many centuries of Russian joy and sorrow. In the field of "enlightenment" he felt that the West had nothing to offer Russia, since Russia possessed all the elements necessary for her own redemption—in particular, the Russian Orthodox Church. While he was against the encroachment of Western "isms," he readily acknowledged Western accomplishments in the field of invention and technique which benefited humanity as a whole, opposing only the importation and adaptation of things intrinsically cultural.

In the final analysis, Dostoyevsky's gallery of characters was composed of lunatics, perverts, epileptics, prostitutes, drunkards, and swindlers—the scum of society, afflicted with all manner of mental diseases. Most of them lived in the city slums or in the provincial metropolis. Dostoyevsky assembled them all, demonstrated their plight, expressed their thought, aroused sympathy in their behalf, subjected them to a spiritual bath, and started them out all over again. To a certain extent he played for them the rôle of the Salvation Army, emphasizing their spiritual welfare rather than their physical necessity.

The same controversy, which is reflected in the works of Dostoyevsky and Turgenev, is being rehearsed in Russia today under a somewhat different nomenclature. The existing clash of opinions between the Right and the Left in the Soviet Union, between those who demand a nationalist orientation ("Nationalist in form, socialist in content."—Stalin), and those who advocate an international platform, constitutes a revival of the struggle between the Slavophiles and the Westernizers. At present—in partial fulfilment of Dostoyevsky's prophecy—the former seem to be gaining ground.

In recent years the works of Dostoyevsky have enjoyed remarkable popularity among the leaders of Nazi Germany. Even a brief analysis of Nazi ideals may help to reveal the basis of this popularity. Dostoyevsky opposed foreign influences in the interest of a national culture; the Nazi leaders do likewise. Dostoyevsky preached a Russian Christianity—the Nazis in their efforts to establish Neo-paganism are in search of a German national God. Dostoyevsky was convinced of the superiority of Holy Russia—as the Nazis boast of the superiority of the Aryan race. Dostoyevsky in his "Russian myth" predicted that Russia would save the world from chaos; the mission of the German Fascists is to save the world from Bolshevism.

But Nazi Germany will find it impossible to reconcile all of Dostoyevsky's teachings with her own platform. He did not expect to save the world through militarism and re-armament, but through the Church and the re-assertion of its culture. For him there was no substitute for the Christ. While elevating the soul of the Russian people almost to a myth, he bore in his heart no hatred toward other races or nationalities. As far as he was concerned, everybody could become Russian. According to the Nazi concept, blood determines that issue, and non-Aryans have been excluded. In the final analysis the Nazis are more particularistic, Dostoyevsky more universal.

BIBLIOGRAPHY

Aikhenwald, U. I., *Dve Jheni: Tolstaya i Dostoyevskaya (Mesdames Tolstoy and Dostoyevsky: Two Wives)*, Berlin, 1925.

Baring, Maurice, *An Outline of Russian Literature*, Home University Library.

Berdyaev, Nicholas, *The Origin of Russian Communism*, N. Y., 1937.

Berdyaev, Nicholas, *Freedom and the Spirit*, N. Y., 1935.

Berdyaev, Nicholas, *Mirosozertsanie Dostoyevskogo (Dostoyevsky's Philosophy of Life)*, Praha, 1923.

Bulgakov, Sergius, *The Orthodox Church*, N. Y., 1935.

Carr, E. H., *Dostoyevsky (1821-1881), A New Biography*, London, 1931.

Dolinin, A. S. (Editor), *Materiali i isledovania (Documents and Special Works)*, Academy of Science, Leningrad, 1937.

Dostoyevsky, A., *Fyodor Dostoyevsky*, Yale University Press, 1922.

Gide, André, *Dostoyevsky*, N. Y., 1926.

Kropotkin, Peter, *Russian Literature*, N. Y., 1905.

Masaryk, T. G., *The Spirit of Russia*, 2 Vols., London, 1919.

Merejkovsky, D., *Tolstoy as Man, with an Essay on Dostoyevsky*, N. Y., 1902.

Mirsky, D. S., *A History of Russian Literature*, N. Y., 1927.

Mirsky, D. S., *Contemporary Russian Literature, 1881-1925*, N. Y., 1926.

Murry, J. M., *Fyodor Dostoyevsky, A Critical Study*, London, 1910.

Netchayev, V. S., *Dostoyevsky and His Family* (in Russian), U.S.S.R., 1939.

Nikolsky, Yuri, *Turgenev and Dostoyevsky* (in Russian), Sophia, Bulgaria, 1921.

Nitobe, Inazo, "Trends of Thought in Present Japan," *The New Orient*, Vol. II, Chicago, 1933.

Nomad, Max, *Apostles of Revolution*, Boston, 1939.

Olgin, M. J., *Guide to Russian Literature*, N. Y., 1920.

Phelps, W. L., *Essays on Russian Novelists*, N. Y., 1916.

Simmons, Ernest J., "Dostoevski in Soviet Russia," *The American Quarterly on the Soviet Union*, Vol. I, No. 2, July, 1938, N. Y.

Tsanoff, R. A., *The Problem of Life in the Russian Novel*, Rice Institute, 1917.

Wiener, Leo, *Anthology of Russian Literature*, Vol. II, N. Y., 1903.

Yarmolinsky, Avrahm, *Dostoyevsky, A Life*, N. Y., 1934.

Lev Nikolayevitch Tolstoy
1828-1910

LEV NIKOLAYEVITCH TOLSTOY was born on September 9, 1828, at Yasnaya Polyana, near Tula, and died on November 20, 1910, at Astapovo, in the province of Riazan. On his father's side, he was a descendant of Peter Andreyevitch Tolstoy (1645-1729), a friend and companion of Peter the Great, who had the distinction of being the first regularly accredited Ambassador to the Porte. Tolstoy's father, born in 1797, served for a short time in the army, and retired in 1824 with the rank of lieutenant-colonel. The writer's mother was Princess Marya Nikolayevna Volkonskaya, the only daughter of Prince Nikolai Sergeyevitch Volkonsky. Count Lev Tolstoy was the youngest one of five children by this marriage.

After his father's death in Moscow in 1837, Tolstoy and his brothers were placed under the guardianship of his aunt, the Countess Osten-Sacken, and in care of Mme. Tatyana Alexandrovna Yergolskaya, a distant relative. In 1840 the Countess died, and the charge devolved upon another aunt, Pelagia Yushkova, who lived in Kazan. Tolstoy was eleven years old when he came under her influence, an influence which he subsequently regarded as anything but beneficial.

French, German, and Russian tutors were engaged for him and his brothers prior to their entrance into the University of Kazan. As a child, Lev showed no marked talent. While his father was still alive, the lad accompanied him on those hunting and shooting expeditions which were the delight and the chief pastime of the Russian nobleman.

In 1843, at the age of fifteen, he entered the University of Kazan, where, in the Oriental Department, he studied Arabic and Turkish. Later in life he studied

Hebrew and Greek. After two years, Tolstoy abandoned the study of Oriental languages and enrolled in the School of Law, where he met with equal discouragement. His restless mind revolted at what he considered the artificiality of academic scholarship. In the course of desultory reading at the university, he studied the works of Jean Jacques Rousseau. The Frenchman's plea for the natural life, honest work, and simplicity only served to convince him of the futility of his academic career. In 1847 he left the University of Kazan without a degree.

Tolstoy returned to his estate at Yasnaya Polyana with high ideas about reform and the amelioration of the condition of his peasants. He owned about 2500 acres of land in the province of Samara, and 300 horses. It is sometimes said, erroneously, that Tolstoy liberated his serfs before the date of general emancipation in 1861. In reality the greater part of them were out on quit-rent *(obrok)*. He soon discovered that the management of a large estate required knowledge and experience in addition to noble aspirations. Weary of the effort, he began to emulate the life of Rousseau rather than his teachings. He indulged in riotous living, gambled away a goodly part of his inheritance, and altogether became a dissolute rake.

In 1851, when the utter futility of this type of life dawned upon him, Tolstoy betook himself to the Caucasus (Piatigorsk), where his brother was stationed with a regiment, and where he hoped to find peace for his restless spirit by living close to nature. At this time the Russian government was disturbed over the lawlessness prevalent among the Caucasian peoples. As an officer, Tolstoy took part in punitive expeditions against the rebellious tribes of the border—his first taste of warfare. Here, too, he began to write. His first manuscript, *Childhood* (1852), was accepted by Nekrasov, editor of *The Contemporary*. Tolstoy was then twenty-four, the same age as Dostoyevsky when the latter published *Poor People*, his maiden effort, in 1846.

Childhood was followed by *The Landlord's Morning, Boyhood,* and *Youth,* in rapid succession. During the siege of Sevastopol (1854-55), in the Crimean War, Tolstoy served under the command of Prince Gortchakov. In the excitement of the time he recorded his experiences in *Sevastopol,* which earned him immediate celebrity. Even the Emperor Nicholas I issued special orders for the protection of the life of the young writer. Tolstoy returned home with valuable experience and impressions to receive an ovation from the social elite of St. Petersburg.

Reform was in the air in Russia, and Tolstoy, still seeking to ameliorate the condition of the peasants, traveled to Germany to study foreign educational methods. Three times between 1857 and 1861 Tolstoy crossed the Russian frontier to visit Germany, Rome, Naples, Florence, Lucerne, and London. In 1860 his brother Nikolai died, an event which made a profound impression on Tolstoy, and which he recorded almost autobiographically in his description of the death of Levin's brother in *Anna Karenina.*

While abroad, Tolstoy was deeply impressed by that novel institution, the kindergarten, to which Fröbel, the great German educationist, was devoting all his energies. Determined to emulate the latter, Tolstoy obtained permission to open a school on his estate, where he sought to put into practice the theories of Rousseau. In his zeal, he also began an educational journal called *Yasnaya Polyana.* The time for opening the school was well chosen; just two months previously (March 3, 1861), the decree for the emancipation of the serfs had been issued.

In 1862 Tolstoy married Sophya Andreyevna Behrs, the daughter of Doctor Andrey Behrs, of Moscow, and settled on his estate at Yasnaya Polyana. She bore him thirteen children, of whom five sons and three daughters reached maturity. Sonya, as he called her, became his devoted literary assistant, his amanuensis, and eventually his "publications manager."

After 1879 Tolstoy's outlook on life and his views on theology underwent a material change. He found his inspiration in the simple faith of the peasant, and began to urge, even for the nobility, a return to the life of the common laborer. He joined his own peasants daily in the fields, striving even to excel them at their work of ploughing or pitching hay. At the same time, he virulently attacked the artificiality of the theology and the elaborate ritualism of the Russian Orthodox Church. Many disciples, calling themselves Tolstoyists, sought to emulate the simple life of their master. Chief among these was Tchertkov, who, for better or for worse, exerted a great influence over Tolstoy in his later years. Finally in March, 1901, when Tolstoy had already abandoned the Orthodox faith for his own creed of Tolstoyism, the Holy Synod issued the edict of excommunication which had been hanging over his head for thirty years.

Tormented by what he and others regarded as the incongruity between his life and his teachings, Tolstoy in 1910, at the advanced age of eighty-two, decided to leave his luxurious home forever, in spite of his precarious health. He was taken ill on the train, contracted pneumonia, and died on November 10, 1910, in the home of the stationmaster at Astapovo.

Tolstoy's literary career may be roughly divided into three periods: the first, from 1852 to 1862, in which he produced *Childhood, Boyhood,* and *Youth* (1852-56), *Sevastopol* (1855) and *The Cossacks* (1860-63) ; the second, from 1862 to 1879, that is, from his marriage to his conversion, during which he wrote his best novels, *War and Peace* (1863-69) and *Anna Karenina* (1873-77) ; and the third, from his conversion in 1879 to his death in 1910. His most important works of fiction during his later years were *The Death of Ivan Ilyitch* (1886), *The Kreutzer Sonata* (1889), and *Resurrection* (1899).

To this final period also belong his chief works on religion and ethics, including *A Harmony and Translation of the Four Gospels* (1881-82), *My Religion* (1883),

What Shall Be Done? (1886), and *The Kingdom of God is Within You* (1893). His critical essay on *What is Art?* (1898) was an outgrowth of his religious convictions.

Most of Tolstoy's dramas were issued posthumously. During his life, only three of his plays were published, namely, *The First Distiller* (1886), *The Power of Darkness* (1886), and *The Fruits of Enlightenment* (1899). All his plays clearly reflect the ideas and the general outlook of the third period.

THE PLOT OF *THE COSSACKS* (1863)

Dimitri Andreyevitch Olenin is a young man without a career, who has frequented all the fashionable resorts in Moscow, who has squandered half his fortune, and who, at twenty-four, has accomplished little or nothing. Since the age of eighteen he has done exactly as he pleased; he believes in little or nothing and loves only himself, in whom he is not yet disillusioned. Vaguely dissatisfied with this purposeless existence, and conscious of past mistakes, Olenin decides to seek "a new life" of happiness and contentment in the Caucasus, then the wild West of Russia, and never again to show his face in society.

Having burned his bridges behind him, Olenin travels to the village of Novomlinsk to live as an officer among the Grebensk Cossacks, a simple people who hunt and fish and defend themselves against the raids of hostile tribesmen. The majestic scenery impressis Olenin; the elemental simplicity and naturalness of Cossack life appeals to him, and he soon feels like a different man. Uncle Yeroshka, a Cossack philosopher, explains to him the simple outlook of the average Cossack, who steals or kills, feasts, and drinks, but wastes little time in pondering over what are for Olenin the perplexing problems of life.

Olenin undergoes a new experience when he falls in love with Maryanna, a simple Cossack girl, whose affections soon appear to be divided between Olenin and Lukashka, her Cossack suitor. Lukashka loves Maryanna, but he has no horse, and in accordance with the traditions of his people, he cannot marry until he buys, steals, or captures one in battle. When Olenin, in a spirit of altruism and self-sacrifice, gives him one, Lukashka suspects his motives.

When Lukashka is seriously wounded in repulsing an enemy raid, it becomes perfectly clear that Maryanna prefers the hero of her own people to the stranger from the north. Olenin, already somewhat weary of the primitive life, returns to Moscow and the world of humbug without Maryanna, and without having found the complete satisfaction he sought in the majestic scenery and among the simple people of the Caucasus.

THE PLOT OF *WAR AND PEACE* (1863-69)

Although this, the national novel of Russia, spreads itself over the pages of four bulky volumes, the story centers about the vicissitudes of two noble families, the Rostovs and the Volkonskys. Their adventures provide Tolstoy with an unparalleled opportunity to describe the Napoleonic battles which culminated in the invasion of Russia in 1812. The scene of action is the whole of Europe, and the book is crowded with the leading figures of that great European drama—Napoleon, Alexander I, Russian, French, and German generals, as well as a host of less prominent people. Such a vast panorama admits of no simple plot.

Prince Andrey Volkonsky, disillusioned in marriage, takes leave of his crotchety old father and his devout sister, Marya, and goes to fight for his country. Count Pierre Bezukhov, likewise disillusioned in his marriage with the voluptuous Princess Elena Kuragina, who was after his money rather than his love, deserts her, and disguised as a peasant, joins the colors with the particular object of shooting Napoleon. He becomes dissolute and is taken prisoner.

Count Nikolai Rostov, in the course of his military experiences, arrives at the estate of the wealthy Princess Marya Volkonskaya in time to protect her from a peasant uprising. He falls in love with her and they marry. His former fiancée and impoverished cousin, Sonya, who has released him, is a companion to the remarkable Natasha Rostova, the vital and charming heroine of this novel.

Natasha, who has just recovered from an impetuous love affair with the mercenary Prince Boris Trubetzkoy, discovers Prince Andrey Volkonsky among the scores of wounded and nurses him back to life. Their resulting engagement is broken when Natasha, just as impetuously, falls in love with Prince Anatol Kuragin, and Sonya barely prevents their elopement. Although Andrey forgives Natasha, he dies shortly after.

Meanwhile, Elena Kuragina divorces her disillusioned husband, Count Pierre Bezukhov, and dies. Bezukhov meets Natasha, falls in love with her, and marries her. She attains complete happiness in her love for her husband and her many children.

THE PLOT OF *ANNA KARENINA* (1873-77)

Anna Karenina is a beautiful and virtuous woman with a romantic soul, who has been married, in accordance with the wishes of her relatives, to Alexey Alexandrovitch Karenin, a celebrated public official twice her age. Karenin is too unemotional, too cold, and altogether too much absorbed in his work to bestow upon Anna the affection she craves.

Anna meets Alexey Vronsky, a handsome, dashing young officer, the favorite suitor of Kitty Shtcherbatsky, who is madly in love with him. Vronsky promptly deserts Kitty for Anna, who, at first, seeks to avoid him for the sake of her younger friend. Undismayed by such rebuffs, Vronsky continues to pursue Anna, who recognizes that he is the very embodiment of all her heart's desires. In him she has found a man who loves her passionately, and one who cares more for her than for his career. For him she is ready to sacrifice her good name, her outstanding social position, to give up her friends, and to leave the son she adores. Too late her husband finds that Anna is no longer faithful.

Alexey Karenin, with a generosity which Anna despises, forgives his wife and surrenders her to Vronsky, who as a wealthy man, surrounds her with every luxury. In the eyes of the world she and Vronsky live in adultery, and Anna is promptly deserted by the friends who formerly flattered and envied her. The helpless Kitty, overcome by humiliation at Vronsky's desertion, hastens to marry a suitor whom she had previously refused, Konstantin Levin. Levin is a wealthy but serious-minded landowner, who seeks to rectify the injustices of the social order, and whose sterling merits, Kitty, blinded by jealousy, does not at first perceive. Only gradually does she find that her love for Levin is a much deeper emotion than her infatuation for Vronsky.

For a time Anna's cup of love is full to the brim, and she, to all appearances, is happy. Her new life is, nevertheless, a lonely one, for her husband continues to frequent social circles which have closed their doors to her. In her dreams she is haunted by memories of the caresses of her husband and her lover, and her moral nature revolts at the adultery. In real life she is soon torn between her love for the son she deserted and her love for Vronsky. Her life is no longer normal and serene.

In time Vronsky's ardor cools, or at least it seems so to Anna. Tortured by jealousy, she begs her husband to divorce her that she may marry Vronsky and hold him. Alexey Karenin refuses, and Anna in her despair, makes life almost unbearable for her lover. After one of their frequent quarrels, Vronsky absents himself on a business trip. Anna, suspicious now of his every move, writes to demand his immediate return. On her failure to receive an answer, she commits suicide. Anna Karenina's unhappy life is terminated when she throws herself beneath the wheels of a train.

THE PLOT OF *RESURRECTION* (1899)

Prince Dimitri Ivanovitch Nekhludov, a youth of nineteen with high ideals of purity and honor, falls in love with Katusha Maslova, a servant in the home of his two elderly aunts. She reciprocates his love, but, because of their youth, they are afraid and ashamed to display their affection.

Nekhludov enters the army, and three years later, while en route to the front during the Russo-Turkish war (1877-78), he meets Katusha again, and his love is rekindled. Nekhludov's military experience, however, has corrupted his idealism, and a wave of passion supersedes the pure idealistic love he felt for her as a youth. He makes his way into her room by stealth and betrays her. The following day he adds insult to injury by pressing into her hand a one-hundred-ruble note. As far as he is concerned the affair is finished.

Shortly before the birth of her child, Katusha is dismissed by the two righteous aunts, who have become aware of her condition. After holding several positions, she finally decides to place her baby in an orphanage where he may receive adequate care. The baby dies en route. In her despair, Katusha enters a house of ill repute, where for seven years she leads a wanton life. Unaware of a plot against his life, she entertains a rich merchant, who, during a drunken stupor, dies mysteriously. Katusha is charged with his murder and imprisoned.

Meanwhile Prince Nekhludov, weary of the army, has settled down to the quiet life of a country gentleman. Called for jury service, he is shocked to find Katusha, the girl he betrayed, among the prisoners. Overcome by fear and remorse, he determines to repair the wrong he has done her. Katusha, innocent of the crime, makes an effective plea for her acquittal, asserting that she believed that she was administering, not poison, but a headache powder, to the merchant in his glass of wine. Her frank manner convinces the jury of her innocence, but, through the technical error of incompetent court officials, she is sentenced to four years at hard labor in Siberia.

Nekhludov, who has maintained silence during the proceedings, realizes that he has again wronged the woman who was once before his victim. He immediately engages counsel to reopen the case and points out the error in the sentence. Remorse for his misdeeds effects a resurrection in his soul. He decides to turn over his entire property to his peasants, to wed Katusha at the first opportunity, and to find peace for his soul by right-ing at least part of the wrong he has done her. An obstacle exists in the form of his engagement to a wealthy but shallow young society belle. Calling at his fiancee's home, he is amazed at the selfishness, arrogance, and narrowness of those with whom he has heretofore associated.

Pending the withdrawal of her sentence, Nekhludov follows Katusha on her journey to Siberia, in the hope of making life more comfortable for her. It is by no means easy for him to win her confidence again, for the coarseness of the prostitute's life has poisoned her very soul, and she suspects his motives. "You've got pleasure out of me in this life, and want to save yourself through me in the life to come." Such is her diagnosis of his repentance. Gradually, however, she is impressed by the sincerity of his efforts to atone for the past, and the woman in her responds. A new love awakens in her heart, one equally capable of self-sacrifice. Realizing above everything else, that Nekhludov does not love, but only pities her, and seeks his own salvation via atonement, she refuses to ruin his life by consenting to a marriage which must end in unhappiness for him, and accepts instead the hand of Simonson, a prisoner of her own class who loves her. Nekhludov, knowing that she loves him, accepts her decision, and once her freedom is assured, returns to his own life a new man, determined to follow the commandments of Christ.

FROM *RESURRECTION*
Book III, Chapter XXI

Standing on the side of the raft, Nekhludov gazed at the wide river. Two images rose in his mind. One was that of the jolting head of the dying and exasperated Kryltzov, the other the picture of Katusha briskly walking along the road by the side of Simonson. The impression of the dying Kryltzov, unprepared for death, was not only sad, but distressing. The impression of Katusha, so cheerful and vigorous, who had found the love of such a man as Simonson and was now treading the straight and solid path of virtue, ought to have been a pleasant one, but somehow Nekhludov didn't find it so. He was unable to shake off a feeling of depression.

A large church bell was ringing in the town, and the metallic sound was borne across the water. Not only the driver who stood beside Nekhludov, but all the other teamsters one after another removed their caps and crossed themselves. Only one old man, short in stature and ragged in raiment, paid no respect to the signal but lifted his head and looked at Nekhludov. Although he was standing very close, the latter had not noticed him before. He wore a patched coat, cloth trousers, and patched shoes down at the heels. A small bag was slung over one shoulder, and his head was covered with a low fur cap much the worse for wear.

"Why are you not saying your prayers, old man?" asked Nekhludov's driver, as he readjusted his cap. "Have you never been baptized?"

"Whom should I pray to?" asked the old man, in an aggressive tone of voice.

"To whom? Why, to God, of course," ironically replied the driver.

"And will you show me where He is, that God of yours?"

There was something serious and determined in the old man's expression, so that the driver, realizing that he was dealing with a strong personality, though he was somewhat abashed, did not wish to seem discomfited in the presence of this audience. He spoke quickly:

"Where? In heaven, of course."

"Have you been there?"

"I may not have been there, but everybody knows that he must pray to God!"

"No one has seen God anywhere, but His only begotten Son who exists in the substance of His Father who has manifested Him," said the old man, frowning sternly and speaking as fast as he could.

"You must be a heathen and pray to a hole in the ground," replied Nekhludov's driver, tucking his whip into his belt and adjusting the harness of one of the horses on the side.

Some one laughed.

"What, then, is your religion, grandpa?" asked an elderly man who stood beside a loaded wagon near the edge of the raft.

"I have no religion, because I have no faith in any one but myself," replied the old man, speaking just as fast, with the same determination as before.

"How can you believe in yourself?" asked Nekhludov, carrying on the conversation. "You might be mistaken."

"Not on your life!" replied the old man, resolutely shaking his head.

"Then why is it that there are different religions?" asked Nekhludov.

"Religions differ because men put their faith in other men and not in themselves. When I used to pin my faith on other men, I wandered about as if I were lost in the Taiga! I was lost, and I was afraid that I should never be able to find my way out. There are all kinds of religions, Sectarians both Old and New, Sabbatarians, Flagellants, Popish and Popeless, the Austriaks, the Milkers, and Eunudrs. Every religion praises itself. And behold, they are all crawling about in different directions like blind puppies. There are many religions, but only one Spirit, which is in me, in you, and in every man, and this means that each man ought to believe in the Spirit that is within him. Then we shall all be united, each man for himself, and everybody will be agreed." The old man spoke in a loud voice and kept looking around, as if he wanted to be heard by as many persons as possible.

"How long have you professed this faith?" asked Nekhludov.

"Me? Oh, a long time. They have been persecuting me for twenty-three years."

"In what way?"

"As Christ was persecuted. They arrest me and drag me into Court, and the priests read from their books, like the Scribes and Pharisees. Once they put me in the madhouse. But they can't do me any harm because I am a free man. 'What is your name?' they ask. They think I am going to call myself by some name, but I am not. I deny everything,—I have no name, no place, no

country; I have nothing. I am just my own self! 'My
name? A man.' 'And how old are you?' I reply, 'I never
count the years, because it can't be done. I always have
existed, and I always shall exist, for ever and ever.' 'Who
are your father and mother?' 'I have no father or mother
except God and Mother Earth.' 'Do you acknowledge the
Czar?' 'Why shouldn't I? He is a Czar unto himself, I
am a Czar unto myself.' 'What use is there in talking to
you?' And I reply, 'I didn't ask you to talk to me!' That's
the way they persecute me."

"And where are you going now?" inquired Nekhludov.

"Wherever God leads me. I work, and if the work
gives out, I beg," concluded the old man and looked about
him exultantly, as the raft neared the opposite shore.
When it had been made fast, Nekhludov took out his
purse and offered the old man some coins, but the latter
refused to take them. "I never accept that sort of gift."

"Then you must forgive me."

"There is nothing to forgive. You've done me no
harm. Food is what I accept," he said.

"No one can harm me," repeated the old man as he
again slung over his shoulder the bag which he had taken
off his back on the raft. Meanwhile Nekhludov's cart
had been taken from the raft and the horses reharnessed.

"I wouldn't talk to him, sir. He is just a worthless
tramp," said the driver to Nekhludov, when the latter,
having fed the ferryman, climbed again on to his cart.

BOOK III, CHAPTER XXV

In spite of the white mantle that now covered the
walls, the porch, and the roof of the jail, in spite of its
brightly lighted windows, the sentinels, and the lantern
at the gate, it looked to Nekhludov even more gloomy
than it had looked in the morning by daylight.

The imposing Inspector came out to the gate, and
after reading the permit given to Nekhludov and the
Englishman, shrugged his broad shoulders in surprise;
but obeying the order he invited the visitors to follow
him. He escorted them first through the yard to a door
on the right, and then they mounted the stairs that led

into the office. Inviting them to take seats he asked them what he could do for them, and when Nekhludov expressed a wish to see Maslova, he sent a warden to fetch her; then he prepared himself to answer the questions which the Englishman, with the aid of Nekhludov as an interpreter, began to ask him: "How many persons was this jail meant to hold? How many are here now? How many men, women, and children? How many are sentenced to hard labor, how many are exiles, and how many followed them of their own free will? How many are sick?"

Nekhludov translated the questions of the Englishman and the replies of the Inspector, hardly conscious of their significance, so agitated was he by the expectation of the impending interview. When, in the middle of a sentence which he was translating for the Englishman, he heard approaching footsteps and saw the door of the office open, and when, as had happened many times before, the warden came in followed by Katusha in her prison garb, her head tied up in a kerchief, he felt a sinking sensation.

"I want to live. I want a family, children of my own, and to live like other men," flashed across his mind, just as with a quick step and downcast eyes Maslova came into the room.

As he rose and took a few steps toward her, he saw that her face was stern and unfriendly. It was the expression he remembered when she had reproached him. She raised and lowered her eyes and turned pale, and her fingers nervously twisted the edge of the jacket.

"Have you been told that your pardon has been granted?"

"Yes, the Inspector told me about it."

"So when the document arrives you will be able to settle where you like. We shall think it over——"

She interrupted him hastily.

"There is nothing to think over; I shall follow Vladimir Vassilievitch wherever he chooses to go."

In spite of her excitement she spoke quickly and distinctly, as though she had learned a lesson, and looked directly into Nekhludov's eyes.

"Indeed?" said Nekhludov.

"Well, Dmitri Ivanovitch, if he wants me to live with him—" she paused and corrected herself, "wants me to be with him—I ought to consider myself very lucky. What more could I expect—?"

"One of two things, either she loves Simonson and has never appreciated the sacrifice which I imagined I was making for her sake, or she continues to love me even while she refuses me and 'burns her ships' by uniting her lot with Simonson's," thought Nekhludov. He felt ashamed of himself and it made him blush.

"Of course, if you love him," he said.

"What's the odds whether I do or not? I am past that sort of thing. And, besides, Vladimir Ivanovitch is a different kind of man."

"Yes, of course," began Nekhludov, "he is a remarkable man, and I think—" She interrupted him again as though she feared lest he might say too much, or that she would not have a chance to say everything she had intended to say.

"You must forgive me, Dmitri Ivanovitch, if I am not doing what you wish me to do," she said, looking into his eyes with that mysterious squinting look of hers. "This seems to be the best way out of it. You have your own life to live."

She was only repeating what he had just been saying to himself, but now he felt quite differently.

"I never expected this," he said.

"What good does it do for you to live here and suffer? You have suffered enough already."

"I have not suffered. I have been happy and I want to go on serving you."

"*We* need nothing," she said, and looked up at Nekhludov. "You have already done a great deal for me. If it hadn't been for you—" she was about to say something more, but her voice quivered.

"You are the last person to give thanks to me," said Nekhludov.

"What's the use for us to square accounts? God will do that for us," she said, and her black eyes shone with the tears that rushed into them.

"What a good woman you are!" he exclaimed.

"I? A good woman!" she answered through her tears, and a pitiful smile lighted up her face.

"Are you ready?" asked the Englishman.

"In a moment," said Nekhludov, and asked her about Kryltzov.

She became calm and quickly told what she knew. Kryltzov's journey had weakened him and he had been placed in the hospital at once. Marya Pavlovna was very anxious and had asked to be allowed to stay with him as a hospital nurse, but was refused.

"May I go now?" she asked, noticing that the Englishman was waiting.

"I will not say good-by. I will see you again," said Nekhludov, holding out his hand.

"Forgive me," she said in a whisper. Their eyes met, and by her peculiar squinting look, her pathetic smile, and the tone of her voice in which she said, not "Good-by" but "Forgive me," Nekhludov understood that the second of his two suppositions was the real cause of her decision,—that she loved him, and knew that by uniting their lives she would ruin his, therefore she released him by remaining with Simonson and was now rejoicing that she had accomplished her purpose and yet suffering because she had to part with him.

She pressed his hand and, quickly turning, left the room. Nekhludov was now ready to go, but glancing at the Englishman he saw him still writing in his notebook. Not wishing to disturb him, Nekhludov took a seat on the wooden settle behind the wall and a great weariness came over him. It was not the weariness one feels after a sleepless night of travel or excitement,—he was simply tired of life. He leaned on the back of the seat, closed his eyes, and at once fell into a deep, heavy slumber.

"Would you also like to see the prisoners' cells?" asked the Inspector.

Nekhludov awoke and was surprised to find himself there. The Englishman had finished his minutes and was ready to visit the cells. Nekhludov, weary and indifferent, followed him.

"Two voices are there: one is of the sea,
One of the mountains; each a mighty voice."

—Wordsworth

Tolstoy and Dostoyevsky, the two Titans of Russian literature, and each "a mighty voice," stand head and shoulders above the rest of their countrymen, assured of a prominent place even in world literature. So different are they, that one might well be regarded as the antithesis, or perhaps even better, the complement of the other. Life itself discriminated between these two literary giants, caressing Tolstoy and chastening Dostoyevsky. Tolstoy enjoyed health and physical vitality above the normal; Dostoyevsky was a frail epileptic. Tolstoy inherited a noble name, great wealth which he increased, and broad acres which he made more fruitful. Dostoyevsky was of comparatively humble origin, while life for him was a perpetual struggle to keep the wolf from the door. Tolstoy wrote at leisure in the midst of affluence, and polished and repolished his work. Dostoyevsky wrote in haste and under pressure, without time for revision. Tolstoy was practically the only Russian author to enjoy relative freedom of speech, his work being regarded with an amazing amount of tolerance by the authorities. Dostoyevsky was banished to Siberia for a minor infraction of the censorship laws, while all his life he remained under the surveillance of the authorities. Tolstoy served in the army as an officer, Dostoyevsky as a common soldier among the convicts of Siberia. Tolstoy left a wealthy home and adoring family in the morning to toil from preference among the peasants; but Dostoyevsky from necessity lived the life of the slum dweller and shared his experiences. The one was charitable out of curiosity and in order to attain experience—the other because of feeling and necessity.

Such diversity of environment was bound to be reflected in the literary work and in the philosophy of life of these two famous writers. Dostoyevsky, for example, introduced the slums and the middle class into Russian literature, while Tolstoy confined himself to green pastures, to the nobility, and the peasantry. The one deified the Russian people, the other lauded to the skies the virtues of the Russian peasant. In this respect Tolstoy has more in common with Turgenev, for he began where Turgenev left off in his *Memoirs of a Sportsman*. But Tolstoy treated the peasants subjectively, while Turgenev viewed their most vital problem, that of serfdom, with remarkable objectivity.

Tolstoy's characters are simple, like the country folk he admired so greatly; Dostoyevsky's are complex. Tolstoy wrote, for the most part, of the sane, the healthy, and the normal individual—Dostoyevsky, of the criminal, the diseased, the insane, and the abnormal. In spite of his dynamic power, Dostoyevsky wrote like a humble man—Tolstoy with authority. "I say unto you," is the predominant tone of Tolstoy's work, particularly in later years. Dostoyevsky underestimated his own greatness. Tolstoy was not only aware of his creative genius, but, by implication, boldly announced to the world his opinion of himself. His ego defied even his own earnest attempts at humility, led him to project his personality into most of his works, many portions of which are autobiographical. Dostoyevsky rarely resorted to autobiography, an exception being his *Memoirs from a Dead House*, although he revealed his own Slavophile views in the person of Shatov and his own epileptic condition in the experiences of Prince Myshkin.

Tolstoy regarded himself as the foremost prophet and teacher of his generation, while Dostoyevsky in reality was both. The former raised disciples; the latter, imitators. Tolstoy was both a great teacher and philosopher, Dostoyevsky, a disciple of Christ and a psychologist. Tolstoy emerged unscathed from his "mission," whereas Dostoyevsky was "crucified" as an idiot and an epileptic. Even posthumously Tolstoy has fared better than his great contemporary. His works were the first of the Russian classics to stage a comeback after the Revolution, while Dostoyevsky's works still await recognition. This is in spite of the fact that the New Russia reflects, under a new nomenclature, more of Dostoyevsky's philosophy than of Tolstoy's.

While Turgenev was a Westernizer and Dostoyevsky a Slavophile, Tolstoy for a time combined the ideologies of both, until at length he established a teaching of his own known as Tolstoyism. In methodology, he was nearer Turgenev, but dogmatically and ideologically he was closer to Dostoyevsky. Like the latter, he repudiated Western civilization, and in particular, Western materialism. The philosophy of each was Oriental, the difference being that Dostoyevsky's was more of an elongation of the Near East plus Russia, whereas Tolstoy's was Russian plus the Taoism of the Far East. While Tolstoy wrote extensively of Reason in his later years, often identifying Reason with God and with Knowledge, the Reason he described emanated from the heart rather than from the head. For Tolstoy finds that Reason is inherent in every man, although often obscured or eclipsed by other factors. In order to reassert that Reason, it was only necessary, in his opinion, to listen to and obey the inner voice of conscience—which is again closer to the heart than to the mind. In brief, Tolstoy's Reason must not be identified with the Practical Reason of Kant. His is Russian Reason, grafted upon Oriental philosophy. In other words, it represents a combination of heart and mind, at times almost constituting an answer to Dostoyevsky's dream.

A significant factor in Dostoyevsky's Slavophilism was the Russian Orthodox Church. To Tolstoy, the Church—and by the Church he meant the Orthodox or Catholic Churches—distorted, institutionalized, particularized, obscured, and debased the Gospel of Christ, and he predicted its downfall. Dostoyevsky, while he admitted certain abuses and shortcomings (*The Idiot, The Brothers Karamazov,* and *Raw Youth*), believed that a rejuve-

nated Orthodox Church constituted the only hope for
the salvation of Russia and of the world, and he predicted
its ultimate triumph. Tolstoy was nearer the Protestant
Church, while Dostoyevsky, in spite of his attacks on
Roman Catholicism, was nearer to it than he realized.
Dostoyevsky dreamed of the universal application of
Russian Christianity, Tolstoy of a universal religion,
which would become the creed of Russia—a Christianity
minus Churchianity. Tolstoy put to the test most of the
world's leading religions. Like Nietzsche, he did not
discard Christianity, but became jealous of the Christ,
and established a creed of his own—Tolstoyism.

Tolstoyism belongs to the later years of Tolstoy's
life, from 1879 to 1910, that is, from the time of his
conversion until his death. These years are sometimes
known as the period of "preaching" or the age of Tolstoy
the Apostle. The essence of Tolstoyism is to be found
in *Confession* and in his subsequent work, most of which
is summed up in *Resurrection*. In fact, all the later works
of Tolstoy, even his dramas, may be termed "confessions"—either confessions about himself, about the Russian nobility, authorities and institutions, or in particular
about the Russian Church from which he was excom-
municated in 1901.

Tolstoyism teaches that there is no God, other than
the moral law inside man. Instead of being motivated
by outward inducement, that moral law moves in obedience to an inward spontaneity. The inner life underlies
the universe. The end or the goal of inner action is inner
peace (happiness). By peace, Tolstoy does not imply
Epicureanism, but the doctrine of imperturbability or
quietism, the essence of which is Taoism. In Tolstoyism,
as well as in Taoism, there are elements of defeatism and
anarchism, and also of domination. The *withdrawal* of
the senses to a point where one no longer sees the things
perceived implies all this. The idea that "To a mind that
is still the whole universe *surrenders*," suggests domination—subjugation, rather than resignation. Thus, in

spite of Tolstoy's later ethical teachings, in which "Resist no evil" occupies the most prominent place, he himself barely practised it. In fact, Tolstoy recognized no authority above himself, for he was neither a disciple nor a follower. He was the founder of Tolstoyism—another creed.

Some critics see in Tolstoy's *withdrawal* a new version of Meister Eckhart's *renunciation (otryeshenie)*, thereby explaining the difference between him and Dostoyevsky on Love, Charity, etc. The German Dominican mystic (1250?-1328?) placed *renunciation* above Love as the highest human achievement. The philosophy of Eckhart was, however, an outgrowth of the scholastic literature of the Middle Ages. In other words, it was more apologetic than mystic. Its main purpose was to explain the indifference of the Father to the tortures of the Son on the cross. In Tolstoy's case, it may have been an unconscious apology for the discrepancy between his teaching and practice. The philosophy of renunciation of the contemporary Russian thinker, Nicholas Berdyaev, is also worthy of note in this respect.

Like his Oriental predecessors, Tolstoy conceived the cosmos as a harmonious entity, in which all men are equal. Friction between the individual and society merely indicated that one or the other was occupying the wrong place. Maintaining peace in the universe involved making the necessary adjustments, that is, seeing that each one found his proper niche. Its accomplishment required a change not only in the outer world and social order, but also in the moral nature or inner man. There are times, according to Tolstoy, when either the individual or the system must undergo a change. In that event, the individual, without hindrance from Church or State, should be permitted to withdraw and to seek his own proper place in the universe.

To Tolstoy, as to the typical Oriental philosopher, all virtues, sciences, and arts were attributes of the *summum bonum*. They emanated from a single source in centrifugal fashion. In his essay on *What is Art?* he expressed no belief in the idea of "Art for Art's sake," but defined it as a part of the *summum bonum,* and the artist as a co-Creator. His cosmos was a unit, with a central Universal Idea. The latter might be called Religion, a Deity, Taoism, Christianity, or Buddhism—anything, in fact, so long as it remained the *way of life,* the norm. Tolstoy's universe, like that of the Orient, was centralized, whereas the Western universe is decentralized. Tolstoy's cosmos was composed of the attributes of the Perfect One, whereas the tendency in the West is toward a distributive rather than an attributive world.

In this light we can understand the Oriental genius, particularly of the Near East, when he declares that religion is the foundation of all foundations, permeating everything. By everything, he means the entire life, including what the Westerner would classify as secular. When religion permeates everything, then to deny any part of it involves crushing the entire structure. In the West, where there is decentralization and distribution, this is not necessarily true. In the West a person may proclaim himself an atheist, yet continue to give to charity, interest himself in social welfare, and carry on his business honestly. From the Oriental standpoint, the individual by his practice of the above-mentioned functions is religious, in spite of his statement to the contrary.

In the Western world we sharply differentiate between things secular and things religious. In the East it is very difficult to draw a line of demarcation between these two realms. Strictly speaking, from the Eastern standpoint, there is even more religion in the West than in the East, if we include sanitation, medicine, etc., as the attributes of religion. Here lies the rub. To Dostoyevsky, Love, Charity, and Self-Sacrifice mark the *summum bonum* of religion, and God is revealed only through these virtues. Tolstoy's attitude, as we have just seen, is vastly different. For him there is no God except the moral law inside man, and the end of good action is inner peace. The truth cannot be preached, according to Tolstoy, but may only be discovered by the individual. Man must be good, because it is the only way for him to find peace (happiness). In this respect Tolstoy is nearer Lao-Tzu (born 604 B.C.) than any other Eastern philosopher and teacher. Tolstoy's *Confession* is the Russian *Tao - teh King*. Tolstoy's religion has no definite name, yet it may have many names. In short, for Tolstoy, it is Tolstoyism; for Lao-Tzu, Taoism.

The Cossacks. The most representative work Tolstoy produced during the first period of his literary career, 1852 to 1862, was *The Cossacks*. Although this novel was published in January, 1863, he first projected it in 1852, wrote it in 1860, and added the finishing touches to it in 1862, prior to his marriage. Tolstoy had no intention of publishing this work for some time. It would, perhaps, have shared the fate of *Hajji Murad*, which appeared posthumously in 1911, had Tolstoy not used it to settle a gambling debt at a time when he was otherwise short of funds.

The Cossacks ranks next in importance to Gogol's *Taras Bulba*. Gogol's narrative was historical, but Tolstoy wrote of the Cossacks of his own day whom he knew in person. Gogol's work was a tale of adventure; Tolstoy's was philosophical in tone. *Taras Bulba* has its vivid climax, leaving the reader a glorious picture of triumphant fierceness of exaltation in the face of actual death. *The Cossacks* closes with an anticlimax, when Olenin returns to his former empty life, without Maryanna, and without having found the "inner peace" he sought in the Caucasus. Gogol's work was epic in tone, whereas Tolstoy's is lyric. Olenin also proved to be a new version of Petchorin in *The Hero of Our Times*.

Tolstoy's greatest contribution in *The Cossacks* was that he revealed the everyday life of the Caucasians, presenting their strong, rather than their weak points, against a magnificent scenic background. His was a sympathetic account and an appreciative understanding of customs which were strange to the Russian people as a whole. Maryanna, Lukashka, and Yeroshka were soon as familiar to Russians as Turgenev's characters in his *Memoirs of a Sportsman*. Tales of the Caucasus have always held a certain fascination for the Russian people. The greatest Russian poets and a few outstanding writers received their literary baptism amidst the scenic grandeur and the picturesque customs of the Caucasus. As we shall see, F. A. Korsh, the founder of the first private theater in Moscow, was a native of the Caucasus; and V. I. Nemirovitch-Dantchenko, who established the Moscow Art Theatre, came from the same region.

In *The Cossacks* we can detect the symptoms of Tolstoy's later philosophy, particularly his preference for the simple life close to nature. In the person of Olenin we find that same restlessness which pursued Tolstoy all his days. For in this autobiographical novel he was just beginning his search for an answer to the riddle of life.

Sevastopol. Tolstoy's three sketches, entitled *Sevastopol* (December, 1854, May, 1855, and August, 1855), also belong to the first period of his literary career. Written while he was on active service at Sevastopol during the Crimean War, these sketches marked Tolstoy's first attack on war in general, particularly upon war between Christians. His descriptions of the horrors of war and his discrimination between real and false heroes were only excelled in his later masterpiece, *War and Peace*. In *Sevastopol*, Tolstoy did for the common soldier what Turgenev in his *Memoirs* did for the serf. He directed attention to the services rendered by the ordinary soldier, who, more often than not, received no recognition of his sacrifice, since all the glory and honor went to false heroes. In Tolstoy's estimation, the common soldier was more patriotic than his superiors who spent most of their time talking about promotion. The army never forgave Tolstoy for this exposure, regarding him as a renegade from his own class.

War and Peace. This bulky novel, together with *Anna*

Karenina, may be termed the product of the "honeymoon period." After his marriage in 1862, Tolstoy conceived plans for writing works of an historical nature. Had it not been for the Countess, however, he would never have been able to give to the world these two masterpieces. In her own handwriting she painstakingly copied and recopied the manuscripts of both novels many times.

Originally Tolstoy intended to write a history or a novel of the Decembrist Movement of 1825, which shook Russia profoundly. This first revolutionary attempt to secure a constitutional government involved the flower of the Russian nobility. Many paid for this revolt with their lives; others were exiled to Siberia, where they laid a foundation for culture in that remote region. The stories and legends about them which circulated throughout Russia, especially among the nobility, provided ideal subject matter for a novel. Tolstoy had only published three chapters of *The Decembrists,* however, when he became absorbed in the reign of Alexander I. His interest gradually focused on the Napoleonic campaigns, and he abandoned the Decembrists for *War and Peace,* a novel which was five years in the making. Tolstoy intended this novel as an introduction and background to the Decembrist Movement—a purpose which it fulfills to the letter, since *War and Peace* ends where the Decembrist Movement begins. It appeared first as a serial, and later in book form in 1869.

War and Peace is justly called the national novel of Russia. It is a colossal prose epic, reflecting the whole range of Russian life at the beginning of the nineteenth century. Once again Tolstoy paid homage to the simplicity and strength of the common people in contrast to the artificiality of the upper classes. Being an officer himself, it was natural that he should devote more space to descriptions of battles than to other phases of Russian life. Nevertheless, one finds here a true reflection of the life of the various classes in Russia—of their life during peace and war, as well as during the aftermath of war;

of the various superstitions and beliefs which were the product of war, as well as of the positive benefits arising from a just struggle.

In this novel, even more than in the Sevastopol sketches, Tolstoy denounced war as an instrument for the settlement of disputes between nations. He tried his level best to minimize the sagacity of the strategists and the heroic exploits of the superior officers. Some critics have seen in this approach the recurrence of an old fatalism in a new guise. But this was not fatalism. Tolstoy merely sought to minimize the achievements of the war lords and the glory of war. Perhaps here, too, he had already acquired a habit, which became more pronounced in after years, of consciously or unconsciously minimizing the achievements of others in his own field—in this case, the army.

While Tolstoy's main purpose was to strip war, particularly imperialistic war, of its vain glory, and to discourage men from seeking a military career, some critics feel that he accomplished just the reverse. Unconsciously, *War and Peace* became the text for patriotism in Russia, and the battles so vividly described and so artistically delineated, served rather as an inducement for men to enter the army than as a deterrent to military service. In spite of his anti-war message, Tolstoy, in this book, said practically nothing in opposition to defensive wars. It was not until later, after his conversion, that he advocated a literal application of the Christian doctrine, "Resist no evil." In this novel, Tolstoy was more objective than in his previous or in his subsequent works. Absorbed in others, he, for the first time, with a few exceptions, left himself entirely out of the picture. In *War and Peace* there are several heroes of equal importance, none of whom is Tolstoy, although Prince Andrey and Pierre Bezukhov no doubt reveal Tolstoy's outlook at that time.

There is a feeling of spaciousness in this novel. It leaves the reader with the impression of being part of a vast audience, watching a performance of the epic of a nation, in which Russians from one end of the country to the other flit across the stage before his eyes.

Anna Karenina. Although this novel was based upon an actual incident which took place not far from Tolstoy's estate, its central idea was a natural outgrowth of *War and Peace.* While Vronsky and Anna, as far as the plot goes, are the main characters, Levin was the soul of the novel as far as Tolstoy was concerned. In fact, Levin was Tolstoy himself—the transitional Tolstoy of the period between *War and Peace* and *Confession.* Levin's ideas on labor and the social order incurred all the hostility from members of the nobility that Tolstoy himself experienced from his own people—even from his own wife, the Countess. Levin, in a rather artificial fashion, put into practice some of his ideas, which Tolstoy himself never succeeded in doing. In studying the personality of Tolstoy and his philosophy, especially after 1879, much attention should be paid to the character of Levin and even to Kitty, his wife. One almost infers that, at times, Tolstoy would have preferred a wife like Kitty to the Countess.

Although Levin is the personification of Tolstoy, there is much of Tolstoy in Vronsky too. Before he met Anna, Vronsky was just a man in a uniform, "un homme comme il faut"; from the bureaucratic standpoint, a man with a chequered past, not unlike Tolstoy prior to his marriage. This was the first time that Vronsky had actually fallen in love. Though an illicit love, it was nevertheless the real thing. Tolstoy shows that even an illicit love might prove a resurrection for a Vronsky, while it meant death for Anna. From the time Vronsky met Anna, his star began to rise, hers to decline. He was resurrected because of her love, and when she had done everything for him within her power, she gave him the last she had to offer—her life. There are indications that Vronsky's love for Anna began to grow cold—not so Anna's. Having given up everything in the world for him, she made Vronsky the center of her universe, and her love became a jealous passion. When she realized that her attitude would only bring him unhappiness, she took her own life.

In this novel, as in *War and Peace,* Tolstoy swung his lash at the military class with its unbalanced code of morals. He did for Anna what Dostoyevsky did for Sonya, although they belonged to different classes. One thing they had in common—adultery. While Dostoyevsky gave Sonya a new start in life, Anna Karenina, because of her position, character, and culture, and owing to the conventional attitude of her class, could not begin life anew. Although Tolstoy himself disapproved of Anna's action, he portrayed her in such a fashion that her sin was almost obscured and eclipsed by her charm and courage. He presented her fall from grace in a most natural manner, as something which might happen to anyone, irrespective of background, rank, or station. As a warning to those who might presume to pass judgment upon one who paid a heavy price for her sin, he prefaced his book with the Biblical injunction, "Vengeance is Mine. I will repay!"

Confession. Subsequent to the publication of a few other works, a drastic change took place in Tolstoy's life. In 1879 he began his *Confession,* in which, for the first time, he preached his new creed of Tolstoyism. This is a theological treatise, in which Tolstoy openly voiced his opinion of the Orthodox Church, and his personal recollections of the inconsistency of his own upbringing with the actual teachings of Christ, although those who reared him posed as Christians. He asserted, here as elsewhere, that the influence of the Church upon true Christianity was detrimental, implying that the Church for Christianity what Buddhism did for Taoism. Just as Taoism degenerated into superstition and mysticism until it consisted of a debased ritual which bore no resemblance to the original teaching of Lao-Tzu, so the ritualistic and other functions of the Christian Church, in his opinion, distorted and degraded the ethical teachings of Christ. In other words, it was in this book that Tolstoy for the first time openly advocated a Christianity minus Churchianity.

The Kreutzer Sonata. After another interval, during which additional publications appeared, Tolstoy produced *The Kreutzer Sonata* in 1889, followed by his explanatory *Afterword* to it in 1890. This short novel caused a sensation, not only in Russia, but throughout Europe. For a time it was even banned in the United States. Without going into details, it may be mentioned that this was the first sex novel in Russian literature. Tolstoy wrote two novels on sex. The other was *The Devil,* published posthumously in 1911. Strangely enough, in this novel, as in *War and Peace,* his achievement was in direct opposition to his intentions. *War and Peace* was intended to discourage the glorification of army life, but it served rather as an inducement to that very thing. The same was true of *The Kreutzer Sonata.* It was a didactic work, a moral novel, against "conventional" marriages. It opened the door to a stream of sex literature in Russia. It seems strange that Tolstoy, the moralist, should pave the way for writers like Artzibashev *(Sanine),* in whom this crude, licentious, abusive approach to the sex problem reached its culmination. *Sanine* was, in more ways than one, "a Russian tragedy." When *The Kreutzer Sonata* was first published it was regarded as an attack on all marriage—which was not true. Tolstoy's attack was directed at light marriages, which he termed legal prostitution.

Resurrection. Tolstoy's last great novel, *Resurrection,* was written in 1899, and sold to the highest bidder to defray in part the expenses of the migration of the persecuted Dukhobors (Christian Communists) to Canada. It was the most loosely constructed novel that Tolstoy has written. He himself acknowledged that he obtained the idea for this work from the resurrection of Raskolnikov, recorded in the epilogue of Dostoyevsky's

Crime and Punishment. Tolstoy's *Resurrection* is a working out of the regeneration Raskolnikov achieved through Sonya's great love, but with an entirely new character, a different crime, and much the same setting.

Dostoyevsky's *Crime and Punishment* was a psychological study of the criminal mind. *Resurrection* is a sociological study of prisons and prisoners. Tolstoy began where Dostoyevsky left off. A consecutive reading of *Crime and Punishment* and *Resurrection* leaves one with two very moving, but quite distinct, experiences— the first a glimpse into the mind of a man; the second, into his heart. Both novels were concerned with criminals. Fundamentally the idea of both novelists was the same—that persons who commit crimes are normal people not unlike ourselves, but who, owing to the injustice and inequalities of their social environment and certain ideologies, run counter to the law and to the legal machinery set up to ensnare them. *Resurrection* tells us much about the prison system and so-called criminal justice, but nothing of the mental and spiritual anguish to which the individual is subjected before his punishment is meted out to him. *Crime and Punishment,* on the other hand, tells what goes on in the mind of one man before and after he commits his crime, but next to nothing about his life in prison. Dostoyevsky brought out the "inner good" in Raskolnikov; Tolstoy related Nekhludov's search for "inner peace." In *Crime and Punishment,* the individual is the center of attention; in *Resurrection,* society predominates. Both novelists revealed some understanding of Russian society: Dostoyevsky, of the lower stratum; Tolstoy, of both the upper and the lower classes.

Resurrection summed up Tolstoy's "confessions." In this final novel, he not only advocated a theory, but through Nekhludov he put his own theories into practice. Tolstoy accepted as gospel truth the old Oriental adage that "The greatest hero is he who can overcome himself," and he believed that the only prerequisite to the practical application of his theories was courage.

In spite of the fact that Nekhludov is Tolstoy himself, he does not hesitate to reveal the limitations of Nekhludov even after his resurrection. It is strongly suggested that all Nekhludov's sacrifices were made from an egotistical motive—in order to achieve inner peace. His trip to Siberia with the convicts, and his proposed marriage with Katusha Maslova, were the price he expected to pay for this inner peace. There was nothing altruistic about it.

Katusha Maslova was infinitely superior to Nekhludov. Although of peasant origin, she had greater moral and spiritual stamina than the Prince. His resurrection was the product of remorse—hers, of love. In not one of the many criticisms of Katusha has justice been done to her. Her love was a Russian love, which it is difficult for the Westerner to grasp—just as it is difficult for him to understand Anna's final sacrifice for Vronsky. When Katusha rejected Nekhludov's proposal of marriage, she did it because she loved him, because she knew he did not love her, and because of the social gulf that separated them. Hers was an unselfish renunciation. He, knowing that she loved him, was obviously relieved at her decision, which he accepted with alacrity at its face value. Nekhludov found "inner peace" at Katusha's expense.

The Nobility and the Peasantry in Tolstoy's Novels. A member of the higher nobility himself, Lev Tolstoy was perhaps the most famous and the most popular portrayer of aristocratic life in Russia. Reared in a cultured environment and accustomed to consort with the elite, he was thoroughly acquainted with the best as well as with the worst traits of his class. In describing the life of the nobility, he confined himself to three groups: the first consisted of statesmen and prominent office-holders—men like Karenin, Oblonsky, and Shtcherbatsky; the second included military officers, such as Vronsky and Nekhludov; and the third was composed of rich landowners, represented by Nekhludov and Levin.

To the casual observer the Russian nobility was a gay, witty people, whose time was spent in search of pleasure. Tolstoy gives us a vivid picture of a class, which in Russia no longer exists, and of which there remain only a few last representatives in exile. In the painting of such scenes he had no superior in Russia.

Tolstoy depicted this class at work and at play. He described their formal balls, as in *Anna Karenina,* where, against a background of beautiful gowns, smart uniforms, gay music, and graceful dances, the love between Anna and Vronsky was born before the very eyes of the distressed Kitty. Time and again he described their intimate informal parties, where at dinners, at homes, and musical evenings, groups of close friends gathered to discuss the latest scandals, political and war news, philosophical questions, literature, music, art, in fact, almost every conceivable subject which was not of an ultraserious nature. Where gossip and light conversation became a fine art, the accomplished hostess dreaded a moment's awkward silence in case it might ruin the entire evening. Tolstoy's novels covered the entire range of the normal activities of his class—not only the balls, but the skating party, where Levin renewed his acquaintance with Kitty; the horse races frequented especially by the officers; the hunting expeditions, which were an integral part of the curriculum of every nobleman; and even the new vogue for tennis.

In Tolstoy's novels we can follow the noble from youth to old age, for he described the education of both men and women of his class. Like himself, the majority of the men attended university for a time even if they did not graduate. They tasted the discipline of army life, and observed its rigid code of honor. Their women were educated for marriage, learning, in addition, music, dancing, drawing, French literature, and languages. It was imperative for the Russian woman of aristocratic origin to marry as soon as possible, with the question of love a minor problem to be settled as satisfactorily as possible after the wedding. Before marriage they met men in society under strained, artificial conditions that did not lead to a real knowledge of character. As Tolstoy indicates in the case of Kitty, it was the height of humiliation and social disgrace for a woman to be dropped by a young man who had paid her any noticeable attention. Both men and women were proficient linguists, and they all spoke French, the smart language of society, although German and English were popular. It was the custom at the evening salons Tolstoy described so well, for both men and women to intersperse foreign words and phrases in their ordinary conversation.

In *Anna Karenina,* perhaps better than elsewhere, Tolstoy revealed the double moral standard for Russian men and women of the aristocracy. The typical nobleman, like Vronsky, was permitted, even expected, to have as many affairs as possible. The more women who fell in love with him, the more popular he became. The typical officer, like Vronsky, or like Olenin in *The Cossacks,* drank too much, gambled for high stakes, conquered as many women's hearts as possible, and in general lived a reckless and extravagant life. Vronsky's code is well illustrated by the following selection from *Anna Karenina:*

" . . . These principles laid down as invariable rules: that one must pay a cardsharper, but need not pay a tailor; that one must never lie to a man, but one may to a woman; that one must never cheat anyone, but one may a husband; that one must never pardon an insult, but one may give one, and so on. These principles were possibly not reasonable and not good, but they were of unfailing certainty, and as long as he adhered to them, Vronsky felt that his heart was at peace and he could hold his head up."

The married aristocrat had to be more discreet about his affairs, when he chose to leave the straight and narrow path, especially if the object of his devotion was a woman of a lower class. In *Anna Karenina,* when Stiva had an affair with the former governess of his children, his wife, Dolly, could not forgive him, not because he had an affair, but because he had one with a woman of an inferior class.

A woman's affairs, even if she were married, were not particularly condemned as long as they did not become a topic for common gossip, and as long as her husband's professional reputation was not injured. When Karenin found out that Anna was unfaithful, he thought, not of the immorality of the situation but only of his own reputation, fearing that this might cost him his career in politics. Anna's friends continued to accept her, even though they suspected her guilt, until she and Vronsky openly admitted their relationship to the world by going off and living together. Then they refused to associate with her any longer. Her women friends were more harsh in their uncompromising condemnation than the men, who might have forgiven her. Vronsky, however, was in a better position than Anna. He lost no respect and no friends, and had he given her up and returned to the army, he could have started again just where he left off, with as good a chance for advancement as before.

In brief, Tolstoy, on the one hand, showed the life of the nobility at its best—its glamor, excitement, luxury, culture, and brilliant social life. The *raison d'être* of the nobility depicted in his major novels was ably summed up by Oblonsky in *Anna Karenina:* "The aim of civilization is enjoyment." But Tolstoy was among the first of the outstanding Russian authors to have the temerity to point out the corrupt and degenerate mode of living tacitly accepted by its members—a constructive criticism. He revealed its shallowness, its incongruous moral code, its extravagance, its unbalanced sense of values, the amount of valuable time wasted on ridiculous pastimes. In his novels he showed that the artificiality, restlessness, and boredom of the average noble demanded a far heavier price than he lavished on his own entertainment. Levin and Nekhludov bore witness to the serious problem of land management which faced the rural nobility, Karenin and Oblonsky to the political wire-pulling necessary in order that the city official might not only retain his position, but secure a better one.

Finally, Tolstoy exposed to the light of day the unhappy condition of any country where a small percentage of the population did none of the labor, yet lived in the lap of luxury, while the vast majority who did all the work lived in miserable poverty, with no educational opportunities and barely enough to eat. Of the three representative groups of the nobility with whom he dealt —the prominent officeholders, the military officers, and the rich landowners—Tolstoy pinned his hopes on the third, believing that they might be instrumental in bringing a new deal to the Russian peasantry.

While Tolstoy painted a vivid portrait of the nobility of his day and generation, the peasants were dearer to his heart, at least in his later years, than any members of his own class. Tolstoy approached the peasants from a different angle than that followed by Gogol, Turgenev, or even Pisemsky. He not only regarded them as human beings, but he was not satisfied until he had placed them on a pedestal, until, in fact, he had almost deified them. Not only did he describe sympathetically their physical conditions, but also their philosophy of life, their ideas, emotions, and opinions, in such a way that he left no doubt but that he was their personal champion. Tolstoy, in other words, approached the peasants subjectively, with the result that one finds a better appreciation of them in his works than in those of any other Russian writer.

In the chapters about Levin and the management of his estate *(Anna Karenina)*, Tolstoy revealed the peasant as an intelligent human being with a quick mind and a fine character. Simple living and hard manual labor had made of him a noble superior creature of lofty thoughts and strong character. Tolstoy believed that luxurious, artificial, idle living weakened a man's character and destroyed his peace of soul: that the most admirable type of existence was one of simplicity and hard work coupled with brotherly love and the practice of the Golden Rule. He thought the peasants came much nearer this ideal of perfection than the aristocracy. Therefore, he wanted to follow Christ's injunction to the rich young ruler, that is, to give up all that he had and become a peasant himself. He believed that since the peasants had more of the inner peace which comes from the attainment of these ideals than the aristocracy, they found greater favor in the eyes of God.

Levin, in *Anna Karenina,* who is really Tolstoy himself, voices his philosophy and thoughts. He has the distinction of being the most ideal landowner in Russian fiction. In his attempt to find some meaning in life, he associated with the peasants at harvesttime, working side by side with them on an equal footing. During the dinner hour, he ate with an old man, and they became good friends. Tolstoy says that Levin "felt much nearer to the old man than to his own brother, and could not help smiling at the affection he felt for him." That night, after a hard day's work, Levin felt more at peace with himself than he had for a long time, and he reached the decision that it was more important to be a competent farmer than a rich but idle nobleman. In this passage, Tolstoy's account of the peasants swinging their scythes is typical of his fine descriptive powers.

Levin did not join the peasants at harvest in any spirit of condescension. The reader feels that he regarded them with an envy and admiration which were entirely new in Russian literature. Because he believed that the life of the peasant was an ideal life—not one to be pitied— he wanted them to be free to acquire land of their own, provided they themselves did not have serfs. Levin, or in reality Tolstoy, was a complete democrat in this respect. Serfdom was already abolished when he wrote

Anna Karenina; it only remained for the aristocratic landowner to share his spoil with the peasants on an equal footing.

In *Resurrection,* Nekhludov attained this aim, by parceling out his land among his peasants. Unfortunately, Nekhludov's peasants had been subjugated and cheated so often by their landlords that they simply failed to understand that he was actually giving them the land, and they regarded his scheme as merely another ruse to extract money from them. It was almost impossible for them to realize that he was doing something for them at no profit to himself, and at first they bluntly refused to accept his offer. Such were the peasants with whom Tolstoy himself had to deal, and whose conditions he sought to alleviate.

To sum up, Tolstoy's literary career is one of the most absorbing in the history of Russian literature. His life was practically coincident with the Golden Age. His literary activity spanned a period of some fifty-eight years, from 1852 to 1910. In versatility, he was unexcelled by any writer of his time. He was not only a novelist, but a short-story writer, an essayist, a dramatist, a theologian, a philosopher, an artist, a preacher, and the founder of a creed of his own. No writer surpassed him in describing the life of the nobility in pre-revolutionary Russia, or in appreciation of the Russian peasantry. His works reflected all the ideas and ideals that prevailed in the Russia of his day and generation. He was the only author in Russian literature who could speak with authority even to his rulers, who could prophesy their downfall, and yet emerge unscathed. In Tolstoy one visualizes the patriarch of old, who raised his powerful voice in protest against the injustice and corruption of his time. In short, Tolstoy was an institution by himself in the Golden Age of Russian literature.

BIBLIOGRAPHY

Baring, Maurice, *An Outline of Russian Literature*, Home University Library.

Birukov, Paul, *Tolstoi und der Orient*, Zurich-Leipsig, 1925.

Birukov, P. I., *The Life of Tolstoy*, London, 1911.

Bunin, Ivan, *Osvobojhdenie Tolstogo (Tolstoy's Liberation)*, Paris, 1937.

Dole, N. H. (Translator), *The Dramatic Works of Lyof Tolstoi*, N. Y., 1923.

Fülöp-Miller, René, *L. N. Tolstoy.*

Garnett, Edward, *Tolstoy*, London, 1914.

Gorky, Maxim, *Reminiscences of Leo Nicolayevitch Tolstoi*, England, 1920.

Gusev, N. N. (Editor), *Tolstoy i o Tolstom (Tolstoy and about Tolstoy)*, Tolstoy Museum, Moscow, 1924-1928.

Howells, W. D., "Lev Nikolayevitch Tolstoy," *Scandinavian and Slavonic Literature*, Columbia University Press, 1928.

Krasni Arkhiv (Red Archive), 5 (84), 1917-37, Moscow, U.S.S.R., pp. 241-45.

Kropotkin, Peter, *Russian Literature*, N. Y., 1905.

Kropotkin, Peter, *Ideals and Realities in Russian Literature*, N. Y., 1916.

Maklakov, B. A., *Tolstoy and Bolshevism* (in Russian), Paris, 1921.

Maklakov, B. A., *About Tolstoy* (in Russian), Paris, 1929.

Maude, Aylmer, *The Life of Tolstoy*, 2 Vols., N. Y., 1911.

Merejkovsky, D., *Tolstoy as Man, with an Essay on Dostoyevsky*, N. Y., 1902.

Mirsky, D. S., *Contemporary Russian Literature, 1881-1925*, N. Y., 1926.

Noyes, G. R., *Tolstoy*, N. Y., 1918.

Olgin, M. J., *Guide to Russian Literature*, N. Y., 1920.

Phelps, W. L., *Essays on Russian Novelists*, N. Y., 1916.

Shestov, Lev, *Dobro v Utchenii Tolstogo i Nitshe (The Good in the Teachings of Tolstoy and Nietzsche)*, Berlin, 1923.

Steiner, C. A., *Tolstoy: The Man and His Message.*

Tolstoy, S. A., *Autobiography of Countess Tolstoy*, N. Y., 1922.

Tsanoff, R. A., *The Problem of Life in the Russian Novel*, Rice Institute, 1917.

Waliszewski, K., *A History of Russian Literature*, N. Y., 1900.

Yarmolinsky, Avrahm, *Russian Literature* (Reading With a Purpose), Chicago, 1931.

Alexander Nikolayevitch Ostrovsky
1823-86

ALEXANDER NIKOLAYEVITCH OSTROVSKY was born on April 24, 1823, in Moscow, and died on July 6, 1886, at Kostroma. He was the son of a merchant, who later became a solicitor *(advocat)* to the merchant class of Moscow, which had not yet discarded the customs, manners, and beliefs that prevailed before the reforms of Peter the Great. As a boy, he had, therefore, ample opportunity to observe and to acquire an intimate knowledge of a class which was practically ignored by his contemporaries. At the same time he developed a passion for the theatre.

Forced to terminate his study of law at Moscow University in 1843, Ostrovsky served for two years in a minor capacity in the Moscow Conscience Court, an apprenticeship which left him with a vivid picture of the seamy side of domestic life. He then served for six years in the Commercial Court, where he continued to come into contact with the merchant class. After leaving the Court in 1851, he devoted the rest of his life to literature. He married an actress.

In 1847 two of his plays appeared: *Pictures of Family Happiness* and excerpts from *It's a Family Affair—We'll Settle It Ourselves* (published in full in 1850). After this debut he attracted considerable attention. The latter play highly offended the merchants, who brought pressure upon the authorities, and Ostrovsky was placed under police surveillance. Five years later he took up his pen again with more success. Yet, for various reasons, Ostrovsky continued to feel the pinch of poverty until shortly before his death.

Thanks to Ostrovsky's effort, the monopoly of the Imperial Theatre was abolished, and the first private theatre was founded in Moscow in 1882. The real founder of this first private theatre was F. A. Korsh, who was born in the Caucasus in 1852. The Korsh Theatre paved the way for the Moscow Art Theatre, established in 1893 by Vladimir Ivanovitch Nemirovitch-Dantchenko, born in the Caucasus in 1858. Just before his death in 1886, Ostrovsky attained the climax of his career as a dramatist, when he was put in charge of the Moscow Imperial Theatres and appointed head of the dramatic school.

Ostrovsky wrote nearly half a hundred plays, forty-one of which were in prose and seven in verse. The most important are *It's a Family Affair—We'll Settle It Ourselves* (1850), *The Poor Bride* (1852), *Poverty is No Crime* (1854), *The Storm* (1859), and *The Forest* (1871).

THE PLOT OF *THE POOR BRIDE* (1852)
A COMEDY IN FIVE ACTS

The widow Anna Petrovna Nezabudkina finds herself unable to cope with the problems which arise following her husband's death. She ardently desires the marriage of her daughter, Marya Andreyevna, so that there may be a man in the family to shoulder her responsibilities. The girl has no particular desire to marry, but her mother gives her no peace, and makes every effort to find her a suitable husband. This proves a difficult task, since Marya's only dowry is her beauty, and she will be, therefore, in a very literal sense, a "poor bride."

Several suitors present themselves, but there is little to recommend them either from the standpoint of personality or property. However, Marya falls in love with one of them, a certain Vladimir Vasilyevitch Merich, and lends a willing ear to his protestations of love. Vladimir's reputation is not of the best, but Marya petulantly refuses to heed the warnings of her friends.

Meanwhile, Platon Markovitch Dobrotvorsky, an old friend of the family, presents as a suitor a certain official, Maxim Dorofeyevitch Benevolensky. Although he is uncouth, immoral, addicted to drink, and is known to accept bribes, Anna Petrovna is entirely satisfied with him. The fact that he is a man of means, and offers to aid her in a lawsuit which threatens to leave her penniless, more than compensates, in her opinion, for his shortcomings. Consequently, she brings great pressure to bear upon Marya, who detests him.

In desperation Marya appeals to Merich to save her from a marriage which is abhorrent to her. Instead of living up to his protestations of love, Merich weakly remarks, that since circumstances are too strong for them, she had better follow her mother's wishes. Overcome with shame, and feeling that she has forced her love upon a man who did not desire it, Marya consents to marry Benevolensky.

Having resigned herself to her fate, she resolves to be a good wife, and consoles herself with the thought that she may be able to lead her husband to a better way of life. She assures her mother that she will be happy and that in any event she will bear no grudge against her.

THE PLOT OF *THE STORM* (1859)
A Tragedy in Four Acts

The scene of this tragedy is laid in a small town on the banks of the River Volga. The central figure is Katerina, the beautiful, but inwardly rebellious young wife of the spineless drunkard, Tikhon. Martha Kabanova, the mother of Tikhon, rules the entire household with an iron hand. Jealous of Tikhon's love for Katerina, she makes life almost unendurable for her daughter-in-law.

In accordance with his mother's orders, and after receiving endless injunctions from her on how to conduct himself, Tikhon leaves home on a fortnight's business trip. In spite of Katerina's pleas, he refuses to let her accompany him, rejoicing that for a time at least he will be free from the uncongenial home environment. Katerina is oppressed by a presentiment of approaching disaster.

On the very night of his departure, Tikhon's giddy young sister, Varvara, arranges a tryst between Katerina and Boris Grigorevitch in the dell below the Kabanov's garden. Boris, the ward of a bullying and miserly merchant by the name of Dikoy, has for some time loved Katerina from a distance, and, although they had never met in privacy, she, in spite of her efforts to remain loyal, returns his affection. They now plan to meet daily during Tikhon's absence.

When Tikhon returns, Katerina, tormented by conscience and terrified by a storm, which to her spells approaching disaster, makes a public confession of her guilt to her husband. The unhappy Boris is banished to China by his uncle, Dikoy, for three years. Katerina, after their final farewell, feeling that death is preferable to a life of misery and disgrace in her mother-in-law's home, throws herself into the Volga.

FROM *THE POOR BRIDE*
ACT V, SCENE xi

Marya Andreyevna: You here, mamma? I'm looking for you. (She goes up to her mother.)

Anna Petrovna: What's the matter, darling; what is it?

Marya Andreyevna: I feel rather ill somehow, mamma. (Sits down on the couch and leans her head against her mother.)

Dobrotvorsky (taking a glass): What's the use, young lady? You must get used to it! To your health! Be rich, and then don't forget us! He, he, he! Your little hand please, young lady. (He kisses her hand.)

Anna Petrovna (drinks): Well, little girl, be happy; don't bear any grudge against your old mother. You'll live a few years, and then you'll find out yourself what children are like. (She kisses her.) Do you like him? I must admit the thing was done pretty quickly. Who knows? You can't tell what he's like.—

Marya Andreyevna (in tears): I like him so-so, mamma. Never mind my crying; that's just because I'm nervous. I think I'll be happy.—

A Voice from the Crowd: Some husbands are fussy, my dear, and like to have you please 'em. Of course, they'll come home drunk most of the time; and then they like to have you tend to 'em yourself, and won't allow any one else near 'em.

Marya Andreyevna: But if I shouldn't be happy, it won't be your fault; you've done everything for me that you could; all that you knew how. I thank you, mamma, and you, Platon Markych. (From the other room music is heard. Benevolensky comes in; Marya Andreyevna goes to meet him and gives him her hand.)

Dobrotvorsky (offering his arm to Anna Petrovna): And you and I, madam, let's dance the polka. (They go out.)

One of the People: Well, is that the bride?

An Old Woman: That's she, my dear, that's she.

A Woman: How she cries, poor dear.

The Old Woman: Yes, my friend, she *is* poor: he's taking her for her beauty.

—Tr. by SEYMOUR and NOYES

FROM *THE STORM*
ACT III, SCENE ii

(Night. A gully, covered with bushes; at the top is seen the fence of the Kabanov's garden, with a gate leading into it. A path leads to the gully.)

Kudriash (enters with a guitar): Nobody here. What keeps her? Well—let's sit down and wait (sits on a rock). Let's banish ennui with a song (sings a Cossack song. Boris enters and Kudriash stops playing.) Well, of all things! A quiet fellow like you out on a spree!

Boris: Kudriash—is that you?

Kudriash: It is I, Boris Grigorevitch!

Boris: Why are you here?

Kudriash: I? Just because I have to be here, Boris Grigorevitch. If I didn't have to, I wouldn't come. Where are you going?

Boris (looking cautiously about): Look, Kudriash: I must remain here, but, if it's all the same to you, won't you find another place?

Kudriash: No, Boris Grigorevitch. I can easily see that this is your first time here, but I have been here so many times that I have worn the path bare. I like you, sir, and I am ready to do you a favor, provided you steer clear of this path at night—lest, God forbid, something worse might come of it. A bargain is better than money.

Boris: What's the matter with you, Vanya? (Ivan)

Kudriash: Don't Vanya me! I know my name is Vanya. You mind your own business, that's all. Find a girl of your own, and have a good time with her, and nobody will bother you. But don't meddle with another fellow's girl! That isn't done here. If you do, the fellows will break your neck. As for me— ... I really can't answer for what I may do! Cut your throat!

Boris: You have no reason to be angry. I've never had any intention of stealing your girl. I'd never have come here, had I not been told to do so.

Kudriash: Who told you?

Boris: I couldn't see. It was dark. Some girl stopped me in the street and told me that I must come to this very place,—to the path behind the Kabanov's garden.

Kudriash: Who could it have been?

Boris: Listen, Kudriash, may I speak to you frankly? You won't gossip?

Kudriash: Speak, don't be afraid! I know how to hold my tongue.

Boris: I don't know a thing about this place, nor about your habits or customs. The fact is—

Kudriash: Perhaps you've fallen in love?

Boris: That's just it, Kudriash.

Kudriash: Well, that's all right. There's no harm in that. Girls go about as they please without any interference from their parents. Only the married women are shut up.

Boris: That's just my trouble.

Kudriash: You don't mean to say that you've fallen in love with a married woman?

Boris: She's married, all right, Kudriash.

Kudriash: Oh, Boris Grigorevitch, put an end to it!

Boris: That's easier said than done! Perhaps you could; you drop one and pick up another. I can't do that. If I love...!

Kudriash: Do you want to ruin the poor woman, Boris Grigorevitch?

Boris: God forbid! God forbid! No, Kudriash, how could I? I wouldn't harm her for the world! I only want to see her, nothing more.

Kudrish: How can you tell what will happen! Don't you know the people here! You know yourself, they would bury her alive!

Boris: Don't say that, Kudriash! Please don't frighten me!

Kudriash: Does she love you?

Boris: I don't know.

Kudriash: Have you ever met her—or not?

Boris: I've only called on them once with my uncle. I see her in church. I meet her on the boulevard. Ah, Kudriash, if you could only see her when she prays! Her smile is like an angel's, and her face is radiant!

Kudriash: Why, it must be the young wife of Kabanov?

Boris: It is she, Kudriash.

Kudriash: Oh! So that's it! Well, permit me to congratulate you!

Boris: Why?

Kudriash: Why? If you have been told to come here, that proves that everything's arranged.

Boris: Has she really told you so?

Kudriash: Who else could it be?

Boris: No, you are joking! It can't be true (clutching at his head)!

Kudriash: What's the matter with you?

Boris: I will go mad with joy!

Kudriash: I agree with you. There's reason enough for losing your mind! But look out—don't get into trouble yourself, or get her into trouble!

Varvara (sings): "Beyond the river, beyond the
    swift river, my Vanya goes,
    There my sweet Vanya goes..."

Kudriash (continues): "To buy goods." (Whistles).

Varvara (comes down the path, hiding her face in her kerchief, and approaches Boris): Stay here, young fellow. Something is in store for you. (To Kudriash) Let's go down by the Volga.

Kudriash: Why so long? I always have to wait for

you. You know how I hate waiting! (Varvara puts her arm around him and they go off together.)

Boris: It's like a dream! What a night—songs—a lover's tryst! There they go, with their arms around one another. This is so new to me, so good and so joyful! And what am I waiting for? I don't know and can't imagine; my heart throbs, and my blood tingles! I don't even know what to say to her! It takes my breath away —my knees are trembling! If my foolish heart should begin to boil all of a sudden, nothing could calm it. Here she comes! (Katerina comes down the path quietly, wrapped in a large white kerchief, her eyes fixed on the ground. Silence.) Is it you, Katerina Petrovna? (Silence.) I don't know how to thank you, really, I don't. (Silence.) If you only knew, Katerina Petrovna, how I love you! (Seeks to take her hand.)

Katerina (in terror, but not raising her eyes): Don't touch me, don't touch me! Oh! Oh!

Boris: Don't be angry.

Katerina: You must go away! Leave me alone, you wicked man! Don't you know that no prayer of mine will ever suffice to expiate this sin. Never! It will weigh upon my soul like a stone!

Boris: Don't drive me away!

Katerina: Why have you come here? Why have you come to ruin me? Don't you know that I am married, that I must go on living with my husband until I die ...

Boris: But you, yourself, told me to come ...

Katerina: Don't you understand that you are my enemy: I have told you—even till I die!

Boris: Better that I had never seen you!

Katerina (with great emotion): What will happen to me? Where can I go? Do you know?

Boris: Calm yourself! (takes her hand) Sit down!

Katerina: Why do you wish to ruin me?

Boris: How could I wish to injure you, when I love you better than anyone else in the world, even better than myself.

Katerina: No, no! You have ruined me!

Boris: Am I such a wicked man?

Katerina (nodding her head) : You have ruined me, ruined me, ruined me!

Boris: Heaven forbid! I would rather perish myself!

Katerina: How can you say that you have not ruined me, when I have left home at night to come to you?

Boris: You came of your own free will.

Katerina: I could not help myself. Otherwise, I wouldn't have come at all. (She lifts her eyes and looks at Boris. Short silence.) I have no will now but yours, don't you see that! (She throws herself on his neck.)

Boris (embraces Katerina) : My life!

Katerina: How I wish I could die now!

Boris: Why die, when life is so good?

Katerina: No, not for me! I know I won't live.

Boris: Please don't say such things, don't hurt me so . . .

Katerina: That's all very well for you—you are a free Cossack, but I! . . .

Boris: Nobody will ever know about our love. Don't you realize that I will protect you!

Katerina: Ah! Why should you pity me, nobody is to blame,—I alone am to blame. Don't pity—ruin me! Let everybody know, let everybody see, what I am doing! (Embraces Boris.) If I was not afraid to sin for your sake, shall I fear what people will say? They say, if one suffers on earth for a sin, it is better hereafter.

Boris: Why think about such things, now that we are so happy!

Katerina: Ah, well! I will have time enough to think and to weep.

Boris: And I was afraid; I thought you were sending me away!

Katerina (smiling) : Send you away! Where? My heart wouldn't let me! If you hadn't come, I should have come myself to you!

Boris: I never even suspected that you loved me!

Katerina: I have loved you so long—to my sorrow! From the moment I first saw you I was no longer the same woman. From the very beginning, I think, if you had beckoned to me, I would have followed you; even to the end of the world, I would have followed you, without even looking back.

Boris: Will your husband be away long?

Katerina: For a fortnight.

Boris: Oh, if that is the case we shall have plenty of time!

Katerina: Very well...and then... (she becomes thoughtful) They will lock me up, and I shall die! But if they don't, I shall find some way to see you. (Enter Varvara and Kudriash.)

Varvara: Well, have you come to an understanding? (Katerina hides her face on Boris' breast.)

Boris: Yes.

Varvara: Now you go for a walk, and we will wait here. When it is time to go in Vanya will shout. (Boris and Katerina go away...Kudriash and Varvara sit down on the stone.)

Kudriash: A fine idea that, to slip out through the garden gate! Just the thing for us.

Varvara: It was my idea.

Kudriash: One can leave such things to you. But suppose your mother finds out?...

Varvara: Oh! She won't! It would never occur to her.

Kudriash: But what if she did?

Varvara: She sleeps soundly now; in the early morning she wakes up.

Kudriash: Yes, but how can you tell? Suppose something wakes her up?

Varvara: Well, what if it does! The gate into the yard is locked on the garden side; she'd have to knock and knock and knock to wake us up to open it. And in the morning we could say that we slept so soundly, we did not hear her. Moreover Glasha is on guard; if something should happen, she will let us know immediately. One must always take risks! How could it be otherwise! All we have to do is to avoid getting into trouble. (Kudriash strums on his guitar. Varvara leans against his shoulder. Disregarding her, he plays quietly.)

Varvara (yawning) : How can we find out what time it is?

Kudriash: It's one o'clock.

Varvara: How do you know?

Kudriash: The watchman has just struck the hour.

Varvara (yawning): It's time to go. Give them a call. Tomorrow we'll slip out earlier, so we'll have more time together.

Kudriash (whistles and then sings loudly):
      "It's time to go home, it's time to go home!
      But I don't want to go home!"

Boris (behind the scene): I hear!

Varvara (rises): Well, good-bye! (Yawns, then gives a cool kiss to Kudriash as if he were an old and intimate friend.) See that you come earlier tomorrow! (Looks in the direction of Boris and Katerina.) That's enough, you are not saying good-bye for ever. You'll see each other tomorrow. (Yawns and stretches. Katerina and Boris run up.)

Katerina: Well, we must go, we must go! (Goes up the path. Katerina turns.) Good-bye!

Boris: Till tomorrow!

Katerina: Yes, till tomorrow! You will tell me your dreams! (She reaches the gate.)

Boris: Without fail! (Kudriash and Varvara sing.)

ACT V, SCENES vi and vii

The Voice: A woman's thrown herself into the river. Fetch a boat! (Kuligin, Ivan and several others run out.)

Tikhon: My God, it's she! (Tries to run off. Mme. Kabanova holds his arm.) Mamma, let me go. I will pull her out, if not, I myself . . . I can't live without her!

Kabanova: I won't let you. As if she's worth risking your life for! Hasn't she brought enough disgrace upon us already? Isn't that enough?

Tikhon: Let me go!

Kabanova: Let others go. If you go, I will curse you!

Tikhon (falling on his knees): Let me just look at her!

Kabanova: You will see her when they find her.

Tikhon (rises and looks in the direction of the people): Hi, old man, do you see anything there?

First Man: It's very dark below—nothing visible. (Noise behind the stage.)

Second Man: I hear a noise but I can't make out what it's all about.

First Man: It's Kuligin's voice.

Second Man: They're walking along the bank with a lantern.

First Man: Here they come. They are carrying her. (Some of the people return.)

One of the Crowd: I tell you Kuligin is a brave fellow! Near here, out in the river—the light you know reflects very far—he saw her dress and dragged her ashore.

Tikhon: Is she alive?

Another Man: How could she be? She threw herself from the cliff, and she must have struck an anchor, poor thing! But she looks as if she were alive. There is just a small wound on her temple. (Tikhon starts to run; he meets Kuligin and the crowd carrying the body of Katerina.)

Kuligin: Here is your Katerina! You can do anything you please with her now. Here is her body, take it! But her soul is not yours any longer! She is now before a Higher Judge, who is more merciful than you. (Lays her body on the ground and departs quickly.)

Tikhon (throwing himself on Katerina's body): Katya! Katya!

Kabanova: Be quiet! That will do! It's wicked to weep for her!

Tikhon: Mamma, it's you who have killed her—you—you—you!

Kabanova: What's the matter with you? Are you out of your mind? Have you forgotten to whom you speak?

Tikhon: You killed her! You! You!

Kabanova: Well, I'll talk to you at home. (Bows low to the crowd.) Thank you, good people for your help. (All bow.)

Tikhon: You are well off, Katya, but why am I left to live and suffer! (Falls on the body of his wife.)

—Tr. by I. SPECTOR

Although in this study of Russian literature our attention has been focused primarily upon the novel, our understanding of Russian life as revealed through that literature would scarcely be complete without some consideration of Ostrovsky, the dramatist. While, in the novel, Turgenev and Tolstoy were depicting the life of the Russian nobility or peasantry, and only incidentally referring to other slices of Russian society, a new class was making a niche for itself in the drama—namely, the Russian merchant *(kupetchestvo)*. Whereas, in the literature we have already discussed, the underlying motives were political, social, philosophical, and idealistic, in the plays of Ostrovsky the economic factor predominates.

If Russian drama may be defined as "life relived," as a genuine transmigration of the souls of characters portrayed, then Ostrovsky is the most representative Russian dramatist. He placed the drama on a par with the novel. What Turgenev did for the serf, and Tolstoy for the nobility and peasantry, Ostrovsky did for the merchant. For almost half a century he dominated the Russian stage. He produced over fifty plays, forty-seven of which he wrote himself, five in collaboration with others, while twelve were translations and adaptations for the Russian stage.

In spite of his popularity in Russia, Ostrovsky's plays are the most difficult to stage abroad. One reason for this is that his language was the vernacular, both regional and local, of the merchant class, and as such it often defies translation. As a result much of the content of his plays has been misconstrued or has failed to be appreciated in the West. In recent years a few of his plays have been translated, but the translator has sometimes departed so far from the original text that his final product contains little or nothing of Ostrovsky. Some translators have felt constrained to transform Ostrovsky's Russian merchants into American Rockefellers, American Babbitts, or American workers.

Three quarters of Ostrovsky's plays deal with the everyday life of the merchant class, with their strong as well as with their weak points. Ostrovsky's approach was clearly revealed in one of his letters:

"Let the Russian be gay rather than sad when he sees himself reproduced on the stage. Let others assume the rôle of reformers if they wish. In order to claim the right to correct the shortcomings of a person without insulting him, it is essential to prove that you are also aware of his strong points. That is exactly what I am trying to do in my comedies."

This approach is particularly well illustrated in his two plays, *The Sleigh* and *Poverty is No Crime*. Because he adopted this methodology even in his comedies, stressing not only the incongruities but also the positive qualities of the Russian merchant class, many Westernizers accused Ostrovsky of Slavophilism. Such was the fate of any writer who attempted to portray the better qualities of Russian individuals or classes. On the other hand, when Ostrovsky had the temerity to champion the cause of the liberal merchant in his struggle with the hidebound traditionalists, many Slavophiles branded him as a Westernizer. As a matter of fact, Ostrovsky belonged to neither political camp. His purpose was to describe the life of the class of which he himself was a product, as it actually was—realistically and naturally. Inasmuch as any group has its merits and defects, it was therefore natural that the rival political camps alternately suspected him of partiality to one or the other.

Ostrovsky's merchant class, from the Russian standpoint, was neither a middle nor an upper class, but comprised the representatives of many classes. Within its ranks were to be found destitute members of the nobility, who, as a last resort, sought to retrieve their fortunes in the business world rather than by the management of their estates. It included the *nouveau riche*, the merchant capitalist, whose success only served to convince him of the power of the Almighty Ruble. Here, too, were to be found many ex-peasants, who had transferred their activities from the seasonal occupation of the farm to the more lucrative world of business, not to mention innumerable clerks and office employees who were the hangers-on of commerce and business. To the nobility described by Turgenev and Tolstoy, the running of an estate or the management of a business was usually a last resort, only to be undertaken in the face of desperate financial reverses, or when life held nothing but bitterness, disillusionment, and defeat. Ostrovsky's merchant class, on the other hand, devoted their lives to business management, and, far from regarding it as a disgrace, they elevated it to an art.

This class had its Russian Rockefellers as well as its Russian Babbitts. When Ostrovsky wrote, the merchant class was mainly responsible for the support of various social and cultural institutions, including art galleries. Its members not only subsidized talented writers, artists, dancers, and musicians, but produced them within their own ranks—as in the case of Ostrovsky himself. They helped to raise the standard of living, not only for their own class, but for others. In fact, their contribution to Russian culture and civilization has never received due recognition. On the other hand, they were also responsible for much bribery and corruption, prostitution, and vice, and for making a god of the Almighty Ruble.

In general, Ostrovsky voiced the sentiment of the liberal merchant. The plays which reflect this best are *The Storm* and *The Poor Bride*. *The Storm*, by general consensus of opinion, is considered one of the best, if not the best, of his many works. Here, as nowhere else, he presented the clash between the older generation of traditionalist merchants, the *samodurs* (domestic tyrants or bullies) like Madame Kabanova and Dikoy, whose roots were fixed in the feudal society of the past, and the younger and more liberal group (Katerina, Boris, Kuligin, Varvara), who strove for freedom of expression,

liberty of action, and a more equitable division of authority. Balked by the *samodurs* from finding any legitimate
outlet for their feelings, they sometimes, as in the case of
Katerina and Boris, mistook license for liberty and indulged in serious lapses from the conventions. Even
Tikhon, once he got beyond the reach of his mother's
caustic tongue, cast everything else to the winds, in order
to crowd as much pleasure as possible into a fortnight
of freedom.

In *The Storm* it was the domestic tyranny of Martha
Kabanova and Dikoy which bred license—a tyranny
which demanded blind unreasoning obedience from the
younger members of the family. This tyranny produced
both mental and physical suffering. Not only did Katerina have to submit to the constant nagging of her shrew-
ish mother-in-law, but she had to endure a beating at the
hands of her husband in accordance with her mother-in-
law's orders—a beating which was supposed to make her
a better wife. She was forced to kneel before her husband
on the eve of his departure on a business trip, and promise not to look at other men during his absence—just as
he had to kneel before his domineering mother and pay
heed to her countless instructions.

The chief object of Ostrovsky's dramas, particularly
of this one, was the destruction of the *samodur*, and the
triumph of honesty, moderation, and genuine goodness.
Unlike Tolstoy, who practically sought to transform the
nobility into a peasantry, or Tchekhov, who sought to
supplant the nobility by a middle class, Ostrovsky was
not seeking the destruction of the merchant class. He
merely wished to rid it of its more undesirable elements,
to eliminate the *samodurs*—in fact, to ethicise the business profession.

In *The Poor Bride* the power of the ruble is ably illustrated. In the first place a bride without a dowry was
a frozen asset in a merchant's family, especially if she
lacked beauty. If she were good looking, she could still
hope to be sold to the highest bidder—to some rough, un-

couth, and none too respectable merchant like Benevolensky. Anna Petrovna Nezabudkina was a product of the older traditionalist generation, for whom wealth covered up a multitude of sins, and who could unhesitatingly sacrifice her daughter to a man like Benevolensky in order to improve her financial position. Marya, representing the younger generation, accepts her mother's choice reluctantly, but unselfishly, in a fine spirit. On the one hand, Ostrovsky shows greed, selfishness, and disregard for human values; on the other, love and self-sacrifice.

To sum up, Ostrovsky gave a faithful description of the practical, materialistic merchant class, which was about to supplant the idealistic nobility. The final triumph of this class is reflected in Tchekhov's plays, particularly in *The Cherry Orchard*.

BIBLIOGRAPHY

Abramovitch, G., and Goloventchenko, F., *Russkaya Literatura (Russian Literature)*, Moscow, 1935.

Carter, H., *The New Spirit of the Russian Theatre*, N. Y., 1929.

Chaliapin, Feodor, *Man and Mask*, N. Y., 1932.

Covan, J. (Translator), *Enough Stupidity in Every Wise Man*, N. Y., 1923.

Garnet, C. (Translator), *The Storm*, London, 1899.

Mirsky, D. S., *A History of Russian Literature*, N. Y., 1927.

Nemirovitch-Dantchenko, V., *My Life in the Russian Theatre*, Boston, 1936.

Noyes, G. R., *Masterpieces of the Russian Drama*, N. Y., 1933.

Noyes, Rapall (Editor), *Plays by Alexander Ostrovsky*, N. Y., 1917.

Olgin, M. J., *Guide to Russian Literature*, N. Y., 1920.

Patouillet, J., *Ostrovski et son théâtre de moeurs russes*, Paris, 1912.

Stanislavsky, Constantin, *My Life in Art*, Boston, 1927.

Vsevolodsky-Gengross, V., *Khrestomatia po istorii Russkogo Teatra (An Anthology of the History of the Russian Theatre)*, Moscow, 1936.

Waliszewski, K., *A History of Russian Literature*, N. Y., 1900.

Wiener, Leo, *The Contemporary Drama of Russia*, Boston, 1924.

Anton Pavlovitch Tchekhov
1860-1904

ANTON PAVLOVITCH TCHEKHOV was born on January 29 (O.S. January 17), 1860, at Taganrog, on the Sea of Azov, and died on July 15 (O.S. July 2), 1904, at Badenweiler, Germany. His grandfather, Yegor Mihailovitch Tchekh, was a serf from the province of Voronezh, where he belonged to a landowner *(pomiestchik)* by the name of Tchertkov, father of Vladimir Tchertkov, the famous disciple of Tolstoy. Long before the abolition of serfdom (March 3, 1861), Tchekh purchased his own freedom and that of his family for 3,500 rubles and became the manager of a large estate. P. E. Tchekhov, father of the famous writer, began his career as a cattle dealer, but later became a clerk in a Taganrog grocery store. After his marriage in 1854, he opened a grocery store of his own.

Anton Tchekhov was the third of six children, five boys and one girl, all of whom were unusually talented, industrious, and devoted to one another. Anton, of course, excelled them all. Although his father was well disposed toward art, music, and education in general, he could offer very little financial support toward the lad's education. Consequently, young Tchekhov, like some of the other members of his family, was forced to work long hours in his father's grocery store. At home the children were subjected to rigorous discipline, and at times they were severely chastised for their pranks. P. E. Tchekhov's favorite hobby was the singing of church hymns in chorus with his family. Needless to say, the ritual of the Orthodox Church was strictly observed in the Tchekhov home.

After attending the local Greek Church School from 1867 to 1869, Tchekhov entered the Taganrog Gymnasium from which he was graduated ten years later in

1879. His scholastic record at the Gymnasium was far from excellent. His worst grades, strangely enough, were in Russian composition, in which he never received more than a C *(troika)*. This poor scholastic record was partly due to extracurricular activities in the theatrical field, but also to long hours of work in his father's store. In 1876, as a result of a business depression, Tchekhov's father sold his property, and the family moved to Moscow.

In 1879 Tchekhov enrolled at Moscow University in the Department of Medicine, from which he was graduated, with the degree of M.D., in 1884. The beginning of his literary career practically coincided with his entrance into the university. His first story, "A Letter from a Don Landowner, Stepan Vladimirovitch N., to His Learned Neighbor, Doctor Frederick," appeared in *The Dragon-Fly*, No. 10, in 1880. From 1880 to 1881 he wrote a lengthy play which was left in manuscript form. He met with greater success in the publication of his short stories and *feuilleton*, which were designed to amuse the public, and which appeared under various pseudonyms, such as Antosha Tchekhone. These included *A Brother of My Brother, A Man Without a Spleen*, and so on. Tchekhov's early literary activities proved remunerative, thereby enabling him to complete his university course. His critics already remarked, in typically Russian fashion, that "it was too bad that such a talented young man should spend all his time making people laugh."

After his graduation in 1889, Tchekhov hung out his shingle, and from the very beginning of his medical practice, he enjoyed a decent income. In the same year, however, he abandoned his private office for a position in a Zemstvo hospital in the city of Voskresensk.

In spite of his comparative success in the medical profession, the *writer* in Tchekhov took possession of, and utterly superseded, the *doctor*. It was not long before he was devoting his entire time to literature. In 1886 he began to contribute to various periodicals, in particular to *Novoye Vremya*, a sensational journal, edited and published by A. S. Suvorin, whose opinions and political views Tchekhov did not share. His novels *Steppe, Fires,* and *Name-Day*, which began to appear about the same time, were a natural outgrowth of his short stories. Tchekhov was a born short-story writer, and the structure of the short story underlies all his other works, particularly his dramas.

In 1890 Tchekhov made a special trip to Sakhalin (Saghalin) to examine the penal colony and the prisons there. Inasmuch as the Siberian railroad was not yet completed, he was forced to travel from Tiumen to the coast by horse, eventually returning by boat to Russia via India, Ceylon, and the Suez Canal. He published his experiences in a series of sketches called *The Island of Sakhalin* (1893). In 1891 he made his first trip to Western Europe, visiting Austria, Italy, and France.

During the cholera epidemic of 1892-93 Tchekhov took an active part in relief work. In spite of his strong predilection for liberal ideas, he continued to shun politics. In 1901 he married an actress of the Moscow Art Theatre, Olga L. Knipper, who assumed leading rôles in several of his plays. Because of his consumptive condition, physicians advised him to transfer his residence to the sunny south. His last years were spent in his villa at Yalta, Crimea, which soon became a literary Mecca for Russian writers and artists. He died at the prime of his literary career on July 15, 1904, during the Russo-Japanese War, at Badenweiler, a small German health resort. His body was brought to Moscow and buried by the side of his father.

Although he was fundamentally a short-story writer, Tchekhov's fame rests on his plays, and he is better known to the world at large as a playwright. His most popular plays, and those which have been most widely discussed are *The Seagull* (1896), *Uncle Vanya* (1897), *The Three Sisters* (1900), and *The Cherry Orchard,* (1904).

THE PLOT OF *THE CHERRY ORCHARD* (1904)

After five years abroad, Lyubov Andreyevna Ranevskaya returns from Paris only to learn that the family estate, with its historic but dilapidated manor house and its beautiful but run-down cherry orchard, is on the verge of being sold to pay the mortgage on the property. Neither Madame Ranevskaya nor her impractical middle-aged brother, Leonid Andreyevitch Gayev, have any constructive program for averting the approaching catastrophe, which is, in reality, the outcome of their own incorrigible extravagance.

Yermolay Alexeyevitch Lopakhin, a former peasant, but now a wealthy merchant, proposes a plan which will not only save the family from bankruptcy, but which, in his estimation, will net them a profit of 25,000 rubles ($12,000) per year from the property. In short, he recommends that they tear down the manor house, cut down the cherry orchard, divide the property into building lots, and lease it for suburban villas. However, Madame Ranevskaya and her brother lend a deaf ear to such a "vulgar" proposition, especially one that involves the destruction of their cherry orchard, which even if it does bear only once in two years, is mentioned in Andreyevsky's Encyclopedia! They prove equally unwilling to sell the cherry orchard to Lopakhin, who offers to buy it for a generous sum, in order that he may carry out the plan they have so unqualifiedly rejected as "absurd." Lopakhin is forced to admit that he has never met anyone "so crazy and unbusiness-like" as Madame Ranevskaya and her brother.

With a little common sense, even with a modicum of mental concentration, it seems obvious that the pending calamity might be averted. Yet neither Gayev nor his sentimental sister can take the situation seriously enough to face realities. Nor can they permit themselves to soil their hands by bargaining with an upstart peasant-merchant. They are content to talk the situation over, to procrastinate, to hope that Dashenka will win the lottery or that something else will turn up, until at length the estate is sold over their heads at auction to none other than the practical "money-grubber," Lopakhin. Coincident with the family's departure, the sound of the axe rings out in the beloved cherry orchard as workers clear the ground for the suburban villas.

As Madame Ranevskaya and her brother bid a sentimental farewell to the estate they accidentally, but with characteristic thoughtlessness, lock the eighty-seven-year-old Firs, a faithful servant, inside the empty and abandoned house.

FROM *THE CHERRY ORCHARD*
EXCERPTS FROM ACTS III and IV

Lyubov Andreyevna: Was the cherry orchard sold?
Lopakhin: Yes.
Lyubov Andreyevna: Who bought it?
Lopakhin: I bought it.
(Pause. Lyubov Andreyevna is stunned. She would fall were she not leaning against the table and the armchair. Varya takes the bunch of keys from her belt, throws them into the middle of the drawing-room floor, and goes out.)
Lopakhin: I bought it! Wait a little, ladies and gentlemen, have patience, my head's swimming, I can't talk. ... (Laughs.) When we arrived at the auction, Deriganov was already there. Leonid Andreich had on hand only fifteen thousand, while Deriganov immediately bid thirty thousand above the amount of the mortgage. I saw I was going to have a tussle with him, and bid forty. He raised to forty-five. I bid fifty-five. So he kept raising me five and I raised him ten.... Well, it was over at last. I offered ninety thousand over the mortgage, and it went to me. The cherry orchard's mine now! Mine! (Roars with laughter.) O Lord my God, the cherry orchard's mine! Tell me I'm drunk, out of my head, or dreaming.... (Stamps his feet.) Don't laugh at me! If only my father and grandfather could rise from their graves and see all these things that have come to pass—how their Yermolay, beaten, illiterate little Yermolay, who used to go barefoot in the winter, has bought an estate— the most beautiful one in the world! I have bought the

estate where my father and grandfather were slaves, where they weren't allowed even to set foot in the kitchen. I'm asleep, this is only a dream, an hallucination. . . . This is the fruit of my imagination, veiled with the mist of uncertainty. . . . (Picks up the keys with a caressing smile.) She threw away the keys, she wants to show that she's no longer housekeeper here. . . . (Jingles the keys.) Well, no matter! . . . (The orchestra is heard tuning up.) Come, musicians, play, I want to hear you! Come, every one, and watch Yermolay Lopakhin swing his ax through the cherry orchard, see the trees fall to the ground! We'll build cottages here, and our grandsons and great-grandsons will see a new life arising here. . . . Let the music play!

(Music. Lyubov Andreyevna falls into a chair and weeps bitterly.)

Lopakhin (reproachfully) : Why, oh, why didn't you listen to me? My poor, dear friend, you cannot return to your home now. (Weeping.) Ah, if only this might swiftly pass by, if only we might swiftly change this unhappy, incoherent life of ours!

Pishchik (in a low voice, taking him by the arm) : She is weeping. Let us go into the ballroom and leave her alone. . . . Come on! . . . (Takes him by the arm and leads him into the ballroom.)

Lopakhin: What's the matter? Mind your notes, musicians! Let my wishes be obeyed. (With irony.) The new proprietor is coming, the lord of the cherry orchard! (He unexpectedly bumps against a table, almost upsetting the candelabra.) I can pay for everything! (He goes out with Pishchik.)

(The ballroom and the drawing-room are empty save for Lyubov Andreyevna, who is huddled in her chair, weeping bitterly. The music plays softly. Anya and Trofimov come in quickly. Anya goes over to her mother and kneels before her. Trofimov remains near the ballroom door.)

Anya: Mama! . . . Mama, are you crying? My dear, good, kind mama, my beautiful mama, I love you. . . . I bless you. The cherry orchard is sold, it is gone, that is true, true, but don't cry, mama. Your life to come is left you, your good, pure soul is left you.... Come with me, come away with me, darling, come away!...We'll plant a new orchard, a more beautiful one; you shall see it, shall understand it; and joy, deep and quiet, shall descend upon your soul like the evening sunlight, and you will smile again, mama. Come, darling, come!

.   .   .   .

Lopakhin: Is every one here? No one left? (He locks the door on the left.) There are some things stored here, we'll have to lock them up. Come on!

Anya: Good-by, old house! Good-by, old life!

Trofimov: Welcome, new life! (He goes out with Anya.)

(Varya casts a glance around the room and goes slowly out. Yasha, and Charlotta, her lap dog in her arms, follow.)

Lopakhin: Until spring then! Come on, my friends! Till we meet again! (Goes out.)

(Lyubov Andreyevna and Gayev are left together. They seem to have been waiting for this moment. They fall into each other's arms and sob softly, restrainedly, as though fearing lest some one hear them.)

Gayev (in despair) : My sister, my sister!...

Lyubov Andreyevna: Oh, my dear orchard, my tender, beautiful orchard! My life, my youth, my happiness, farewell! Farewell!

Anya's voice (joyously, appealingly) : Mama!...

Trofimov's voice (joyously, and with ardor) : Yoohoo!

Lyubov Andreyevna: To look at the walls, at the windows, for the last time!...Our dead mother loved to walk to and fro in this room....

Gayev: My sister, my sister!

Anya's voice: Mama!

Trofimov's voice: Yoo-hoo!

Lyubov Andreyevna: We're coming!... (They go out.)

(The stage is empty. One can hear keys turning in the locks of all the doors, the carriages roll away. Then the sound of an ax striking against wood, a sad and lonely sound, rings out amid the stillness. Footsteps are heard. Firs emerges from the door on the right. He is dressed as usual in a waiter's jacket and white waistcoat, with slippers on his feet. He is ill.)

Firs (going over to the door and pulling at the knob) : Locked! They've gone away.... (Sits down on the sofa.) They've forgotten me.... No matter.... I'll sit here a little while.... And I suppose Leonid Andreich didn't put on his fur coat and went off in a light one.... (Sighs anxiously.) I never looked to see.... Young and green! (Mutters something unintelligible.) So life has gone by —just as though I'd never lived at all.... (Lies down.) I'll lie here a little while.... You've no strength in you, nothing's left, nothing.... Eh, you're a ... lummox! (Lies motionless.)

(A distant sound is heard, like the melancholy twang of a string, breaking in the heavens. It dies away. Silence, save for the dull sound of an ax chopping, far off in the orchard.)

—Tr. by C. C. Daniels and G. R. Noyes.

Although Anton Tchekhov was a prolific writer of short stories, novels, and plays, practically all his ideas are summed up in his last drama, *The Cherry Orchard,* A Comedy in Four Acts, published in 1904. Technically speaking, and from a universal standpoint, *The Three Sisters* (1900) is perhaps his masterpiece; but from an historical point of view *The Cherry Orchard* is much more significant. For that reason we have confined our discussion to this play.

In general, *The Cherry Orchard* was more popular and more widely discussed than any of Tchekhov's previous writings. The main reason for its phenomenal success was that it voiced the prevailing political, economic, and social sentiment of the Russian people. This play appeared during the Russo-Japanese War, and almost on the eve of the Revolution of 1905, when the common platform of all political parties was the urbanization (industrialization) of Russia. By general consensus of opinion there were far too many villages and "cherry orchards" in Russia, when what the country actually needed was cities, factories, railroads, machinery, and a vast program of industrial development.

For the benefit of the Western reader it may be pointed out that the Russian village of the period in question was not a European village or an American farming community. Many of them were several hundred miles from a railroad station, while the roads leading to them were unpaved and often impassable. There were no libraries, no clubs, no daily newspapers, and very little connection with the outside world. In such an atmosphere people vegetated in boredom. A stranger from town, more particularly from Moscow, was sure to become an absorbing center of interest for the entire community. Most of the enterprising people marooned in these villages, like the "Three Sisters," spent their time planning how to get out, how to get to Moscow, the land of dreams. Some left of their own free will—others, because of the mismanagement of their estates, were forced out by the Lopakhins. To understand Tchekhov better, one should read Turgenev's *A Month in the Country*, where the theme, the negative side of country life, is the same, minus the Lopakhins, who have not yet appeared on the scene.

Tolstoy idealized the peasant and the simple naturalness of village life. In Tchekhov we see that too much village life retards the material progress of Russia. His plays mark a distinct reaction against the idealism of Tolstoy—a reaction which expressed the general sentiment of the people. In *The Cherry Orchard*, more than in any other contemporaneous work, this clash between ruralism and urbanization, between the impractical, traditionalist, and often impoverished members of the nobility, and the impatient, ruthless businessman, is faithfully depicted. Tchekhov makes it quite apparent that a new era is beginning and that the architect of the industrial age is the merchant capitalist.

In this play Madame Ranevskaya and her brother Gayev represent the unbusinesslike, impractical, decadent members of the "House of Gentlefolk," who have retained but the shadow of the former glamor which surrounded the nobility of Anna Karenina, and who contribute to the vegetation and stagnation of other classes by supporting "superfluous people" in idleness. On the other hand, Lopakhin, who seems to have stepped out of the pages of Ostrovsky, stands for the new prosperous merchant class, not far removed from serfdom, which inherits the family estates of the Ranevskys, destroys the cherry orchards, together with all that they stood for symbolically and otherwise, and replaces them with suburban villas, the symbol of the new age.

In *The Cherry Orchard* the star of the Lopakhins is in the ascendancy—that of the Ranevskys is setting. The reader is confronted with a clash between sentimentalism on the one hand, and dollars and cents on the other; between static life and dynamic life; between culture and civilization; between that which was old and familiar and that which is new and unknown. The new way had a stronger appeal because the old way had been tried and found wanting. The new way promised concrete returns in the shape of higher wages, shorter hours, better living conditions, popular education, and so on, at the expense of the Oblomovs, dilapidated manors, and run-down cherry orchards. The dissatisfied elements, therefore, pinned their hopes on industrialization, or, as they called it, urbanization, which promised all this in return for the sacrifice of a group which was numerically insignificant.

While it seems apparent that Tchekhov's sympathies lay with the Lopakhins, of which class he himself was a product, nevertheless, he was fair enough and objective enough to lay bare the strong and the weak points of both sides in the struggle. The crude methods of Lopakhin reveal the destructive element latent in him. At times his coarseness assumes such proportions that one wonders which the merchant capitalist wanted more—a new world of his own making, or revenge for the injustice and inequalities of the past—perhaps both. On the other hand, the sentimental Ranevskys, who cherished every stick and stone of the ancient and decrepit manor house, thoughtlessly abandoned the eighty-seven-year-old footman, Firs, who had served the family for forty years. When Firs discovered his predicament, his first thought was not for himself, but for his master and whether he had remembered to wear his fur coat. Like Turgenev, Tchekhov, perhaps consciously, points out that the serf may reveal a nobler spirit than his master.

In *The Cherry Orchard*, the clash between the old and the new ends with the defeat of the old and the triumph of the new. The merchant capitalist, whose victory was foreseen by Gontcharov, whose leadership was sought by Turgenev and whose representatives take precedence in the works of Ostrovsky, finally in *The Cherry Orchard*, displaces the old nobility. The triumph of Lopakhin is also the triumph of the Stolzes and the Solomins, while the defeat of the Ranevskys is likewise the defeat of the Oblomovs and the Lavretskys.

The merchant capitalist dealt his death-blow with the axe that cut down the cherry orchard—a blow that was heard throughout Russia—and which proved to be the first signal of the approaching revolution. For the Revolution of 1905 was not, in the final analysis, a social revolution. It put the merchant capitalist in the saddle, where he remained until 1917. Strangely enough, it was his children who provided the leaders for the 1917 revolution; and it was this very class, which, by its contributions to the revolutionary money chests, blindly dug its own grave. The merchant capitalists were ousted, not by the axe, but by firing squads and "liquidation."

Abroad, and particularly in England, Tchekhov became the most popular of the Russian dramatists—even upon occasion a rival of Shakespeare. There are several reasons for this. In the first place, Tchekhov, with his humorous short story, broke new ground in Russian literature from the standpoint of the foreigner. By showing that the Russian could laugh as well as sigh, he was for them like a ray of light in "the monotonous gloom" of Russian literature. In Europe, moreover, the short story enjoyed an immense popularity, and in Russia, where it had reached its nadir, Tchekhov elevated it to an art. Furthermore, his dramas, though less amusing, expressed a reaction against sentimentality which coincided with English taste at the beginning of the twentieth century. The attention of the English public may have been attracted to the dénouement of his plays, particularly in the case of *The Three Sisters* and *Uncle Vanya*, which are somewhat reminiscent of Goldsmith's *Deserted Village*. To be sure, in the latter, the depopulation of the countryside was bemoaned as a tragedy, whereas in Tchekhov it is welcomed, but the milieu is the same. Finally, the merchant capitalist, depicted by Tchekhov, was an even more familiar figure in the industrial centers of Western Europe than in Russia itself. To the Englishman, as well as to Tchekhov, he was a practical man who stood for material progress.

In brief, Tchekhov's works, especially *The Cherry Orchard*, mark the transition between the downfall of the "House of Gentlefolk" and the advent of the proletariat—sometimes called Russia's "Twilight Period."

BIBLIOGRAPHY

Barkshy, Alexander, *The Path of the Modern Russian Stage*, London, 1916.
Carter, H., *The New Spirit of the Russian Theatre*, N. Y., 1929.
Chaliapin, Feodor, *Man and Mask*, N. Y., 1932.
Elton, Oliver, *Chekhov*, Oxford University Press, 1929.
Fovitzky, A. L., *The Moscow Art Theatre and Its Distinguishing Characteristics*, N. Y., 1922.
Garnett, C. (Translator), *Letter to Olga L. Knipper*, N. Y., 1926.
Garnett, C. (Translator), *Letters of Anton Chekhov*, London, 1920.
Gerhardi, William, *Anton Chekhov, A Critical Study*, London, 1923.

Glinka-Volzhsky, A. (Editor), *A. P. Tchekhov* (in Russian), Moscow, 1934.

Koteliansky, S., and Tomlinson, P. (Translators and editors), *The Life and Letters of Anton Tchekhov*, 1925.

Mirsky, D. S., *Modern Russian Literature*, London, 1925.

Nemirovitch-Dantchenko, V., *My Life in the Russian Theatre*, Boston, 1936.

Noyes, G. R., *Masterpieces of the Russian Drama*, N. Y., 1933.

Sayler, Oliver, *The Russian Theatre*, N. Y., 1922.

Stanislavsky, Constantin, *My Life in Art*, Boston, 1927.

Toumanova, A., *Anton Chekhov, The Voice of Twilight Russia*, Columbia University Press, 1937.

Vsevolodsky-Gengross, V., *Khrestomatia po istorii Russkogo Teatra (An Anthology of the History of the Russian Theatre)*, Moscow, 1936.

Wiener, Leo, *The Contemporary Drama of Russia*, Boston, 1924.

Znosko-Borovsky, *The Russian Theatre from the Beginning of the Twentieth Century* (in Russian), Praha.

Leonid Nikolayevitch Andreyev
1871-1919

LEONID NIKOLAYEVITCH ANDREYEV was born on August 21, 1871, at Orel, in Central Russia, the birthplace of Turgenev, and died on September 25, 1919, in Finland, at the age of forty-eight. His mother, née Anastasia Nikolayevna Poskovskaya, from whom he derived much of his artistic talent, was of Polish descent. His father, a surveyor by profession, died when Leonid was still a student in the Gymnasium, leaving his family in a state of abject poverty.

Although Andreyev's scholastic record was poor, and his deportment at the Gymnasium far from exemplary, he was a voracious reader. At a very early age he became conversant with the works of most of the outstanding Russian writers. In the face of insuperable financial obstacles he continued his education at St. Petersburg and Moscow universities, eventually receiving his diploma in law from the latter institution in 1897. For days at a time in St. Petersburg, Andreyev felt the pinch of hunger, while in Moscow he increased a precarious livelihood by painting portraits of his fellow students. As an artist he displayed much talent, but remained essentially an amateur. During these early years of intense struggle for subsistence Andreyev three times contemplated suicide as the only solution of his difficulties.

Andreyev displayed no aptitude for the law, and after losing his one and only civil case, he became a police court reporter for the Moscow *Courier* without attracting any particular attention. In 1898, however, when he published his first story in the same paper, he aroused the interest of Maxim Gorky, who encouraged and assisted him. The appearance of Andreyev's first collection of stories in 1901 placed him on a par with Gorky, made his name a byword, and his books best-sellers. Within a short time 250,000 copies of his collected stories were sold. This phenomenal record might almost be said to have been surpassed, when, with the publication of *King Hunger* in 1907, the entire edition of 18,000 copies was sold in four hours. Andreyev's choice of titles, like *The Red Laugh, King Hunger,* and *The Pretty Sabine Women,* to a Russian public accustomed to *Rudin, The Brothers Karamazov,* and *Anna Karenina,* were sensational, and may have served to augment his book sales. Even beyond the borders of Russia, Andreyev's name was better known than those of many of his contemporaries, translations of his works having appeared in all European languages. In 1906 he sought relief from the distractions of city life in his country home at Terioky, Finland, some thirty miles from Petrograd. In the same year his first wife died.

The last five years of Andreyev's life served rather as an anticlimax to his rapid rise from poverty to international fame. With the outbreak of the Great War in 1914, his artistic output came to an end. In spite of *The Red Laugh* (1904), which exposed the horrors of war, he was engulfed in the wave of patriotism which swept over Russia, and became a convert to the Allied cause, believing it to be the cause of justice and humanity. The correspondent in him triumphed over the literary artist, and he produced war literature of a propagandist nature. When the Revolution broke out Andreyev was haunted by forebodings of evil and approaching starvation. He was elected to the Constituent Assembly convoked by Kerensky on the eve of the Bolshevik Revolution. To the end of his days he never forgave the Bolsheviks their "betrayal" of the Allied cause in the Treaty of Brest-Litovsk. His uncompromising hatred of the new regime embittered his last years in Finland. These were years of hardship, of physical and mental suffering, of chronic insomnia and financial stress, during which he occupied himself primarily with his diary. Consistently enough, he rejected Gorky's offer, on behalf of the Soviet Government, to purchase his works to ease the financial strain. Death came on September 25, 1919, while he was planning a trip to America. His funds were insufficient to cover his funeral expenses.

Although Andreyev was a prolific writer, his fame rests chiefly on his twenty-eight plays, the best known of which are *Savva* (1906), *King Hunger* (1907), *Black Masks*, (1908), *Anathema* (1909), *The Pretty Sabine Women* (1912), and *Professor Storitsyn* (1912). Of these, *Anathema* best reflects his own philosophy and the mood of the Russian intelligentsia in the trying years subsequent to the Revolution of 1905.

THE PLOT OF *ANATHEMA* (1909)
A Tragedy in Seven Scenes

Anathema, as the etymological derivation of the name implies, is the Devil (Satan), adversary of man. In the prologue we find him standing outside the iron gates of Eternity, where "dwells the Beginning of every being, the Supreme Wisdom of the universe." From this point of vantage, he calls on Someone, a silent Guardian, to open the gates for an instant, that he may have a glimpse of Eternity with which to illumine the path of life, since the Devil and man alike grope in darkness. But the Guardian, his face hidden beneath a dark cover, bars the entrance.

In anger, Anathema vows to return to earth and ruin the soul of a righteous Jew, David-Leizer, in order to prove the injustice and futility of existence. David-Leizer, the victim of the Devil, is not a Job, a Prometheus, a Faust, or the Adam of Imre Madách, but an insignificant Jewish shopkeeper dying of poverty in a Russian ghetto. Nor is Anathema a conventional Devil, a Mephisto in red, with horns and tail, but, on the contrary, he seems more human than man himself.

Anathema appears to David-Leizer in the person of a lawyer to announce that the poverty-stricken Jew has inherited an immense fortune from his brother who died in America. Instead of hoarding his wealth like a miser, David-Leizer divides it among the poor and the outcasts. His fame spreads far and wide, he is honored and revered, and when the report is circulated that he performs miracles, people come from the ends of the earth to worship and be cured.

The Jew's unselfish attempt to help his fellow man results in strife and bloodshed. His millions prove inadequate for the task he has undertaken, and the mob stones him to death because he fails to work miracles to clothe and feed them and to bring back the dead to life.

Anathema, in the epilogue, once more approaches the Guardian of the iron gates, and challenges Someone to answer his queries as to whether David-Leizer by his life and death has not manifested "the powerlessness of love," and has not created "a great evil which could be numbered and weighed." The Guardian, in a fashion somewhat reminiscent of Job (Chapter XLII), finally replies that David-Leizer has attained immortality, but Anathema will never know the secret of the world order.

FROM *ANATHEMA*
THE EPILOGUE

Anathema: Why are there no trumpets here? Why no celebration? Why are these old and rusty gates closed? And why does no one hand me the keys? Is it proper in decent circles to meet thus an eminent guest, the reigning prince of the earth, which is friendly to us? Only the doorkeeper is here, apparently asleep, and no one else. It is bad—bad!

(He bursts into laughter, and stretching himself wearily, sits down upon a rock. He speaks humbly and with an air of fatigue.)

But I am not vainglorious. Trumpets, flowers, and shouting—all this is uesless! I myself heard at one time how the people trumpeted glory for David-Leizer, but what has come of it?

(He heaves a sigh.)

It is sad to think of it.

(He whistles mournfully.)

You have surely heard of the misfortune that has come upon my friend David-Leizer? I remember when I last chatted with you,—you did not know this name then. ... But do you know it now? It is a name to be proud of! When I left the earth, the entire earth in a million of hungry throats called this glorious name, shouting: "David is a deceiver! David is a traitor! David is a liar!" Then it seemed to me that some of the people reproached also another one—for my honest friend, who died an untimely death, did not act so incautiously in his own name.

(The Guardian is silent. And Anathema shouts now with an air of real triumph, breathing malice.)

The name! Call the name of him who has ruined David and thousands of people! I, Anathema, have no heart, my eyes have dried up from the fire of Hell, and there are no tears in them, but if the tears were there I would have given them all to David. I have no heart, but there was an instant when something live trembled in my chest, and I was frightened: I wondered whether a heart could be born. I saw how David was perishing and thousands of people with him, I saw how his spirit, grown dark, curled up piteously like a dead worm in the sun, was hurled down into the abyss of non-existence, into my abode of darkness and death. ... Tell me, are you not the one who has ruined David?

Guardian of the Entrances: David has attained immortality, and he lives forever in the deathlessness of fire. David has attained immortality, and he lives forever in the deathlessness of light, which is life.

(Dumfounded, Anathema falls to the ground and lies motionless for an instant. Then he lifts his head, which is as angry as that of a serpent. He rises and speaks with the calm of boundless wrath.)

Anathema: You lie! Forgive me my daring, but you lie. Surely your power is immense—and you can give immortality to a dead worm that has turned black from the sun. But would that be just? Or do the numbers lie to which you too, must submit? Or do all the scales lie, and is all your world nothing but one lie,—a cruel and mad game of laws, a malicious laugh of a despot at the dumbness and submissiveness of the slave?

(He speaks gloomily, in the grief of deathless blindness.)

Anathema: I am tired of searching. I have grown tired of life, of aimless tortures—of the quest after the ever elusive. Give me death, but do not torment me with ignorance; answer me honestly, even as I am honest in my uprising as a slave. Did not David love? Answer. Did not David give his soul away? Answer. And did they not stone David, who had given his soul away? Answer.

Guardian: Yes. They stoned David, who had given his soul away.

Anathema (smiling darkly): Now you are honest and you answer me with modesty. Without having stilled the hunger of the hungry, without having restored sight to the blind, without having brought to life those who had died innocently,—having stirred up dissension and dispute and cruel bloodshed, for the people have already risen against one another and are committing violence, murder, and plunder in the name of David,—did not David manifest the powerlessness of love, and did he not create a great evil which could be numbered and weighed?

Guardian: Yes. David has done that which you say; and the people have done that of which you accuse them. And the numbers do not lie, and the scales are correct, and every measure is what it is.

Anathema (triumphantly): You say that!

Guardian: But that which you do not know, Anathema, is not measured with a measure, and is not calculated in numbers, and is not weighed on scales. Light has no boundaries, nor is there any boundary for the glow of fire—there is a red fire, and there is a yellow fire, and there is a white fire, in which the sun burns like a yellow straw,—and there is still another unknown fire, whose name no one knows—for there is no limit to the glow of fire. Having died in numbers, having died in measures and in weights, David has attained immortality in the deathlessness of fire.

Anathema: You lie again!

(He flings himself about on the ground in despair.)

Oh, who will help the honest Anathema? He is being deceived eternally. Oh, who will help the unfortunate Anathema? His immortality is deception. Oh, weep, you who have grown fond of the Devil; wail and grieve, you who strive for truth, who honor wisdom,—Anathema is being deceived eternally. When I win, he takes it away from me. When I come out victorious, he fetters the conqueror in chains, he pricks out the eyes of the ruler, and to the haughty he gives the traits of a dog, a wagging and quivering tail. David, David, I was a friend to you, —tell him that he lies.

(He puts his head down on his outstretched arms, like a dog, and wails bitterly.)

Where is the truth? Where is the truth? Where is the truth? Was it not crushed with stones? Is it not lying in the ditch together with the carrion? Oh, the light has died out from the world! ... Oh, the world has no eyes! ...The crows have pecked them out.... Where is the truth? Where is the truth? Where is the truth?

(Plaintively.)

Tell me, will Anathema ever learn the truth?

Guardian: No.

Anathema: Tell me, will Anathema ever see the gates open? Shall I ever see your face?

Guardian: No. Never. My face is open, but you see it not. My speech is loud, but you hear it not. My commands are clear, but you know them not, Anathema. And you will never see, and you will never hear, and you will never know, Anathema, unfortunate spirit, deathless in numbers, ever alive in measure and in weight, but as yet unborn to life.

(Anathema leaps to his feet.)

Anathema: You lie,—silent dog, you who have robbed the world of the truth, you who have barred the entrances with iron! Farewell; I like a fair game, and I pay when I love. And if you will not pay, I shall cry before the whole universe: "Help! I have been robbed!"

(He bursts into laughter. Whistling, he retreats a few steps, and turns around. He speaks unconcernedly.)

Anathema: I have nothing to do, so I roam about the world. Do you know where I am going now? I shall go to the grave of David-Leizer. Like a grieving widow, like the son of a father who had been murdered from behind the corner by a traitor's blow,—I shall sit down on

David-Leizer's grave and shall weep so bitterly, and cry so loudly, and call so terribly, that not one honest soul will remain that would not curse the murderer. Insane from grief, I shall point to the right and to the left. . . . Was not this the one who killed him? Did not that one betray? I shall cry so bitterly, I shall accuse so sternly, that all on earth will become murderers and hangmen, in the name of Leizer, in the name of David-Leizer, in the name of David, who brought joy to mankind! And when from the heap of corpses, of filthy, foul-smelling, and disgusting corpses I shall announce to the people that you are the one who killed David and the people,—they will believe me.

(Bursts into laughter.)

For you have such a bad reputation—of a liar, a deceiver, a murderer. Good-by.

(He goes off laughing. His laughter resounds once more from the depths. And then everything relapses into silence.)

—Tr. by HERMAN BERNSTEIN

If the Russian State was autocratic, Russian literature was democratic. If the official Russian Church was a blind tool in the hands of absolutism, Orthodoxy, Russian Christianity, was the paragon of Christianity. Up to Andreyev, Russian literature had championed the cause of the oppressed and the persecuted. It had found a niche in its Pantheon for the serf and later for the peasant, for the "poor folk," for the prostitute, the criminal, the "lower depths," and the "possessed." Russian literature raised them to a place among the mighty. Whatever we may think of the old regime in Russia, it was that Russia which produced this literature. What the State and the Bureaucracy polluted, Russian writers cleansed and made an attempt to expiate, by creating a better understanding of and deeper sympathy for the plight of the unfortunate.

There was still another group which awaited sympathetic treatment in Russian letters, and that was the persecuted Jewish minority. The champions of the "poor

folk," the peasants, and the "lower depths" had so far
neglected the Jew, while Slavophilism contributed still
further to his misery. This hitherto neglected task fell
to the lot of Leonid Andreyev. In *Anathema,* as well as
in some of his other works, Andreyev sympathetically
portrayed the lot of this persecuted race. Had the World
War and the Revolution not intervened, it would have
been highly interesting to follow the political and bureaucratic response to this new literary appeal on behalf of
another slice of Russia's oppressed. That there existed
such a trend among the Russian intelligentsia is evident
from the fact that during the World War, when anti-
Semitism was rife in the Russian army, a new periodical
Shield, appeared in 1916, under the editorship of Gorky,
Andreyev, and Sologub. This periodical contained nu-
merous studies, essays, short stories, and poems on the
Jew. In addition to its celebrated editorial staff, a galaxy
of brilliant Russian authors actively contributed to the
Shield, including Artzibashev, Balmont, Ivan Bunin, a
recent Nobel prize winner, Korolenko, Merejkovsky, and
Alexei Tolstoy.

When Turgenev needed a strong leader, he turned to
the foreigner and selected the Bulgarian Insarov for his
novel, *On the Eve.* Andreyev's heroes are for the most
part to be found in the grave or in the madhouse. His
most positive character was David-Leizer, the Jew, in
Anathema. His choice of a hero was by no means accidental, for Andreyev intended to prove to the persecuted
Jewish minority that the Russian intelligentsia was
aware of their mistreatment at the hands of the authorities, and that the sentiments of the Russian bureaucracy
were not truly representative of the attitude of the Russian people. The better to prove his case, Andreyev did
not select a Biblical name for his hero, which would
have been too abstract, but a typical name from the
Russian ghetto.

Before he fell a victim to the nefarious scheme of the
"Devil," David-Leizer's outward appearance and living

conditions would have attracted no particular attention, although they might have added weight to the arguments of the anti-Semite. Just as Turgenev discovered under the soiled rags of the peasants a beautiful soul, so Andreyev found in the depths of the Jewish ghetto, his David-Leizer. Through the experiences of David-Leizer, he demonstrated to the world, that there are Jews, who, far from being greedy for gain, are ready to share an American fortune with the outcasts and the unfortunate, regardless of nationality, race, rank, or station; that while the David-Leizers become the victims of pogroms, and are stoned to death by the ungrateful mob, their deeds and their sufferings bring them the reward of immortality.

It was this play, *Anathema*, and the message contained therein, that placed Leonid Andreyev among the Russian classical writers. For if we analyze the Golden Age of Russian Literature, we immediately notice that only those writers became immortal, who espoused the cause of the weak, the insulted, and the injured. The others, in spite of material contributions along other lines, were seldom classed with the mighty. One play of this type was sufficient to raise the other works of Andreyev to the ranks of the classics.

In general, Andreyev was closer to Dostoyevsky than to any other Russian writer, having written much in the vein of *The Idiot* against different backgrounds. Of the two, Andreyev was the greater skeptic—Dostoyevsky had greater faith. Andreyev's nearest approach to Dostoyevsky was in *The Red Laugh* (1904) and *The Seven Who Were Hanged* (1908). The two opening words of *The Red Laugh*, "Horror" and "Madness," became household words throughout Russia. The soldier's Manchurian diary contained a sentence almost prophetic in nature:

"It was in the sky, it was in the sun, and soon it was going to overspread the whole earth—that Red Laugh."

These words of Andreyev almost constitute a prediction of the World War and its aftermath.

While *Anathema* was the first sympathetic plea for the Jewish minority in Russia, it also reflected the disappointment, the bitterness, and the disillusionment of the Russian intelligentsia after the Revolution of 1905. It was not just a spooky story as Lev Tolstoy implied, but a true reflection of the mood of a Russian intelligentsia which had reached the crossroads and knew not which way to turn. Many already questioned whether the fight for progress and freedom was worth while— whether any real benefits were likely to result from such a change. Just as David-Leizer became a martyr to the mob he clothed and fed because he failed to work miracles, many leaders of the 1905 Revolution, who championed the oppressed, were later stoned and betrayed by the very people they sought to assist. This dénouement discouraged thinking men, who began to doubt the value of self-sacrifice for the benefit of humanity.

Anathema was Andreyev's attempt to find out whether it was worth struggling, not necessarily living, for a better life and a better social order. Like Anathema himself, Andreyev's inquisitive mind sought to penetrate the iron gates of uncertainty (eternal mystery), of baffling obscurity (eternal silence), and to establish whether or not there was even a faint ray of hope for the future. Like many of his contemporaries, his reason demanded knowledge rather than blind faith, in order to cope with insuperable obstacles. The message of Anathema was, that in spite of the mob's ingratitude, in spite of the seeming futility of his unselfish efforts to help mankind, David-Leizer nevertheless obtained immortality. Even while he admitted the difficulty, for him the practical impossibility, of grasping the secret of the world order and the justice of its rewards and punishments, he reached the conclusion that a good cause was worth while.

There is no doubt but that Andreyev merits a more extensive treatment than it has been possible to allot to

him here. The main purpose of this work is to indicate
the new ground which each author broke in Russian literature and his contributions to political, social, and
economic conditions. In our opinion Andreyev's *Anathema*, with a few indirect references to his other works,
is sufficient to accomplish this purpose.

BIBLIOGRAPHY

Bernstein, Herman (Translator), *Anathema*, by Leonid Andreyev,
    N. Y., 1923.
Bernstein, Herman (Translator), *The Sorrows of Belgium*, by
    Leonid Andreyev, N. Y., 1915.
Kaun, Alexander, *Leonid Andreyev, A Critical Study*, N. Y., 1924.
Kuntz, Joshua, *Russian Literature and the Jew*, Columbia Uni-
    versity Press, 1929.
Manning, Clarence A., "Leonid Nikolayevich Andreyev," *Scandi-
    navian and Slavonic Literature*, Columbia University Press,
    1917.
Meader, C. L., and Scott, F. N. (Translators), *Plays by Leonid
    Andreyeff*, N. Y., 1918.
Mirsky, D. S., *Contemporary Russian Literature*, N. Y., 1926.
Noyes, G. R., *Masterpieces of the Russian Drama*, N. Y., 1933.
Olgin, M. J., *Guide to Russian Literature*, N. Y., 1920.
Phelps, W. L., *Essays on Russian Novelists*, N. Y., 1916.
Vsevolodsky-Gengross, V., *Khrestomatia po istorii Russkogo Teatra
    (An Anthology of the History of the Russian Theatre)*, Mos-
    cow, 1936.
Wiener, Leo, *The Contemporary Drama of Russia*, Boston, 1924.
Zilboorg, Gregory (Translator), *He Who Gets Slapped*, by Leonid
    Andreyev, N. Y., 1922.
Znosko-Borovsky, *The Russian Theatre from the Beginning of the
    Twentieth Century* (in Russian), Praha.

Maxim Gorky

1868-1936

MAXIM GORKY, whose real name was Alexey Maximovitch Pyeshkov, was born on March 28, 1868, at Nizhni Novgorod, and died on June 18, 1936, at Gorky (named after him), near Moscow. His father, an upholsterer, died when Gorky was only four years of age. The lad was placed under the care of his grandfather, Kashirin, a merchant and the owner of a dyeing establishment. At seven he was sent to school, but an attack of smallpox soon put an end to his scholastic career. In 1878, when his mother died, he was apprenticed to a shoemaker. At the age of twelve, while working for a draftsman, he ran away to join the crew of a Volga steamer as cook's helper. From this cook, Smury by name, Gorky acquired his passion for literature and his thirst for knowledge. On his return he tried his hand for a time at the painting of icons. In 1883, when he was still only fifteen, he served the Nizhni Novgorod Fair Theatre, first as an extra, then as a watchman.

In the summer of 1884 Gorky left Nizhni Novgorod for the University of Kazan, under the false impression that education was dispensed there free of charge. Not having enough money to matriculate, he worked in a bakeshop for a salary of three rubles a month ($1.50). In a fit of despondency he attempted to commit suicide at the age of nineteen. He tried all sorts of odd jobs, becoming a public porter, a fruit vendor, and finally, in 1889, at the age of twenty-one, a lawyer's clerk. To this lawyer, A. I. Lanin, he was greatly indebted for his cultural development.

In 1891, Gorky, with a group of outcasts and vagabonds, tramped through South Russia until he reached Tiflis (Caucasus), at that time a hotbed of revolutionary

activity. Here he was arrested three times for his revolutionary leanings. While working on the railroad at
Tiflis, he published his first short story, *Makar Chudra*
(1892), at the age of twenty-four (like Dostoyevsky and
Tolstoy). Although it attracted little attention, Gorky,
the erstwhile Jack-of-all-trades, persisted in his career
as a writer. The story which finally started him on the
road to fame was "Chelkash" (1895), published in *Russ-
koye Bogatstvo*. Within a few years he became so popular that, in 1901, a collection of his works, *Sketches and
Stories*, was reprinted in five volumes in a fifth edition.
In the early stages of his literary career Gorky owed a
great deal to the assistance of Tchekhov and Korolenko.

In 1902, when Gorky was elected an honorary member
of the Imperial Academy of Science, the Government
vetoed his appointment. As a protest against this arbi-
trary action Tchekhov and Korolenko resigned from the
Academy. In 1903 six volumes of his works appeared in
fine, large editions. However, his play, *The Lower Depths*
(1902), of which fourteen editions appeared in one year,
brought Gorky his most spectacular success. Outside of
Russia, after 1901, when his first two tales appeared in
English, Gorky's fame spread with amazing rapidity.
His works were translated into every European language.
In Russia alone, by 1936, they were available in 101
languages and dialects.

After the suppression of the Revolution of 1905,
Gorky, at the height of his popularity, traveled through
Europe and visited the United States in search of funds
for the cause of Russian freedom. In America, where he
was at first received with open arms, the intrusion of a
moral issue of a personal nature—the legal status of a
woman whom Gorky considered his wife—ruined his
mission. Gorky was turned out of his hotel, and Mark
Twain refused to preside at a banquet in his honor.
Gorky's bitterness over this dénouement found vent in
a series of American stories under the suggestive title,

The City of the Yellow Devil (1907). He sailed for Italy and made his home on the island of Capri.

In 1909 Gorky established at Capri, practically at his own expense, a school for the training of Russian revolutionary leaders. One of his pupils was Joseph Stalin. In 1913 the Tsarist Government permitted his return to Russia. After the outbreak of the October (N.S., November 7th) Revolution in 1917, Gorky lent his support to the Soviet cause. In 1921, however, following a disagreement with Lenin on certain issues, he left the U.S.S.R. for Germany, where he continued his literary activities. In 1928, at the beginning of the first Five Year Plan, he was invited to return to Russia for his sixtieth birthday celebration. He died at Gorky on June 18, 1936. Some months later, in the spring of 1938, certain former high Soviet officials were accused of Gorky's assassination.

Most of Gorky's work has been written in the vein of his drama, *The Lower Depths,* which was staged for the first time on December 31, 1902, and his novel, *Mother,* published in 1906. Gorky's talent lay in the portrayal of the underworld he knew so well, and the revolutionary movement prior to the World War. To this type of work he owes his niche among the writers of the classical age. When he selected other themes he met with only indifferent success.

Among Gorky's best short stories are: *Chelkash* (1895), *Konovalov* (1896), *Orlov and His Wife* (1897), and *Twenty-six Men and a Girl* (1899). His most outstanding novels, novelettes, and other narratives are: *Foma Gordeyev* (1899), *My Childhood* (1913), *In the World* (1915), *Recollections of Tolstoy* (1919), *My University Days* (1923), *Notes from a Diary* (1924), and *Klim Samgin* (1928—translated into English as *The Bystander,* 1930, *The Magnet,* 1931, *Other Fires,* and *The Specter,* 1938). This last novel deals with pre-Revolutionary Russia and the formation of Soviet Russia. A list of his dramas includes: *The Middle Class* or *Petty Bour-*

geois (1900), *The Lower Depths* (1902), *A Country House* (1903), *Children of the Sun* (1904), *The Barbarians* and *Enemies* (1906), *The Last* (1908), *Queer People* and *Vassa Zheleznova* (1910), *The Zykovs* and *Children* (1913), *The Old Man* (1915, translated into English as *The Judge), Cain and Artema* (1921), and *False Coin* (1927).

THE PLOT OF *THE LOWER DEPTHS* (1902)

In a basement night lodging Gorky assembles the dregs of Russian society, including: Vasily Pepel, a born thief; Nastya, a sentimental prostitute, who weeps over sensational love stories; a one-time baron, turned wastrel; Satin, a philosophical card-sharper; a drunken actor; Andrey Kleshch, a gloomy locksmith who wants to work and despises the others who won't, and his wife, Anna, who is in the last stages of consumption; a peddler of dumplings and an erstwhile Tartar prince. The characters tend to vegetate, or at the most to quarrel, in their sordid surroundings.

Vasilisa, the proprietor's domineering young wife, who despises her scoundrel of a husband, has contracted a liaison with Pepel, the thief. Having grown weary of her, Pepel transfers his affections to her younger sister, Natasha. The vicious Vasilisa vents her spleen upon Natasha, but eventually seeks to bargain with Pepel, promising to facilitate his marriage with her sister, if he, in return, will rid her of her husband. He refuses, and Vasilisa takes her revenge by upsetting the samovar and scalding Natasha. In the scuffle which follows, Pepel knocks Kostylev, the proprietor, down, and accidentally kills him. The triumphant Vasilisa accuses her one-time lover of the murder of her husband, but Natasha implicates both of them in the conspiracy, and they are imprisoned. During the course of the narrative the long-suffering Anna dies of consumption.

The one redeeming character of the play is the vagabond pilgrim, Luka, a kindly old man, whose advent produces an immediate effect upon this assembly of human derelicts, and whose simple philosophy of life may be summed up in two injunctions: "Respect one another" and "Be good to one another." He comforts the dying consumptive, rouses the actor from his drunken stupor, and even encourages Pepel, the thief, to begin a new and honest life. After his departure, the lodgers, particularly Satin, recall his kindliness and his simple faith, although they promptly revert to their former mode of life. The drunken actor, despairing of a cure, hangs himself to a lamp post—an incident which causes only a brief interruption in an evening's carousal.

THE PLOT OF *MOTHER* (1906)

The scene is laid in a cheerless factory town in Russia, where a small group of socialists have consecrated their lives to the liberation of the workers from ignorance and oppression.

Until the death of her brutal husband, the Mother, Pelagueya Nilovna Vlasova, a silent, timid, submissive creature, lives in constant fear of blows, but she accepts her melancholy lot with stolid resignation. Her son, Pavel, begins to drink like his father and his fellow workers, but he soon becomes absorbed in "forbidden" socialist literature, from which he hopes to find out the truth about the workingman's life and teach it to others.

Pavel's home serves as a meeting place for an oddly assorted group of young revolutionists, including Natasha, whose wealthy father has turned her out of doors for associating with the socialists; Yakov Somov, son of the factory watchman; the embittered Nikolay Vyesovshchikov, son of a thief, who is known as the village misanthrope; the likeable Ukrainian (Little Russian) with a revolutionary past; and the stern, unyielding Sashenka, who has disowned her father, a prominent landowner. Gradually the Mother's heart warms to these young people, and she grows in courage and understanding of the new movement. Their meetings increase, with the inevitable result that the house is searched by the authorities, and some of the members imprisoned for distributing socialist literature among the factory employees.

Pavel, the intellectual leader of the group, is already a marked man. He is imprisoned, once for inciting the factory workers to strike, once for leading a May-Day parade. His Mother, having become the heart of the movement, takes his place, and continues, now by one ruse, now by another, to distribute the forbidden literature to the workers.

After a farcical trial, Pavel, with some of his comrades, is exiled to Siberia. Sashenka, who loves him, expects to follow him soon. At the railroad station, the Mother, on her way to distribute her son's last speech to the masses, is finally caught with the tell-tale literature. She is beaten and choked to death as she attempts to deliver her final message for the good of the cause.

FROM *THE LOWER DEPTHS*

Satin (striking the table with his fist): Keep still! You're all swine! You blockheads—keep still about the old man! (More calmly.) Baron, you're the worst of all!... You don't understand anything... and you tell lies! The old man was not a charlatan. What is truth? Truth is *man!* He understood that... and you don't! You people are dull as brickbats.... I understand the old man.... Yes, I do! He used to lie... but it was out of pity for you, devil take you! There are lots of men who lie out of pity for their neighbor.... I know that! I've read books! They lie beautifully, with inspiration, in a way that arouses you!... There is a comforting lie, an atoning lie.... A lie justifies the weight that has crushed the arm of the laborer... and accuses men who die of hunger.... I know about lies! If a man is weak of soul ... and if he lives by the sap of other men, then he needs a lie.... A lie supports some men, it gives a refuge to others.... But if a man is his own master... if he is independent and does not prey on his neighbor, then what use has he for a lie? Lies are the religion of slaves and masters.... Truth is the God of the free man!

Baron: Bravo! Finely said! I agree! You talk . . . like a gentleman!

Satin: Why shouldn't card-sharpers talk well sometimes, if gentlemen . . . talk like card-sharpers? Yes . . . I've forgotten a lot, but I still know a few things! The old man? He was clever! . . . He acted on me like acid on a dirty old coin. . . . Let's drink his health! Fill my glass!

(Nastya pours out a glass of beer and passes it to Satin.)

Satin (grinning) : The old man lives his own life. . . . He looks at everything with his own eyes. Once I asked him: "Grandfather, what do men live for?" (Trying to speak with Luka's voice and imitating his mannerisms.) "Eh, men live for a better man, my dear fellow! Just for instance, a lot of carpenters are living, and they're all the scum of the earth. . . . And then among them is born a carpenter . . . a carpenter the like of whom the earth never saw before; he surpasses them all, and he has no equal among carpenters. He gives his own form to all carpenter's work . . . and all at once he moves the whole work twenty years forward. . . . In just the same way all other men . . . locksmiths, for example . . . shoemakers and all other working men . . . and all peasants . . . and even the gentry: they all live for a better man! Everybody thinks that he's just passing his life for himself, but it turns out that it's for a better man! For a hundred years . . . and maybe for even more they live for a better man!"

(Nastya stares fixedly at Satin's face. Kleshch stops working on the accordion and also listens. The Baron, hanging his head, drums softly on the table with his fingers. The Actor, leaning out from his place on the stove, cautiously prepares to descend to one of the bunks.)

Satin: "Everybody, my dear fellow, everybody that exists, lives for a better man! And so we should respect every man. . . . We don't know who he is, why he was born, and what he can do. . . . Maybe he was born to bring us happiness . . . to be of great benefit to us. . . . Above all, we should respect the babes . . . the little children! Little children need room! Do not hinder the babes from living. . . . Respect the babes!"

(A pause.)

Baron (pensively) : Hm! Yes! For a better man? That . . . reminds me of our family. . . . An old stock . . . of the times of Catherine . . . nobles . . . warriors! . . . émigrés from France. . . . They were in the state service, and kept mounting higher. . . . Under Nicholas I my grandfather, Gustav Debil . . . occupied an important post. . . . Wealth . . . hundreds of serfs . . . horses . . . cooks. . . .

Nastya: You lie! There wasn't any such thing!

Baron (jumping up) : Wh-at? We-ell . . . go on!

Nastya: There wasn't any such thing!

Baron (shouting) : A house in Moscow! A house in St. Petersburg! Coaches . . . coaches with coats of arms!

(Kleshch takes the accordion, rises, and walks to the side of the room, whence he watches the scene.)

Nastya: There weren't!

Baron: Shut up! I say . . . dozens of footmen!

Nastya (with enjoyment) : There we-eren't!

Baron: I'll kill you!

Nastya (preparing to run away) : There weren't any coaches!

Satin: Quit it, Nastya! Don't tease him!

Baron: Just wait, you slut! My grandfather—

Nastya: There wasn't any grandfather! There wasn't anything!

(Satin guffaws.)

Baron (sitting down on a bench, exhausted by anger) : Satin, tell her . . . tell that trollop. . . . What—are you laughing too? Don't you believe it either? (He yells with despair, beating his fists on the table.) That was all true, devil take you both!

Nastya (triumphantly) : Aha, so you're howling? Now do you know how a man feels when they won't believe him?

Kleshch (returning to the table) : I thought there was going to be a fight.

Tatar: O-oh, people silly! Very bad!

Baron: I . . . I cannot allow myself to be mocked at! I have proofs—documents, you devil!

Satin: Throw 'em away! And forget about your

grandfather's coaches. . . . You won't drive far in a coach of the past.

Baron: But how does she dare!

Nastya: Do-o tell! Don't I dare!

Satin: You see she does dare! How's she any worse than you are? Though in her past you may be sure she didn't have even a father and mother—not to speak of coaches and a grandfather.

Baron (calming down): Devil take you! . . . You . . . know how to reason calmly. . . . But I . . . seems that I have no character.

Satin: Get one. It's a useful article. . . . (A pause.) Nastya, have you been going to the hospital?

Nastya: What for?

Satin: To see Natasha.

Nastya: The idea! She left there long ago. . . . Left and—disappeared! There's no trace of her.

Satin: So—she's gone for good.

Kleshch: It's interesting to see who'll put the other in the worst hole: Vaska, Vasilisa; or she him.

Nastya: Vasilisa'll get off! She's sly. But they'll send Vaska to prison with hard labor.

Satin: For murder in a scuffle, prison is all you get.

Nastya: Too bad! Hard labor would be better for him. . . . I'd like to send all of you . . . to hard labor . . . to sweep you off, like dirt . . . somewhere into the pit!

Satin (startled): What's the matter with you? Have you gone crazy?

Baron: I'll give her one on the ear . . . for her impudence!

Nastya: Try it! Just touch me!

Baron: I'll try it all right!

Satin: Quit! Don't touch her! . . . Don't do wrong to a man! I can't get that old man out of my head! (Guffaws.) "Don't do wrong to a man!" . . . But what if once on a time they did me wrong and—it's lasted all through my life! What can you do about it? Forgive? Not a bit. Nobody.

Baron (to Nastya): You should understand that I'm not your sort! You're filth!

Nastya: Oh, you poor boob! You...you live on me like a worm lives on an apple!

(The men burst out laughing in unison.)

Kleshch: Oh...the fool! Little apple!

Baron: A man can't...get angry....She's just an idiot!

Nastya: Are you laughing? You lie! You don't think it's funny!

Actor (gloomily) : Let 'em have it!

Nastya: If I...only could...I'd give it to you (taking a cup from the table and throwing it on the floor) like that!

Tatar: Why break dishes? Eh, eh...silly girl!

Baron (rising) : No, I'm going to teach her...good manners right away!

Nastya (running away) : Devil take all of you!

Satin (calling after her) : Hey! That's enough! Who are you scaring? What's the matter anyhow?

Nastya: Wolves! Hope you croak! Wolves!

Actor (gloomily) : Amen!

Tatar: Oo-oo! Russian woman is bad woman! Bold ...free! Tatar woman, no! Tatar woman know the law!

Kleshch: She ought to be thrashed.

Baron: W-wretch!

Kleshch (trying the accordion) : It's ready! But the owner hasn't come back yet.... The lad's on a spree.

Satin: Now take a drink!

Kleshch: Thanks! But it's time to rest my bones.

Satin: Are you getting used to us?

Kleshch (after taking a drink, goes to a bunk in the corner) : So-so.... Men are the same everywhere.... At first you don't see that.... Later, you take a look and find out that all men...are not a bad lot!

(The Tatar spreads something or other on a bunk, kneels, and begins to pray.)

Baron (calling Satin's attention to the Tatar) : Look!

Satin: Let him alone! He's a good fellow...don't hinder him! (Guffaws.) I'm in a pleasant humor today. ...Devil knows why!

Baron: You're always in a pleasant humor when you've had a drink....And sensible too!

Satin: When I'm drunk ... I like everything. ... Yes I do. ... He's praying? Fine! A man may believe or not believe—that's his business! Man is free ... he pays for everything himself: for faith, for unbelief, for love, for intelligence. Man pays for everything himself, and therefore he is free! ... Man—that is truth! What is man? ... Not you, nor I, nor they—no! Man is you, I, they, the old man, Napoleon, Mohammed ... all in one! (With his finger he outlines in the air the figure of a man.) Do you understand? Man is huge! In him are all beginnings and all ends. ... All is in man, all is for man! Man alone exists; all else is the work of his hands and of his brain! Ma-an! That is magnificent! That has a proud sound! Ma-an! We must respect man! Not pity him ... not humiliate him by pity ... we must respect him! Baron, let's drink to the health of man! (Rising.) It is good to feel oneself a man! I'm a jailbird, a murderer, a card-sharper: oh, yes! When I walk the street, people look at me as at a swindler ... and they move aside and look round at me ... and they often say to me: "Scoundrel! Charlatan! Get to work!" Work? What for? To be well fed? (Guffaws.) I've always despised men who are too anxious to be well fed. That's not the point! Man is higher! Man is higher than a full belly!

Baron (shaking his head): You reason about things. ... That's good. ... Most likely that warms the heart. ... That's not in me. ... I don't know how! (Looks around and speaks in a low, cautious voice.) Sometimes, my boy ... I'm afraid. Do you understand? I'm cowardly. ... Because—what comes afterwards?

Satin (pacing the room): Rubbish! Whom should a man be afraid of?

Baron: Let me tell you: From the earliest time that I can remember ... I've always had a sort of fog in my noddle. I never understood anything at all. I feel ... sort of out of place. ... It seems to me that all my life I've done nothing but change my clothes. ... And what for? I don't understand! I went to school, wore the uniform of the Nobleman's Institute ... and what did I study? I don't remember. ... I married; put on a dress coat, and then a dressing gown ... but I got a wretched sort of wife—and what for? I don't understand.... I squandered all I had—wore a sort of gray jacket and rusty-brown trousers.... But how did I get ruined? I never noticed how.... I served in the Department of Finance ... wore a uniform and a cap with a cockade ... embezzled government money.... Then they dressed me in prison garb.... Finally I put on these duds.... And it all ... seems like a dream.... Well? This is funny.

Satin: Not very.... Stupid is how it strikes me.

Baron: Yes ... I think it's stupid myself.... But ... I must have been born for some purpose, I suppose?

Satin (laughing): Probably.... "Man is born for a better man!"

(Nodding his head.) That's a fine idea!

—Tr. by G. R. Noyes and A. Kaun

FROM *MOTHER*
Part I, Chapter XX

"Comrades!" the voice of Pavel was heard. "Soldiers are people the same as ourselves. They will not strike us! Why should they beat us? This our truth is necessary to them, too. Just now they do not understand this; but the time is nearing when they will rise with us, when they will march, not under the banner of robbers and murderers, the banner which liars and beasts order them to call the banner of glory and honor, but under our banner of freedom and goodness! We ought to go forward so that they should understand our truth the sooner. Forward, comrades! Ever forward!"

Pavel's voice sounded firm, the words rang in the air distinctly, but the crowd fell asunder; one after the other the people dropped off to the right or to the left, going toward their homes, or leaning against the fences. Now the crowd had the shape of a wedge, and its point was Pavel, over whose head the banner of the laboring people was burning red.

At the end of the street, closing the exit to the square, the mother saw a low, gray wall of men, one just like the other, without faces. On the shoulder of each a bayonet was smiling its thin, chill smile; and from this

entire immobile wall a cold gust blew down on the work-
men, striking the breast of the mother and penetrating
her heart.

She forced her way into the crowd among people
familiar to her, and as it were, leaned on them.

She pressed closely against a tall, lame man with a
clean-shaven face. In order to look at her, he had to
turn his head stiffly.

"What do you want? Who are you?" he asked her.

"The mother of Pavel Vlasov," she answered, her
knees trembling beneath her, her lower lip involuntarily
dropping.

"Ha-ha!" said the lame man. "Very well!"

"Comrades!" Pavel cried. "Onward all your lives.
There is no other way for us! Sing!"

The atmosphere grew tense. The flag rose and rocked
and waved over the heads of the people, gliding toward
the gray wall of soldiers. The mother trembled. She
closed her eyes, and cried: "Oh—oh!"

None but Pavel, Andrey, Samoylov, and Mazin advanced beyond the crowd.

The limpid voice of Fedya Mazin slowly quivered in
the air.

" 'In mortal strife—' " he began the song.

" 'You victims fell—' " answered thick, subdued
voices. The words dropped in two heavy sighs. People
stepped forward, each footfall audible. A new song, determined and resolute, burst out:

"You yielded up your lives for them."

Fedya's voice wreathed and curled like a bright
ribbon.

"A-ha-ha-ha!" some one exclaimed derisively.
"They've struck up a funeral song, the dirty dogs!"

"Beat them!" came the angry response.

The mother clasped her hands to her breast, looked
about, and saw that the crowd, before so dense, was now
standing irresolute, watching the comrades walk away
from them with the banner, followed by about a dozen
people, one of whom, however, at every forward move,
jumped aside as if the path in the middle of the street
were red hot and burned his soles.

"The tyranny will fall—" sounded the prophetic song
from the lips of Fedya.

"And the people will rise!" the chorus of powerful
voices seconded confidently and menacingly.

But the harmonious flow of the song was broken by
the quiet words:

"He is giving orders."

"Charge bayonets!" came the piercing order from
the front.

The bayonets curved in the air, and glittered sharply;
then fell and stretched out to confront the banner.

"Ma-arch!"

"They're coming!" said the lame man, and thrusting
his hands into his pockets made a long step to one side.

The mother, without blinking, looked on. The gray
line of soldiers tossed to and fro, and spread out over the
entire width of the street. It moved on evenly, coolly,
carrying in front of itself a fine-toothed comb of sparkling
bayonets. Then it came to a stand. The mother took
long steps to get nearer to her son. She saw how Andrey
strode ahead of Pavel and fenced him off with his long
body. "Get alongside of me!" Pavel shouted sharply.
Andrey was singing, his hands clasped behind his back,
his head uplifted. Pavel pushed him with his shoulder,
and again cried:

"At my side! Let the banner be in front!"

"Disperse!" called a little officer in a thin voice,
brandishing a white saber. He lifted his feet high, and
without bending his knees struck his soles on the ground
irritably. The high polish on his boots caught the eyes
of the mother.

To one side and somewhat behind him walked a tall,
clean-shaven man, with a thick, gray mustache. He wore
a long gray overcoat with a red underlining, and yellow
stripes on his trousers. His gait was heavy, and like the
Little Russian, he clasped his hands behind his back. He
regarded Pavel, raising his thick gray eyebrows.

The mother seemed to be looking into infinity. At
each breath her breast was ready to burst with a loud
cry. It choked her, but for some reason she restrained
it. Her hands clutched at her bosom. She staggered from

repeated thrusts. She walked onward without thought, almost without consciousness. She felt that behind her the crowd was getting thinner; a cold wind had blown on them and scattered them like autumn leaves.

The men around the red banner moved closer and closer together. The faces of the soldiers were clearly seen across the entire width of the street, monstrously flattened, stretched out in a dirty yellowish band. In it were unevenly set variously colored eyes, and in front the sharp bayonets glittered crudely. Directed against the breasts of the people, although not yet touching them, they drove them apart, pushing one man after the other away from the crowd and breaking it up.

Behind her the mother heard the trampling noise of those who were running away. Suppressed, excited voices cried:

"Disperse, boys!"

"Vlasov, run!"

"Back, Pavel!"

"Drop the banner, Pavel!" Vyesovshchikov said glumly. "Give it to me! I'll hide it!"

He grabbed the pole with his hand; the flag rocked backward.

"Let go!" thundered Pavel.

Nikolay drew his hand back as if it had been burned. The song died away. Some persons crowded solidly around Pavel; but he cut through to the front. A sudden silence fell.

Around the banner some twenty men were grouped, not more, but they stood firmly. The mother felt drawn to them by awe and by a confused desire to say something to them.

"Take this thing away from him, lieutenant." The even voice of the tall old man was heard. He pointed to the banner. A little officer jumped up to Pavel, snatched at the flag pole, and shouted shrilly:

"Drop it!"

The red flag trembled in the air, moving to the right and to the left, then rose again. The little officer jumped back and sat down. Nikolay darted by the mother, shaking his outstretched fist.

"Seize them!" the old man roared, stamping his feet. A few soldiers jumped to the front, one of them flourishing the butt end of his gun. The banner trembled, dropped, and disappeared in a gray mass of soldiers.

"Oh!" somebody groaned aloud. And the mother yelled like a wild animal. But the clear voice of Pavel answered her from out of the crowd of soldiers:

"Good-by, mother! Good-by, dear!"

"He's alive! He remembered!" were the two strokes at the mother's heart.

"Good-by, mother dear!" came from Andrey.

Waving her hands, she raised herself on tiptoe, and tried to see them. There was the round face of Andrey above the soldiers' heads. He was smiling and bowing to her.

"Oh, my dear ones! Andriusha! Pasha!" she shouted.

"Good-by, comrades!" they called from among the soldiers.

A broken, manifold echo responded to them. It resounded from the windows and the roofs.

The mother felt some one pushing her breast. Through the mist in her eyes she saw the little officer. His face was red and strained, and he was shouting to her:

"Clear out of here, old woman!"

She looked down on him, and at his feet saw the flag pole broken in two parts, a piece of red cloth on one of them. She bent down and picked it up. The officer snatched it out of her hands, threw it aside, and shouted again, stamping his feet:

"Clear out of here, I tell you!"

A song sprang up and floated from among the soldiers:

"Arise, awake, you workingmen!"

Everything was whirling, rocking, trembling. A thick, alarming noise, resembling the dull hum of telegraph wires, filled the air. The officer jumped back, screaming angrily:

"Stop the singing, Sergeant Kraynov!"

The mother staggered to the fragment of the pole, which he had thrown, and picked it up again.

"Gag them!"

The song became confused, trembled, expired. Somebody took the mother by the shoulders, turned, and shoved her from the back.

"Go, go! Clear the street!" shouted the officer.

About ten paces from her, the mother again saw a thick crowd of people. They were howling, grumbling, whistling, as they backed down the street. The yards were drawing in a number of them.

"Go, you devil!" a young soldier with a big mustache shouted right into the mother's ear. He brushed against her and shoved her onto the sidewalk. She moved away, leaning on the flag pole. She went quickly and lightly, but her legs bent under her. In order not to fall she clung to walls and fences. People in front were falling back alongside of her, and behind her were soldiers, shouting: "Go, go!"

The soldiers got ahead of her; she stopped and looked around. Down the end of the street she saw them again scattered in a thin chain, blocking the entrance to the square, which was empty. Farther down were more gray figures slowly moving against the people. She wanted to go back; but uncalculatingly went forward again, and came to a narrow, empty by-street into which she turned. She stopped again. She sighed painfully, and listened. Somewhere ahead she heard the hum of voices. Leaning on the pole she resumed her walk. Her eyebrows moved up and down, and she suddenly broke into a sweat; her lips quivered; she waved her hands, and certain words flashed up in her heart like sparks, kindling in her a strong, stubborn desire to speak them, to shout them.

The by-street turned abruptly to the left; and around the corner the mother saw a large, dense crowd of people. Somebody's voice was speaking loudly and firmly:

"They don't go to meet the bayonets from sheer audacity. Remember that!"

"Just look at them. Soldiers advance against them, and they stand before them without fear. Y-yes!"

"Think of Pasha Vlasov!"

"And how about the Little Russian?"

"Hands behind his back and smiling, the devil!"

"My dear ones! My people!" the mother shouted,
pushing into the crowd. They cleared the way for her
respectfully. Somebody laughed:

"Look at her with the flag in her hand!"

"Shut up!" said another man sternly.

The mother with a broad sweep of her arms cried out:

"Listen for the sake of Christ! You are all dear people, you are all good people. Open up your hearts. Look
around without fear, without terror. Our children are
going into the world. Our children are going, our blood
is going for the truth; with honesty in their hearts they
open the gates of the new road—a straight, wide road
for all. For all of you, for the sake of your young ones,
they have devoted themselves to the sacred cause. They
seek the sun of new days that shall always be bright.
They want another life, the life of truth and justice, of
goodness for all."

Her heart was rent asunder, her breast contracted,
her throat was hot and dry. Deep inside of her, words
were being born, words of a great, all-embracing love.
They burned her tongue, moving it more powerfully and
more freely. She saw that the people were listening to
her words. All were silent. She felt that they were thinking as they surrounded her closely; and the desire grew
in her, now a clear desire, to drive these people to follow
her son, to follow Andrey, to follow all those who had
fallen into the soldiers' hands, all those who were left
entirely alone, all those who were abandoned. Looking
at the sullen, attentive faces around her, she resumed
with soft force:

"Our children are going in the world toward happiness. They went for the sake of all, and for Christ's truth
—against all with which our malicious, false, avaricious
ones have captured, tied, and crushed us. My dear ones
—why it is for you that our young blood rose—for all
the people, for all the world, for all the workingmen,
they went! Then don't go away from them, don't renounce, don't forsake them, don't leave your children on
a lonely path—they went just for the purpose of showing you all the path to truth, to take all on that path!
Pity yourselves! Love them! Understand the children's

hearts. Believe your sons' hearts; they have brought forth the truth; it burns in them; they perish for it. Believe them!"

Her voice broke down, she staggered, her strength gone. Somebody seized her under the arms.

"She is speaking God's words!" a man shouted hoarsely and excitedly. "God's words, good people! Listen to her!"

Another man said in pity of her:

"Look how she's hurting herself!"

"She's not hurting herself, but hitting us, fools, understand that!" was the reproachful reply.

A high-pitched, quavering voice rose up over the crowd:

"Oh, people of the true faith! My Mitya, pure soul, what has he done? He went after his dear comrades. She speaks truth—why did we forsake our children? What harm have they done us?"

The mother trembled at these words and replied with soft tears.

"Go home, Nilovna! Go, mother! You're all worn out," said Sizov loudly.

He was pale, his disheveled beard shook. Suddenly knitting his brows he threw a stern glance about him on all, drew himself up to his full height, and said distinctly:

"My son Matvey was crushed in the factory. You know it! But were he alive, I myself would have sent him into the lines of those—along with them. I myself would have told him: 'Go you, too, Matvey! That's the right cause, that's the honest cause!'"

He stopped abruptly, and a sullen silence fell on all, in the powerful grip of something huge and new, but something that no longer frightened them. Sizov lifted his hand, shook it, and continued:

"It's an old man who is speaking to you. You know me! I've been working here thirty-nine years, and I've been alive fifty-three years. To-day they've arrested my nephew, a pure and intelligent boy. He, too, was in the front, side by side with Vlasov; right at the banner." Sizov made a motion with his hand, shrank together, and said as he took the mother's hand: "This woman spoke the truth. Our children want to live honorably, according to reason, and we have abandoned them; we walked away, yes! Go, Nilovna!"

"My dear ones!" she said, looking at them all with tearful eyes. "The life is for our children and the earth is for them."

"Go, Nilovna, take this staff and lean upon it!" said Sizov, giving her the fragment of the flag pole.

All looked at the mother with sadness and respect. A hum of sympathy accompanied her. Sizov silently put the people out of her way, and they silently moved aside, obeying a blind impulse to follow her. They walked after her slowly, exchanging brief, subdued remarks on the way. Arrived at the gate of her house, she turned to them, leaning on the fragment of the flag pole, and bowed in gratitude.

"Thank you!" she said softly. And recalling the thought which she fancied had been born in her heart, she said: "Our Lord Jesus Christ would not have been, either, if people had not perished for his sake."

The crowd looked at her in silence.

She bowed to the people again, and went into her house, and Sizov, drooping his head, went in with her.

The people stood at the gates and talked. Then they began to depart slowly and quietly.

Maxim Gorky, like Tchekhov, believed that the future of Russia lay in further industrialization rather than in agricultural development. Both writers resented Tolstoy's idealization of the peasantry, and traced much of the wretchedness and misery in Russia to peasant influence. Tchekhov, however, hitched his chariot to the merchant capitalist, as his agent for urbanization, whereas Gorky lined himself up with the urban workers—the proletariat. Moreover, Gorky, unlike his contemporaries, demanded a change through revolution, rather than by education and evolution. In literature he did for the urban "serf" what Turgenev did for the rural serf.

While Gorky is better known as the classic interpreter of Russian proletarian culture, he evinced his real talent

in the portrayal of the Russian underworld. In his idealization of the underworld Gorky undoubtedly sounded a
new note in Russian literature. He was the uncrowned
king of the Russian *bosyak* (tramp or hobo) before he
became the writer-laureate of the proletariat. Not all of
his works—and he was a prolific writer—reflect Gorky.
The Gorky who found a niche for himself among the
writers of the classical age was the Gorky who championed the underworld and interpreted the pre-war Russian proletariat. Although this Gorky belongs essentially to the Golden Age, he was not a genius of the same
caliber as Turgenev, Dostoyevsky, and Tolstoy. He was
a man of great talent.

No other author, prior to Gorky, has given us such a
characteristic and sympathetic description of the Russian *bosyak*. Gorky's tramps differ sharply from the
members of the American underworld, or from those of
any other country, except perhaps Germany and Italy.
This partly explains the popularity of his works in these
two countries. The Russian underworld described in *The
Lower Depths* was not made up of racketeers, gunmen,
and bootleggers, driving high-powered automobiles and
wearing tuxedos and dress shirts. It was composed
rather of "creatures that once were men." For the most
part these human derelicts were victims of the social
order, rather than violators of the law. Their chief
weapon was their fists—or as a last resort, a knife. They
were invariably penniless. Kopecks, when they had them,
burned holes in their pockets. Except for thieves and
robbers, this underworld constituted an army of unem-
ployed and unskilled laborers, who wandered from place
to place in search of work. So true to life was Gorky's
portrayal of this slice of Russian society, that his name
became a byword in the mouth of every tramp, and he
was recognized as the patron of the underworld. To
upbraid a hobo for his laziness, might well bring the
retort: "You never can tell—I might become a Gorky!"

The Lower Depths. By assembling the various types

of the Russian underworld in a basement night lodging, Gorky, in his play *The Lower Depths*, was able to sum up his ideas concerning them. Although of diverse antecedents, barons, Tartar princes, thieves, prostitutes, or card-sharpers, they have this in common—that they are the victims of the social order, and they meet here on a plane of equality. Such a play, for the majority of people, broke new ground in Russian drama.

Originally this play was entitled *Na Dnye Zhizni* (The Lower Depths of Life) ; but, at the suggestion of V. I. Nemirovitch-Dantchenko, Gorky dropped the last Russian word. The play was first produced at the Moscow Art Theatre on December 31, 1902, and its thirty-fifth jubilee was held at the close of 1937. Germany, especially, went wild over the play. From 1903 to 1904 it enjoyed an uninterrupted run of 500 nights in Berlin alone. English translations have appeared under various titles: *In the Depths, A Night Shelter, Submerged, Down and Out*, as well as *The Lower Depths*.

While in Tchekhov's plays, the idle-rich nobility and other "superfluous" people vegetate in boredom in the Russian village, Gorky's hoboes vegetate in idleness and trivialities, sometimes reluctantly, in the dark damp basements where they seek a temporary lodging. In spite of their sordid surroundings, Gorky's heroes still have faith in a better future. They do not spend their time cursing the system or lamenting their misfortunes. The pinnacle of their discussion, as led by Luka, the vagabond pilgrim, and his interpreter, Satin, the cardsharper, is "the better man." Far from being crushed in spirit, some of them regard their wretched conditions as the price of their freedom. To Tchekhov's idle-rich, life spelled boredom; while physically better off than Gorky's tramps, they were spiritually crushed. The human failures of Gorky's underworld, in spite of their environment, are spiritually the stronger of the two. They still have hope; they take life as it comes, sometimes in happy-go-lucky fashion; they sing, and they keep their faith in humanity. Man to them is the norm. Whether he turns out to be a carpenter, a card-sharper, a Napoleon, or a Mohammed, he is still a man, free and deserving of respect. Strangely enough they would prefer "a better man," even a better underworld. Gorky's philosophy of "the better man," expressed by Luka and Satin, almost approaches Tolstoy's "inner peace."

In other words, Gorky discovered a world in the underworld. His implication is clear enough—that tramps or hoboes with such beautiful souls should not be lost to humanity because they are the victims of an unjust social order. In this field Gorky had no predecessor, and herein lies his chief contribution to Russian literature.

Mother. Less artistic, but of greater political significance, was his proletarian novel, *Mother.* This was the first novel subsequent to the 1905 Revolution to portray the life of the urban worker in the factory, at home, at political meetings, on parade, and so forth. While it truly reflects the life of the proletariat during the period in question, there were few mothers like Pelagueya Vlasova. Although it seems quite evident that Gorky wished other mothers to emulate her, he has given us a portrait of the ideal, rather than of the real, proletarian mother.

If we did not know that Gorky's novel was produced in Russia in 1906, we could never guess that it ran the gauntlet of the world's most rigid censorship. This novel was an open challenge to the Government—an appeal to the worker to emulate the Vlasovs, and by force or revolution, to bring about the new social order. Gorky did not mince words in the appeals of his agitators. In a country where freedom of speech exists, speeches like those of Pavel would be regarded as soapbox oratory, or casually dismissed as Red propaganda. But in Russia, during the period in question, the activities of the Vlasovs and their supporters constituted a serious menace to the old regime. Yet this book could be found in every library, accessible to anyone capable of reading it. This was chiefly due to the efforts of the Russian intelligentsia, in welcoming into Russian literature a real proletarian novel, without altogether subscribing to the ideas expressed in it.

Gorky's *Mother* is by no means a work of art. It is rather a political document of the tumultuous years from 1905 to 1906. As we have already intimated, Gorky is really at home only in the underworld. In the world he is less of an artist and more of a propagandist. *The Lower Depths* is a sociological study—*Mother,* a political tract.

In short, Gorky did for the tramp and for the proletarian what Tolstoy did for the peasant, Andreyev for the Jew, and Turgenev for the serf. He idealized him. The impression derived from a study of his works is that he stands at the head of a great mass of humanity, seeking recognition and a new deal. With Gorky began the era of the domination of the proletariat.

The works that Gorky produced after the Revolution, except for his autobiographical trilogy, are of transient significance. They are outside the scope of this study, since they are not and will not be ranked with the classics.

BIBLIOGRAPHY

Desnitzky, V. A., and Balukhaty, *Gorky* (in Russian), Moscow-Leningrad, 1937.

Dillon, E. J., *Maxim Gorky, His Life and Writings,* London, 1903.

Fovitzky, A. L., *The Moscow Art Theatre and Its Distinguishing Characteristics,* N. Y., 1922.

Johnston, Charles, "Maxim Gorky (Alexei Maximovich Pyeshkov)," *The World's Best Literature,* N. Y., 1917.

Kaun, A., *Maxim Gorky and his Russia,* N. Y., 1931.

Kropotkin, Peter, *Russian Literature,* London, 1905.

Leger, Louis, *La Russie intellectuelle,* Paris, 1914.

London, Kurt, *The Seven Soviet Arts,* Yale University Press, 1938.

Lourié, Ossip, *La psychologie des romanciers russes,* Paris, 1905.

Mencke, Rudolph, *Maxim Gorki,* Hamburg, 1908.

Mirsky, D. S., *Modern Russian Literature,* London, 1925.

Nemirovitch-Dantchenko, V., *My Life in the Russian Theatre,* Boston, 1936.

Noyes, G. R., *Masterpieces of the Russian Drama*, N. Y., 1933.

Olgin, M. J., *A Guide to Russian Literature*, N. Y., 1920.

Ostwald, H., *Maxim Gorky*, London, 1905.

Persky, Sergyev, *Contemporary Russian Novelists*, Boston, 1913.

Petrone, Igino, *La visione della vita e l'arte di Massimo Gorki*, Napoli, 1903.

Phelps, W. L., *Essays on Russian Novelists*, N. Y., 1922.

Reavey, G., and Slonim, M., *Soviet Literature—An Anthology*, N. Y., 1934.

Sayler, Oliver, *The Russian Theatre*, N. Y., 1922.

Stanislavsky, Constantin, *My Life in Art*, Boston, 1927.

Vsevolodsky-Gengross, V., *Khrestomatia po istorii Russkogo Teatra (An Anthology of the History of the Russian Theatre)*, Moscow, 1936.

Wiener, Leo, *The Contemporary Drama of Russia*, Boston, 1924.

Znosko-Borovsky, *The Russian Theatre from the Beginning of the Twentieth Century* (in Russian), Praha.

Conclusion

THE VARIOUS patrons of the divergent classes, groups, and races which make up the Pantheon of Russian literature have now been accounted for. Before the bar of history each patron can display his scales, in which the good qualities of serf, peasant, "poor folk," "the lower depths," the Jew, the tramp, and the proletarian, as the case may be, overbalance the seamy side. After each has found his place in the sun, there still remains one vacant niche for the Russian intelligentsia. The Russian intelligentsia have not, as yet, found any ambassador or intercessor to present their case. Although they were chiefly responsible for building this Pantheon, in doing so they neglected their own group. There is not a single work in Russian literature which gives a real appreciation of the intelligentsia. So far only the negative side of the picture has been presented. The various classes which the intelligentsia have raised to immortality in Russian literature, have, in their turn, stoned their benefactors and made of them a legitimate target for abuse and contempt. Although Gorky heaped coals of fire on the heads of the intelligentsia for their inertia, before his death, he had already begun to express some appreciation of their contribution to the cause of the weak and the oppressed. So far he has had no successors. It is to be hoped that Gorky's beginning will be emulated, and that due recognition will be accorded to those who produced the Golden Age of Russian Literature. This belated recognition would constitute a real contribution to Russian culture, as well as to World Literature.

Notes

1. *Tale of the Host of Igor.* In 1795 Count A. I. Mussin-Pushkin, an amateur antiquarian, bought a large collection of manuscripts from a former archimandrite of the Spasso-Yaroslav monastery. This collection contained the "Tale of the Host of Igor, Igor, the Son of Sviatoslav, the Grandson of Olga." Like many old Russian manuscripts it lacked punctuation and word separation.

The Russian historian, N. M. Karamzin, published the first account of the *Tale of the Host of Igor* in French in a Hamburg magazine, *Spectateur du Nord,* in October, 1797. He praised the artistic significance of the poem, which he attributed to an anonymous Russian author of the twelfth century. This brief notice by Karamzin paved the way for extensive and intensive research on the historical background and general interpretation of the manuscript. At least two hundred outstanding studies have appeared to date. In 1797 a special copy was prepared for Catherine the Great. Finally Mussin-Pushkin, in collaboration with others, published a modernized version in 1800. In 1812, during the Napoleonic invasion, Mussin-Pushkin's vast library, including the original manuscript of the *Tale of the Host of Igor,* was destroyed by fire. The text in use today differs materially from the original.

The plot of the poem was based upon the historic fact of the abortive campaign of Prince Igor Sviatoslavitch (1151-1202), his brother Vsevolod, his young son Vladimir, and his nephew Sviatoslav against the Polovtsi. Igor undertook the campaign independently, April to May, 1185, without the collaboration of the other Russian princes. At first he made successful inroads upon the Polovtsi steppes, but eventually he and his companions were captured and imprisoned. Igor soon escaped, and his son Vladimir returned two years later with his wife, the daughter of the Khan Kontchak.

The Tale of the Host of Igor is a battle song, undoubtedly composed by an eyewitness of the campaign against the Polovtsi in 1185. It was written for the most part in *kinah* meter, after the fashion of the Song of Deborah and David's lamentation on the death of Saul and Jonathan. Its influence upon classical Russian literature can scarcely be overestimated.

2. *Nakaz.* The first draft of the *Nakaz* or *Instructions* of Catherine the Great was published in part, 1767-68, in four languages (Russian, French, German, and Latin). Because the liberal and progressive tone of the document alarmed the higher bureaucracy, Catherine was dissuaded from giving it wide publicity. She therefore published only part of the Instructions and permitted a somewhat restricted distribution of the rest. This was her life work. *The Minor* reflects that part of the *Nakaz* which sought to raise standards among the bureaucratic personnel by making education the criterion for rank in the government service.

3. *Moscow Art Theatre.* The Moscow Art Theatre was established by V. I. Nemirovitch-Dantchenko and K. S. Stanislavsky in June, 1897. The first performance, that of *Tsar Fyodor Ivanovitch* by A. K. Tolstoy, took place on October 27, 1898. On the evening of October 26, 1938, the U.S.S.R. celebrated the fortieth anniversary of the theatre with a gala performance of this play. Nineteen of the original actors were still alive, and several of them assumed the same roles as in 1898. The company by this time included 310 actors. The influence of the Moscow Art Theatre is world wide.

Index